BlackBerry© Storm™
9500 *Made Simple*

Written for the
Storm 9500, 9510, 9520, 9530 and all
95xx Series BlackBerry Smartphones

Another in the
Made Simple™
Guide Book Series

By
Martin Trautschold
Gary Mazo

Formerly BlackBerry Made Simple

BlackBerry® Storm™
9500 *Made Simple*

This book is intended to help owners of the BlackBerry Storm™ 9500, 9510, 9520, 9530 and related 95xx Series BlackBerry smartphones.

If you have a different BlackBerry Model, then version where you found this book. If you cannot locate this published guide, please check out our electronic versions at www.MadeSimpleLearning.com

Published by
CMT Publications, Inc.
25 Forest View Way
Ormond Beach, FL 32174

ISBN-10: 1-4392-1756-4
ISBN-13: 978-1-4392-1756-6
Published Date: January 30, 2009

Published in the United States of America

10 9 8 7 6 5 4 3 2 1

Trademark Acknowledgements

Images
BlackBerry images courtesy of Research In Motion, Ltd. (www.blackberry.com)

Contact Us
Contact the authors at
 info@blackberrymadesimple.com
For Free Email Tips, and the Electronic Version ("E-book") in Adobe PDF format, please visit
 www.MadeSimpleLearning.com

Tired of reading?   Rather watch the video?

Check out our Extensive Library of BlackBerry Video Clips
We have developed more than 200 separate "Video Clips" viewable on your personal computer (and soon on your BlackBerry) that bring to life the information found in this book. Each clip will is about 3-5 minutes long and will show you on the screen exactly how to do the setup, tips and tricks! We also will add new Video Clips all the time. To learn more, please visit:
http://www.MadeSimpleLearning.com

Contents at a Glance

Detailed Contents

Detailed Contents

Videos are an easy and effective way to learn: www.MadeSimpleLearning.com

Detailed Contents

Videos are an easy and effective way to learn: www.MadeSimpleLearning.com

Authors & Acknowledgements

 **Martin Trautschold** is the Founder and CEO of BlackBerry Made Simple (soon to be known as "Made Simple Learning"), a leading provider of BlackBerry Training Videos and Books. He has been a successful entrepreneur in the Smartphone training and software business for the past 8 years. With BlackBerry Made Simple, he has been helping to train thousands of BlackBerry users with short, to-the-point video tutorials. He has also co-authored five BlackBerry-related "Made Simple" guide books. He recently worked with co-author Gary Mazo on a similar book for the BlackBerry Pearl™ 'Flip' 8200 Series and the BlackBerry 8800/8300 Curve™. Martin and Gary teamed up with Kevin Michaluk, founder of CrackBerry.com to write a part-serious, part-funny, but wholly entertaining guide to BlackBerry addiction called: "CrackBerry: True Tales of BlackBerry Use and Abuse."

Martin began his entrepreneurial life with a BlackBerry wireless software company which he co-founded with his brother-in-law, Ned Johnson. Together, they spent 3 years growing it and then sold it, the company's flagship product "Handheld Contact" is still being developed, marketed and sold by the new owners. Martin also has 15 years experience managing complex technology and business projects for consulting, technology and energy firms in the US and Japan. He holds a Bachelor of Science in Engineering Degree from Princeton University and an MBA from the Kellogg School at Northwestern University. In his "free time" he enjoys spending time with his wife, Julie, and three children. Occasionally, he tries to sneak a few hours to ride his bicycle with friends in Ormond Beach, Florida. Martin can be reached at martin@blackberrymadesimple.com.

> I would like to thank my co-author Gary Mazo for his tireless effort in helping to make this book a success. This book is much more comprehensive due to his efforts. Special thanks goes out to all the BlackBerry Made Simple customers who have asked great questions and shared their tips, many of which are in this book! I would also like to thank my wife, Julie and my daughters for their support over the many months of writing, re-writing and editing.
>
> -- Martin Trautschold

 **Gary Mazo** is a writer, a College Professor, a gadget nut and an ordained rabbi. Gary joined BlackBerry Made Simple in 2007 and has co - authored the last four books in the BlackBerry Made Simple Series. He serves as VP of the company as well. Along with Martin and Kevin Michaluk from CrackBerry.com, Gary co-wrote "CrackBerry: True Tales of BlackBerry Use and Abuse" - a book about BlackBerry addiction and how to get a grip on one's BlackBerry use. Gary also teaches at the University of Phoenix – teaching Writing, Philosophy, Technical Writing and more. Gary is a regular contributor to CrackBerry.com – writing product reviews and adding Editorial Content. Gary is also the Director of Kollel of Cape Cod – a cutting edge Jewish Educational institution/Congregation in Marstons Mills, Massachusetts. He holds a BA in Anthropology from Brandeis University. Gary earned his M.A.H.L (Masters in Hebrew Letters) as well as ordination as Rabbi from the Hebrew Union College-Jewish Institute of Religion in Cincinnati, Ohio. He has served congregations in Dayton, Ohio, Cherry Hill, New Jersey and Hyannis, Massachusetts.

His first book, entitled "And the Flames Did Not Consume us" achieved critical acclaim and was published by Rising Star Press in 2000.

Gary is married to Gloria Schwartz Mazo and between them, they have six children. Gary can be reached at: gary@blackberrymadesimple.com.

This book is only possible due to the support of several individuals in my life. First, I would like to thank Martin Trautschold for giving me the opportunity to join him in this project. Next, I want to thank my wife, Gloria and our kids; Ari, Dan, Sara, Bill, Elise and Jonah – without whom I would not have the support to pursue projects like this one.

-- Gary Mazo

Other BlackBerry & Smartphone Learning Products

Formerly BlackBerry Made Simple

www.MadeSimpleLearning.com
Smartphone Training Videos & Books

Books:
CrackBerry: True Tales of BlackBerry® Use and Abuse
BlackBerry Pearl™ 'Flip' 8200 *Made Simple*
BlackBerry Bold™ 9000 *Made Simple* (*coming soon*)
BlackBerry Curve™ 8900 *Made Simple* (*coming soon*)
BlackBerry Pearl *Made Simple* for 8100 Series BlackBerry smartphones
BlackBerry 8300/8800 Series *Made Simple*
BlackBerry *Made Simple™* for Full Keyboard BlackBerry smartphones
(87xx, 77xx, 75xx, 72xx, 6xxx Series)
BlackBerry *Made Simple™* for 7100 Series BlackBerry smartphones
(7100, 7130, 71xx Series)

Video Training
(Viewed On Your Computer)
We offer a full library of over 200 3-minute video training clips for:
All popular BlackBerry models with new videos issued every month to keep up with the latest models.

CardVideos™
Video Training You Watch on your BlackBerry®
Full Training library on the Pearl 8100, Curve™ 8300, Series and 8800 Series and coming soon on the Bold™ 9000, Pearl™ 8200 Series, Curve™ 8900 Series BlackBerry devices.

Videos pre-loaded on a Media Card to pop into your BlackBerry and learn on-the-go, from your Media icon.

Quick Reference Guide

GETTING SETUP

The items below will help you get up and running with your BlackBerry.

To Do This...	Use This...	Where to Learn More
Find Your Setup Icons	**Setup FOLDER**	Press and click on this icon to see your other Setup Icons
Email Setup, Date/Time, Fonts, Wi-Fi and more.	**Setup Wizard**	Page 41
Setup or change Your Internet Email	**Setup Internet E-mail**	Page 43
Setup your Bluetooth headset	**Setup Bluetooth**	Page 327
Share Addresses, Calendar, Tasks and Notes with your Computer	**BlackBerry Desktop Manager (for Windows™)** **PocketMac™ for BlackBerry (for Apple™ Mac™)**	Page 60 See Free Videos at www.MadeSimpleLearning.com Page 85
Add memory to store your Music, Videos and Pictures	**Media Card** © SanDisk Corp.	Adding it: Page 286 Using: Page 314
Load up your Music, Pictures and Videos	Win or Mac **Mass Storage Mode**	Page 288
Fine-tune your Internet Email Signature & More	**Your Wireless Carrier Website**	See list of websites on page 52

STAYING IN TOUCH

Use these things to stay in touch with friends and colleagues on your BlackBerry.

To Do This...	Use This...	Where to Learn More
Read & Reply to Email	**Messages**	Email –page 188 PIN Messaging –page 270 Attachments – page 197
Send & Read SMS Text and MMS Messages	**SMS (& MMS)**	See page 260
Get on the Internet / Browse the Web	**Browser**	Page 336
Call Voicemail	**Press & Hold '1'**	Page 149
Start a Call Dial by Name View Call Logs	Green Phone **Phone & Call Logs**	Basics – Page 146 Advanced - Page 165
Dial by Voice	**Voice Dialing**	Page 163
Send an Instant Message to another BlackBerry user	**BlackBerry Messenger**	Page 270
Use your Favorite Instant Messengers	**AOL, Google, Yahoo, Windows Messenger**	Page 283
Flying on an Airplane, need to turn off the radio	**Manage Connections**	Page 378
Maximize your Battery life to talk, message, and play more!	**Battery Life Tips**	Page 384

STAY ORGANIZED WITH YOUR BLACKBERRY

Use these things to stay in organized with your BlackBerry.

To Do This...	Use This...	Where to Learn More
Manage Your Contact Names & Numbers	Contacts / Address Book	Basics – Page 207 Add New - Page 209
Manage your Calendar	Calendar	Page 223 Sync to PC - Page 60 Sync to Mac – Page 85
Manage your To-Do List	Tasks	Page 244 Sync to PC - Page 60 Sync to Mac – Page 85
Take notes, store your grocery list and more!	MemoPad	Page 250 Sync to PC - Page 60 Sync to Mac – Page 85
Cannot type a note? Leave yourself a quick Voice Note!	Voice Note Recorder	Page 369
View & Edit Microsoft™ Office™ Word, Excel and PowerPoint	Word to Go, Sheet to Go, Slideshow to Go	Page 198
Calculate your MPG, a meal tip, and convert units!	Calculator	Other Applications Page 366
Set a wakeup alarm, use a countdown timer or stopwatch	Clock	Page 367
Store all your important passwords	Password Keeper	Page 370
Find lost names, email, calendar entries and more	Search	Page 371

BE ENTERTAINED WITH YOUR BLACKBERRY

Use these things to have fun with your BlackBerry!

To Do This...	Use This...		Where to Learn More
Quickly get to all your Music!		**Music**	Page 293
Play Music, Videos and watch Pictures		**Media**	Music – Page 293 Videos – Page 324 Ring Tones – Page 304 Pictures – Page 314 Voice Notes – Page 369
Snap Pictures of Anything, Anytime!		**Camera**	Page 304
Capture Video of anything, anytime!		**Video Camera**	Page 320
Take a Break and Play a Game		**Games FOLDER**	Page 352
Use the built in Text-Based help *(What, you can't find it in this book!)*		**Help**	Page 116

PERSONALIZE YOUR BLACKBERRY

Use these things to personalize your BlackBerry.

To Do This...	Use This...		Where to Learn More
Change your Phone Ringer, if emails vibrate or buzz and more...	Sounds (No...	Profiles (Sounds)	Page 138
Change your Background Homescreen Picture	Media	Media / Pictures	Use Pictures – Page 133 Use Camera – Page 305
Change your Font Size	Options	Options	Screen / Keyboard Page 119
Change your programmable Convenience Keys	Options	Options	Screen / Keyboard Page 134
Change your "Theme" – Entire Look & Feel	Options	Options	Theme Page 129

ADD & REMOVE SOFTWARE ICONS

Use these things to add capabilities your BlackBerry.

To Do This...	Use This...	Where to Learn More
How to add new Icons and Programs	Browser / Browser	Page 349
Find all the icons you download	Downloads / Downloads FOLDER	Page 351
How to remove Icons and Programs	Options / Options	Advanced Options > Applications Page 354

LEARNING YOUR BLACKBERRY:
THE SCREEN, BUTTONS, AND MORE

Lock Key
Locks the touch screen
Tap again to unlock

 # unopened Messages

Missed Calls

Repeat Notification Light

Mute Key
Mute Phone/Ringer or
Pause Music & Video
playback

Battery Strength

Bluetooth®

Wireless Strength
1-5 Bars / OFF / X

Active Sound Profile
How Phone, Email,
Calendar, Task Alarms
more notify You - Ring,
Vibrate or Mute
TIP: Change your Ringtone
"Set Ringtones/Alerts" >
"Phone"

Headphone Jack

1XEV Wireless Data
GSM (no data, voice only)
1X / GPRS (low speed)
1XEV / EDGE (high speed)

Homescreen Image
Background (Menu Key >
Options to change this
picture)

Volume Up & Down Keys

GPS Indicator
E911 only without 3 signal signs

Left Convenience Key
May be PTT or Voice Dial
(Set in Options > Screen/Keyboard)

Homescreen

TIP: Press your Home
Screen anywhere in
the picture to see all
your icons.

USB Cable & Charger Socket
Socket to plug in the
USB cable or the power
charger.

Your Top Icons
Customize to Top 4, 8, or
12 by pressing Menu key
> Options – Homescreen
preferences

Right Side Convenience Key
May start Camera
(Set in Options >
Screen/Keyboard)

Green Phone Key ("Send")
Start phone call, see call
logs, Press & hold to Dial
by Name

Red Phone / Power ("End")
Tap to power on, Press &
hold to power off, End
phone call,
Multi-task jump to home
screen

Menu Key
Click to see all icons
or menus. TIP: Press and hold
to see multi-tasking window.

Escape / Back
Press to backup or exit

READING YOUR TOP STATUS BAR

Understanding when your Phone, Email, Instant Messaging, Web Browsing and other wireless data services are working. Check out our "Fixing Problems" chapter on page 376 for help with getting this working.

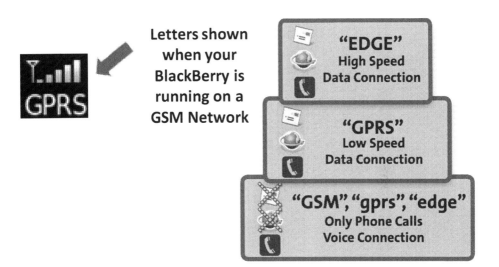

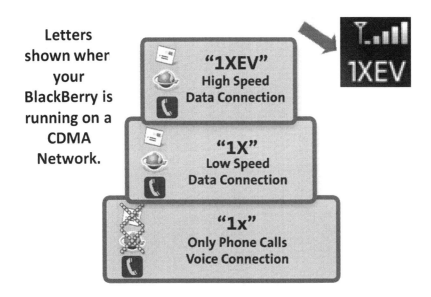

YOUR BLACKBERRY: LEARNING TOUCH SCREEN GESTURES

The BlackBerry Storm™ is the first BlackBerry with a Touch Screen. RIM, the maker of the BlackBerry, has included some innovations which they have called SurePress®. The entire screen actually can be pressed in (or 'clicked') giving you positive feedback that you are clicking the image of a button or key shown on the screen. If you have used an older BlackBerry model, then this touch screen will take a little getting used to because there is no trackball, trackwheel or physical keyboard. With a little patience and practice as you work through this first section of the book you will soon become comfortable doing things with your Storm™.

You can pretty much do anything on your Storm™ by using a combination of:

- Touch screen 'gestures,' (see next page)
- Pressing any soft keys on the screen,
- Using the four navigation buttons on the bottom of the BlackBerry, and,
- Pressing the 'Convenience keys' on the sides (See page 134)

Here is a summary of the basic touch screen gestures:

- **Lightly Touch** – To highlight an icon, menu item or other item on the screen.

- **Touch and Hover** – To see the name of a specific icon.

- **Press and Click** – To start an icon, select a menu item, or select an answer.

- **Swipe across** – To move to the next email message or day in your calendar.

- **Scroll up/down** – To see what is above the top or below the bottom of the screen.

- **Multi-Touch** – Tap the beginning and end of text that you want to cut or copy.

Read the following pages for a full graphical display of exactly how to get around and 'master' your BlackBerry® Storm™.

BASIC TOUCH SCREEN GESTURES

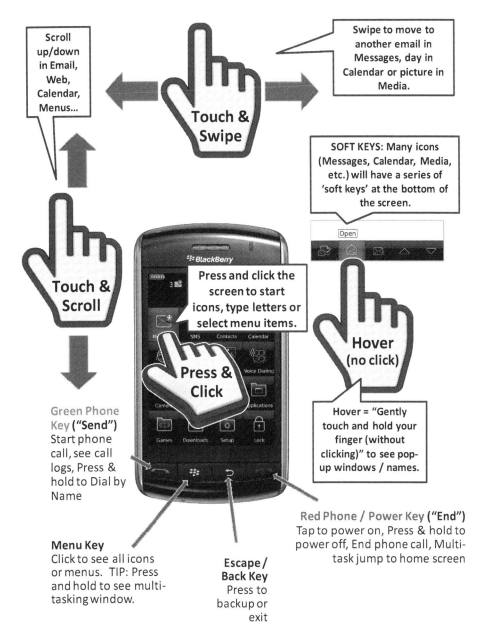

Scroll up/down in Email, Web, Calendar, Menus...

Swipe to move to another email in Messages, day in Calendar or picture in Media.

Touch & Swipe

SOFT KEYS: Many icons (Messages, Calendar, Media, etc.) will have a series of 'soft keys' at the bottom of the screen.

Touch & Scroll

Press and click the screen to start icons, type letters or select menu items.

Press & Click

Hover (no click)

Hover = "Gently touch and hold your finger (without clicking)" to see pop-up windows / names.

Green Phone Key ("Send") Start phone call, see call logs, Press & hold to Dial by Name

Menu Key Click to see all icons or menus. TIP: Press and hold to see multi-tasking window.

Escape / Back Key Press to backup or exit

Red Phone / Power Key ("End") Tap to power on, Press & hold to power off, End phone call, Multi-task jump to home screen

STARTING ICONS

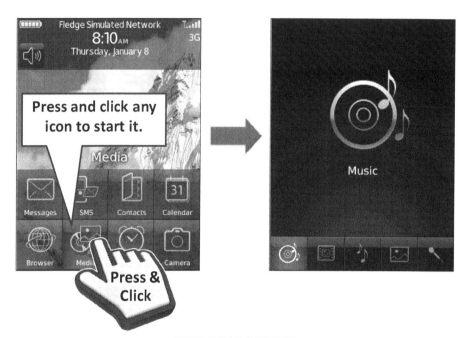

SELECTING MENUS

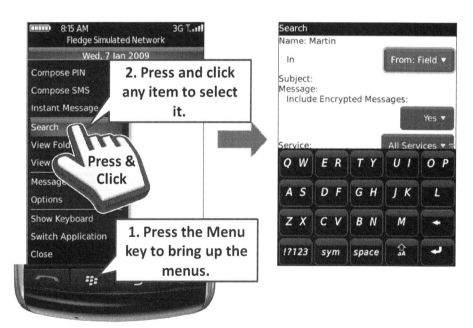

CLICK ON MANY THINGS FOR SHORT MENUS

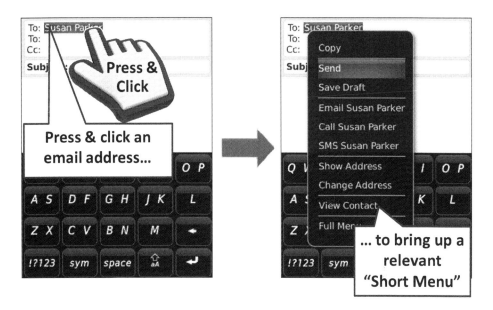

HOVER FOR POP-UP INFORMATION

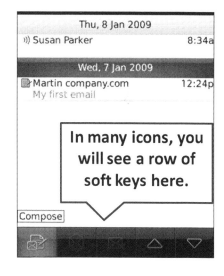

SWIPE GESTURE – MOVE TO NEXT DAY, PICTURE, EMAIL, ETC.

Gently touch and slide your finger.
Moves to the next/previous day, or email, etc.

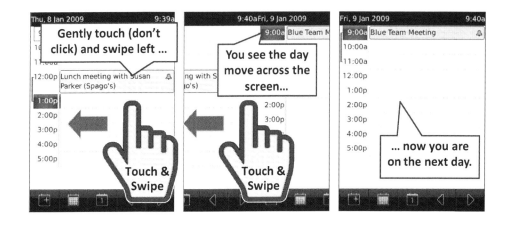

HIDING AND SHOWING THE KEYBOARD

When you hide the keyboard, many times, you will see the "Soft Keys"

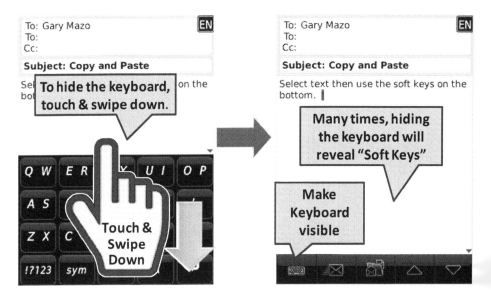

Videos are an easy way to Learn: www.MadeSimpleLearning.c

MULTI-TASKING OR APPLICATION SWITCHING

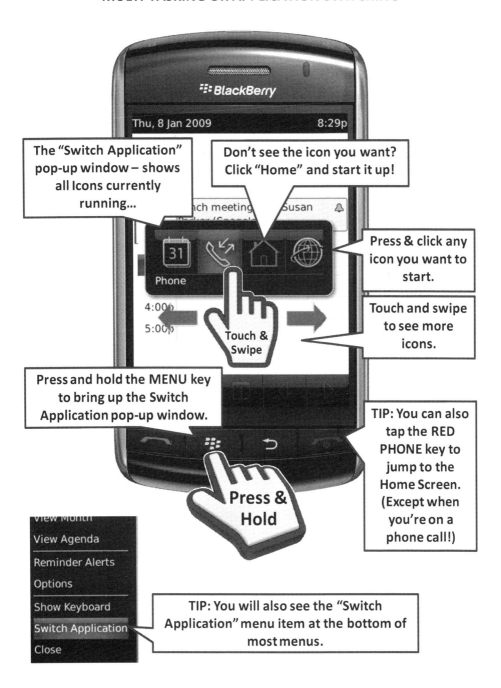

The "Switch Application" pop-up window – shows all Icons currently running...

Don't see the icon you want? Click "Home" and start it up!

Press & click any icon you want to start.

Touch and swipe to see more icons.

Press and hold the MENU key to bring up the Switch Application pop-up window.

TIP: You can also tap the RED PHONE key to jump to the Home Screen. (Except when you're on a phone call!)

Touch & Swipe

Press & Hold

View Month
View Agenda
Reminder Alerts
Options
Show Keyboard
Switch Application
Close

TIP: You will also see the "Switch Application" menu item at the bottom of most menus.

SCROLLING UP AND DOWN THE SCREEN

Use in Messages (Email), Web Browser, Menus and more…

Scrolling Up: Start at bottom, tap and slide up

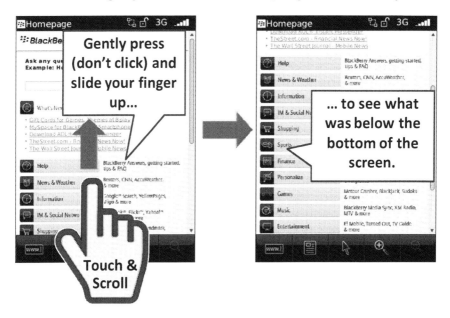

Scrolling Down: Start at top, tap and slide down

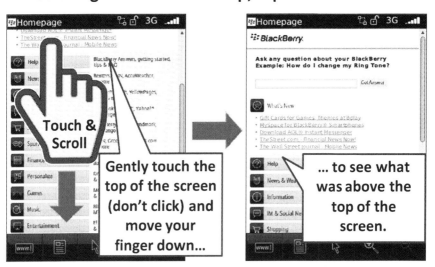

SCROLLING AND TAP TO SHOW/HIDE CONTROLS OR SOFT KEYS

Scroll Up/Down Menus

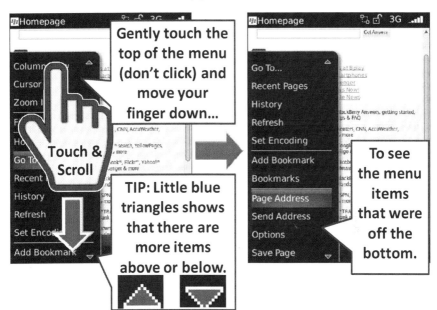

Gently touch the top of the menu (don't click) and move your finger down...

Touch & Scroll

TIP: Little blue triangles shows that there are more items above or below.

To see the menu items that were off the bottom.

Tap to Reveal More Controls in Media Player & Web Browser

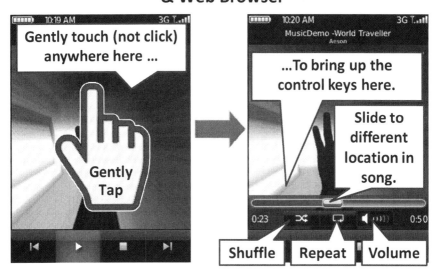

Gently touch (not click) anywhere here ...

Gently Tap

...To bring up the control keys here.

Slide to different location in song.

Shuffle   Repeat   Volume

MANY WAYS TO TYPE ON YOUR BLACKBERRY

Are you a keyboard lover?   See page 134 to learn how to set one of your convenience keys to instantly open your keyboard just about anywhere!

With SureType™, you press every key just once and the words appear as clickable choices...

With Multitap, press once for the 1st letter, twice for the 2nd and so on...

Press the Menu key to Switch between SureType™ and Multitap typing modes.

Select one of these menu options.

Enable Multitap

Enable SureType

Simply turn the Storm™ sideways (Landscape) for the full QWERTY keyboard with a single letter on each key.

TIP: You can set your default Portrait keyboard in the Options icon > Screen/Keyboard.

"Landscape" (Horizontal) Orientation

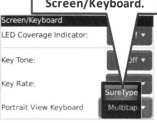

TYPING WITH SURETYPE™ (PORTRAIT)

With SureType™ you press every key just once and watch for suggestions

The number & basic
Symbol keyboard:

To type 'THE' you would
Press TY once = "T"
Press GH once = "H"
Press ER once = "E"

If you see the word you
want, then press and click
it to select it... or just
keep typing.

TIP: Press and hold
the !?123 key to lock.

Press the !?123
key to see
numbers and
basic symbols.

TIP: Many times the
'guess' is correct near the
end of the word, so don't
choose too early.

TIP: Press and
hold a letter
for
UPPERCASE.

Press the 'sym' key to see
symbols not on main keyboard.

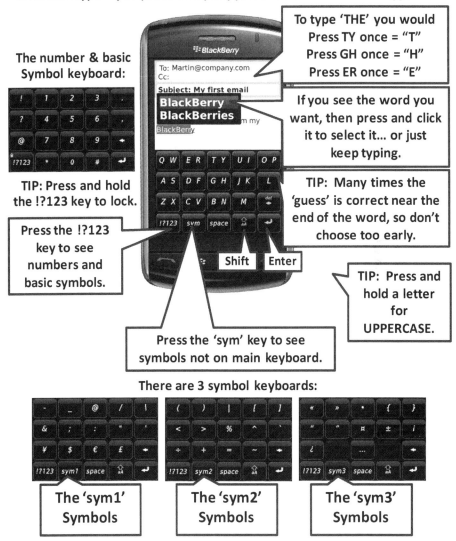

There are 3 symbol keyboards:

The 'sym1'
Symbols

The 'sym2'
Symbols

The 'sym3'
Symbols

TYPING WITH MULTITAP (PORTRAIT)

With Multitap, you press every key one, two, three or four times to get the desired letter or symbol

The number & basic Symbol keyboard:

TIP: Press and hold the !?123 key to lock.

Press the !?123 key to see numbers and basic symbols.

To type 'THE' you would
Press TUV once = "T"
Press GHI twice = "H"
Press DEF twice = "E"

TIP: Have a difficult word to type? Simply rotate the BlackBerry sideways to see the full QWERTY keyboard. (1 letter/key)

TIP: Press and hold a letter for UPPERCASE.

Press the 'sym' key to see symbols not on main keyboard.

There are 3 symbol keyboards:

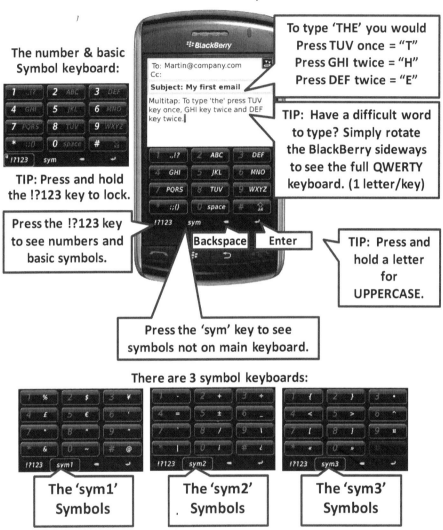

The 'sym1' Symbols

The 'sym2' Symbols

The 'sym3' Symbols

TYPING WITH THE FULL QWERTY KEYBOARD (LANDSCAPE)

Simply turn the Storm™ sideways (Landscape) for the full
QWERTY keyboard with a single letter on each key.
A great way to increase speed and accuracy.

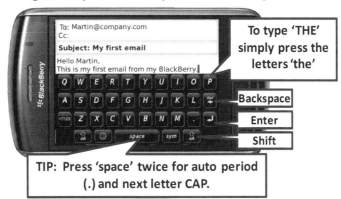

To type 'THE'
simply press the
letters 'the'

Backspace

Enter

Shift

TIP: Press 'space' twice for auto period
(.) and next letter CAP.

The numbers & basic symbols keyboard:

TIP: Press and
hold any letter
for
UPPERCASE.

Press the !?123
key to see
numbers and
basic symbols.

TIP: Press and
hold the !?123
key to lock.

The symbol keyboard:

Press the 'sym' key to see
symbols not on main keyboard.

SAVING TIME WITH THE SPACE KEY

- Use the **SPACE** Bar when typing:

  Email Addresses
  - Type:
    - susan **SPACE** company **SPACE** com

  Web Addresses
  - Get the dot "." in the address:
  - Type:
    - www **SPACE** google **SPACE** com

TIP: Save time typing emails by pressing the SPACE key twice at the end of each sentence. You will get an automatic period and the next letter will be UPPERCASE!

SELECT, COPY & PASTE TEXT WITH MULTITOUCH MODE

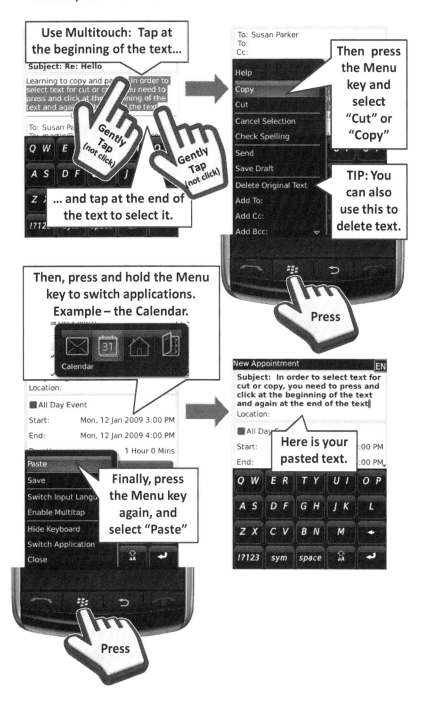

Use Multitouch: Tap at the beginning of the text...

Gently Tap (not click)

Gently Tap (not click)

... and tap at the end of the text to select it.

Then press the Menu key and select "Cut" or "Copy"

TIP: You can also use this to delete text.

Press

Then, press and hold the Menu key to switch applications. Example – the Calendar.

Here is your pasted text.

Finally, press the Menu key again, and select "Paste"

Press

Introduction

Congratulations on your BlackBerry!

In your hands is perhaps the most powerful and revolutionary Smartphone available – the first ever Touch Screen BlackBerry.

It was in 2001 that the BlackBerry name came into the market place. One popular story is that the keys on the very early devices looked like "seeds" to some of the creators. The looked at various "seeded fruit" and decided that the "BlackBerry" would be a friendly and inviting name for the device.

Perhaps the origin of the name is less important than understanding the Philosophy. One thing to understand from the outset is that this is not just a "phone." The BlackBerry is a computer – a sophisticated messaging device that does a bunch of things at the same time – and a phone.

The BlackBerry takes most of the major needs that we have – information, communication, constant contact, accessibility and more and puts them in one device that can do just about everything.

Always on – Always Connected™

Perhaps nothing sums up what a BlackBerry can do (which virtually no other device can do) than the idea that you are always connected. Your BlackBerry will "Push" your email (up to 10 different accounts) right into your hand – all the time – all day and all night. Now, you can put limitations on that – but the reason it is sometimes called a "CrackBerry" is that once you experience this – you might very well not want to limit it at all!

TIP: Need help curbing your BlackBerry desires? Check out "CrackBerry: True Tales of BlackBerry Use and Abuse" – www.crackberrybook.com or from www.amazon.com.

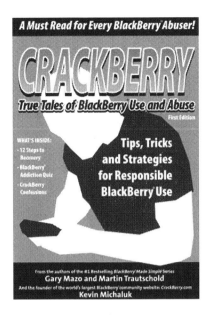

You may be used to turning your old cell phone on and off and only checking it to see if you missed a call. Your BlackBerry stays on all the time – even when it is in "standby mode," it is still on. You will find yourself looking at it not only to see if you missed a call, but to see what emails have come in, who is sending you an instant message, who just posted a note on your Facebook page, what time is your next appointment, what do you need to pick up at the store – in short, your life can be managed from your BlackBerry.

Things this powerful are not always easy to grasp – at first

Your BlackBerry is grouped into the category of things called "Smartphones" by many. A BlackBerry, however, is really....a BlackBerry – more than a "Smartphone" by any other name, because it does so much so well.

The "Pros" of that are clear – in your hand is probably the most capable and most complicated technology available today.
The "Cons" are that the BlackBerry, especially the first touch screen model, is not always "intuitive" at first use. For some, this is frustrating – they want their BlackBerry to do what their old phone did – in just the same way.

Like a computer, your BlackBerry has a unique Operating System (OS) that is proprietary and only found on other BlackBerry devices. Your "Storm" takes the OS one step further and adds an innovative new "Touch" technology which takes a little getting used to.

Introduction

Take your time – this is not a device to pick up for an hour and then throw down in frustration – there is a lot to learn here. Remember when you got your first Windows™ or Mac™ computer? We didn't know what a "window" was let alone where to find things or how to just type a letter – it took time. With the BlackBerry – like most other things in our lives – the more we invest in learning the more we will ultimately get out of these devices.

Get to know those four keys along the Bottom of your BlackBerry

The Green Phone Key

This is the easiest way to make your first few phone calls – it works just like other "Dumb" phone green keys – but you have more options.
Depending on your wireless carrier, pressing this button give you the dial pad and three buttons at the top – the Call log button shows you all your incoming and outgoing calls stored in the Phone's memory and there is a button that can open your Contacts.

The MENU key (BlackBerry Button)

That key with the BlackBerry logo is really the doorway to all the possibilities of your device. In every application, pushing that button brings up a menu with all your possibilities. From the basic "Homescreen," pushing that button brings up all the other icons.

TIP: Tapping in the middle of the Homescreen will show you all your icons.

From a Contact – pushing the MENU key allows you to call, email, SMS or communicate in other ways with that particular contact. Just try pushing it in every program you open to see the myriad of possibilities.

TIP:

Hold the MENU key for two seconds and you will see all your open programs in a little bar across the screen. Now, you can just find the program you want to "Jump" to and press and click on it to "Switch" the application.

Check out the Multi-Tasking section on page 255.

The Escape (or Back) Key

This key does just what its name suggests – it goes back to where you were before. It also prompts you to "Save," "Delete" or "Discard" things you might be working on. If you do something wrong, or find yourself wanting to get back to where you were just a second ago – just press this key.

The Red Phone Key

This is your "End" key with which you are no doubt familiar with from your old phone. You can "End" your calls, ignore calls and do other familiar actions with the Red Phone key.

You can also "**Multi-Task**" using the **Red Phone key. Just press it (when not on a call)** and you jump right to the Homescreen.

Say you are writing an email and needed to check the calendar or wanted to schedule a new event.

1. Press the Red Phone key to jump to the Homescreen.
2. Start the calendar to check your schedule.
3. Press the Red Phone key again to return to the Homescreen.
4. Press and click on the Messages icon to return exactly to where you left off composing your email message.

How cool is this phone?

NOTE: The following is reprinted from www.CrackBerry.com from Gary Mazo's series entitled "BlackBerrius Maximus."

"BlackBerrius Maximus – Storm Edition"

I'm getting too old for this! I can recall times in my life where I "camped out" to be part of something important or just something cool. In college, I drove from Boston down to New York to camp out in Central Park to see Simon and

Garfunkel's big reunion concert and then again for a No Nukes concert with Springsteen and the gang. That was a long time ago. I did go to CompUSA when Windows 95 came out – at midnight – for the big launch. In later years, I took my kids to the midnight launch of the Harry Potter books – but this was different.

I live in New England. It is almost December. I am 45 years old. Nevertheless, there I was on a very cold November morning, standing in the freezing cold at the closest Verizon store – in Hyannis, MA at 7:30 AM. Now, I had done my homework the day before; I read on line that supplies would be short and that this local store would have only 35 BlackBerry Storms (or so I was told.)

I was not so surprised to see the line out the door. What did surprise me was that the other folks in line said there were only 20 devices at this store. Now, understand that this is the flag ship store for all of Cape Cod, MA – 20 units? They handed out green sheets of paper with numbers on it – I got number #19. There was a whole parking lot of people walking towards the store and only one unit left – at least to take home *that* day.

So, I waited, happy that I was getting a Storm – but freezing. Then it dawned on me what I was doing. I was waiting outside a Verizon store for a new BlackBerry!

There was a growing camaraderie out there in the cold. Grown men and women marveled that they were up early and out in the cold in the worst economic downturn in recent history – all ready to drop at least $250 + on a relatively untested new technology – the first BlackBerry touch screen. Most people there had Treos or Motorola Q's or other "lesser" Smartphones in their hands. I must say, there was not an iPhone user in the bunch! There were a few BlackBerry users looking for the upgrade – each one rationalizing how spending this kind of dough was justified.

The doors opened and the party began. I mean it was a party…a zoo. The store was flooded with Verizon employees – each with a smile. Brian, the "data guy" was walking around showing people in line the Storm.."Wanna try it?" he said, giving everyone a chance to salivate and pass the time. We all started talking BlackBerry – people had tons of questions. New BlackBerry users wanted to know everything – seasoned BlackBerry veterans wanted to make sure they could still do all their familiar BlackBerry things.

We all signed in – very orderly and calm. The Verizon folks came with coffee and donuts and walked around. The screen told you your place in line and I watched and waited. Then it happened….the "CrackBerry moment" I had been waiting for.

I was "Talking Berry" with Brian and dropped a card letting him know I was in the BlackBerry biz, showing him our training stuff and he was very interested. Then I met Susan, the District Manager. We talked BlackBerry and I had a similar conversation with her. I mentioned that I write for CrackBerry.com and her face lit up. "Wait," she said…."you are writing the book with Kevin. The BlackBerry Addiction book." "Oh, my God – I know you. I can't wait for that book." Then she stared deep into my eyes for a moment – it was an "aha" moment – an epiphany of sorts…"that means…." She continued…"You…..You are…BlackBerrius Maximus." BINGO! I had hit pay dirt – she knew me, she knew us – the CrackBerry faithful. I was almost famous and it was clear the reach of CrackBerry.com was huge.

I talked with Susan for at least half an hour – we talked shop – all BlackBerry – all fun. I watched her and I watched the other Verizon employees. They had done their homework – they were answering questions well and they were having fun at this early hour getting people set up on their new BlackBerry Storm Smartphones. Even when they ran out, they handled it well – they took names, numbers and addresses and talked about shipping them overnight, etc. There were no riots – even the people who couldn't get their Storms lingered, wished those of us who "got lucky" that day congratulations and looked at our devices.

I saw a bunch of tired, stressed out grownups acting a lot like a child who receives their first new bike. There were lots of smiles and lots of people literally running to their cars to get home and set up their new BlackBerry. I think there will be lots of new CrackBerry.com nation members as well.

I was prepared to be disappointed, frustrated and feeling like a jerk for standing in line in the cold – but the opposite happened. I was incredibly impressed with Susan and her crew from Verizon and it has been quite some time since I felt like I had the absolute newest and coolest device in my possession. This device is so slick, so sexy and so new and cool it might even need its own name. I'm thinking of calling mine "Angelina," but I'm not sure my wife will like that so much. What are you naming yours?

So, how do I like it? Is it everything it is hyped up to be? I can do pretty much everything I would hope to be able to do on this device. I can take great pictures with the 3.2 MP camera. I can stream Stereo Bluetooth in the car; I can play games that are tailored for the accelerometer in the Storm. I can browse the web with a "real" web browser, I can respond to all my mail and messages – all while "clicking" the screen. This is the coolest BlackBerry yet!

Unique Features on the BlackBerry Storm

Your BlackBerry has many shared features with the BlackBerry family and some unique features as well.

Key Features

- Unique Touch Screen Design
- SurePress™ Keyboard
- Camera (3.2 mega pixel) with Flash and Auto Focus
- Media Player (Pictures, Video and Audio)
- Video Recording
- 3G Capable

Touch Screen and SurePress ®

Having a Touch Screen is nothing new these days. What separates the Storm from the rest is that Research in Motion has made a touch screen that supports different types of gestures and touches. The screen also "Press and clicks" when pressed giving the user tactile feedback previously impossible in a touch screen device.

Social Networking Built-In

Use your Storm for accessing your Facebook ® page, YouTube ®, Flikr® and virtually every IM program. Keep in touch with everyone in the ways you like most.

SurePress™ Keyboard

A new design that allows you to "Press" or "Press and click" the keyboard when selecting anything from a "link" in your browser to the correct letter when typing – simply amazing!

Media Card – Expansion Memory Card

Your Storm comes bundled with an 8 GB Micro SD card which allows you to story thousands of pictures or music tracks or videos or a combination of all three.

Chapter 1:
Setup Wizard & Email Setup

IMPORTANT! Before You Read Any Further!

Before you even use the Setup Wizard or anything else, please take a few minutes to check out our "Quick Reference Guide" pages, if you have not already done so, earlier in this book. They are meant to help you find lots of useful things in this book as well as some great beginner and advanced time-saving tips and tricks to get up and running quickly.

Easy Cross Reference - Icons and What they Do – Page 13

Learn the screen, buttons and more - Page 18

Learn the touch screen 'gestures' – page 20

Learn about all three keyboards for typing - page 28

Understand when Email and Web work - page 19

How to Select, Copy & Paste Text – page 33

The Setup Wizard

When you first turn on your BlackBerry, you will likely be presented with the Setup Wizard. If you "Ignored" or "Closed" it, you can get back to it by locating and press and clicking on the Setup Wizard Icon. You may need to

press and click on the Setup Folder in order to find the Setup

Wizard Icon: ![Setup Wizard]

You will be presented with screens similar to the ones below. Go ahead and follow the steps suggested, they will give you a good jump start on getting your BlackBerry setup and learning some of the basics.

Just press and click on any field, like date, time or time zone to make an adjustment and then scroll down to press and click on "Next"

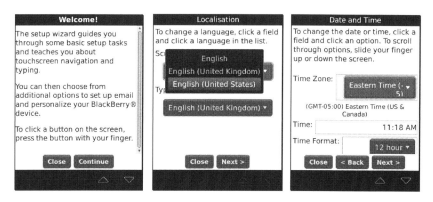

Now, you will see a couple of screens covering the basics of "Navigation" (See page 19)

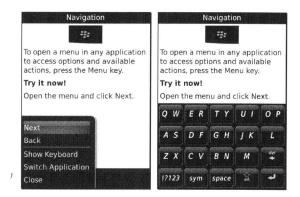

And about SureType® Multi-tap and full keyboard typing. (See page 102 for Typing tips)

Finally, you will see a screen similar to this one to the right. (You may see a few different items listed.)

Email setup – continue reading below

Set up Bluetooth® – see page 327

Import SIM Card Contacts – page 207

Font – see page 128

Help – see page 116

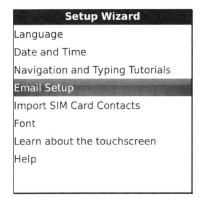

Email Setup

Your BlackBerry is designed to retrieve your email from up to 10 different email accounts and, if you are connected to a BlackBerry Enterprise Server, one corporate email account. When your BlackBerry receives your email, all your messages will be displayed in your Messages inbox.

You can setup your basic email right from your BlackBerry – even your automated email signature "Sent from my (carrier name) BlackBerry", you can also login to your carrier's website to this as well. See page 51.

If you want to setup your BlackBerry to work with email coming from a BlackBerry Enterprise Server, skip to page 58.

Personal or Internet Email Setup

You can setup your Personal or Internet Email from at least two places:

The Setup Wizard and the Email Settings Icon.

From the Setup Wizard Icon, select the Email Setup screen. Accept all user agreements. To continue, press and Click "**I Agree**."

THE BLACKBERRY INTERNET SERVICE END USER AGREEMENT IS SET OUT BELOW. IF YOU ARE UNABLE TO READ THE ENTIRE AGREEMENT ON YOUR BLACKBERRY WIRELESS HANDHELD

I Disagree   I Agree

Now you will be taken to the Email Setup website, as if you had just pressed and clicked directly on this icon:

Choose **"Add"** to setup your BlackBerry to send and receive email from an existing email account you already own. (Usually you will choose "**Add**")

Choose **"Create"** to create a brand new "BlackBerry only" email account that is tied to this BlackBerry. (Press and Click the button.)

Email Accounts
An email address does not currently exist for your BlackBerry device.

Add an existing email account
(e.g. Yahoo!®, Gmail®)

Add

Create a BlackBerry email account
(username@vzw.blackberry.net)

Create

Close

If you chose "Add" then you may be presented with a screen similar to this one. Select your type of email account or choose "Other" if you don't see your account type listed.

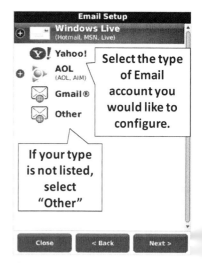

Email Setup
Windows Live
(Hotmail, MSN, Live)

Yahoo!
AOL
(AOL, AIM)
Gmail®
Other

Select the type of Email account you would like to configure.

If your type is not listed, select "Other"

Close   < Back   Next >

Press and click on "**Add**" (you will see any existing email accounts you have already setup to go to your BlackBerry)

Now type your Email account name (using your full email address like name@gmail.com) and Password, then press and click "**Next**" to attempt the login.

If everything is correct, then you will see a screen similar to this one:

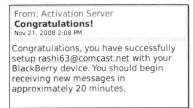

From: Activation Server
Congratulations!
Nov 21, 2008 2:08 PM

Congratulations, you have successfully setup rashi63@comcast.net with your BlackBerry device. You should begin receiving new messages in approximately 20 minutes.

TIP: Press and click on "Show Password" if you are having trouble typing your password correctly.

Having trouble entering your email address or password?

Turn the BlackBerry 90 degrees to **landscape mode** to get a full keyboard to more accurately and easily type your email address and password.

Once each email account is setup correctly, you will see an "Activation" email message in your Messages inbox and within 15-20 minutes, email should start flowing in to your BlackBerry.

Trouble with Email Setup?

Sometimes email will not get setup right away. This could be as simple as a wrong character in your email address or password. Always try retyping them a few times before doing anything else. One other common problem is that your Email server is not setup for POP3 access, or you need to go into the "Advanced Settings" to enter some specific information. Please contact your email provider and verify that you can use your email to "integrate to a BlackBerry using POP3 service". The technical support personnel at your email provider should be able to help you. Or you can contact your wireless carrier technical support.

Manually Setting up Advanced Mail Settings

During the email setup process you may receive an error message telling you that the account could not be configured.

You can either re-enter your email address & password or select to "Provide the settings." If you know the email server settings, then you can choose this option to fine-tune email setup.

We will choose this manual configuration option and click next.

Then you need to choose whether this is a work or personal email account.

After choosing "**Personal Email**," you will see this screen:

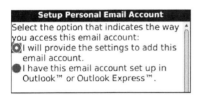

In order to configure your email settings, you must select the top option "I will provide the settings…".

NOTE: The other option ("Outlook™ or Outlook Express™") will either not allow you to enter your settings or bring you to the same "Provide the settings Screen" shown below.

Choosing "**Work Email**" will give you this screen:

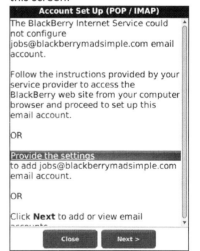

Then, if you know the settings (email server, email name, etc.) tap the "Provide the Settings" link in the middle of the screen to get to the

To the right is the same "Provide the Settings" screen that you will get to from either the Personal or Work options above.

Enter your email address, user name, password and email server information. You should contact your email provider if you need help with any of these items.

Finally, click "Next" to complete your setup. Check your settings if the BlackBerry cannot complete setup. Otherwise, you will receive a 'Successfully Configured' email account message and start receiving email within 15-20 minutes.

"Provide the Settings" screen below. Otherwise, click "Next" to get back to your list of email accounts.

TIP: If you are not sure of your email settings, open up your computer mail client (e.g. Outlook on your computer) and go to your "Accounts" menu and highlight the account you are trying to set up on the BlackBerry. Or, if you use just internet based email, then contact your service provider and explain you are trying to setup your BlackBerry to receive email.

If you are still having trouble with email setup, then please contact your email service provider and possibly your BlackBerry wireless carrier (Phone Company) technical support.

What to do with an *"Invalid Account. Please Validate"* message?

From time to time, you may see either on your BlackBerry Email Setup icon or when you login to your wireless carrier's web site an invalid email account such as shown below. This may happen if you have changed your email account password, or sometimes it just happens if the system encounters an unforeseen error – through no fault of your own!

Correcting this Invalid Account on the web using your Computer:

Login to your BlackBerry Wireless Carrier's web client (see page 52 for list of sites).

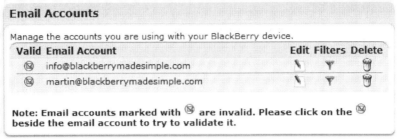

To Validate your Email Account:

Edit

Simply click on the "EDIT" icon ↖️, enter your information, including your password and "SAVE" your changes. Then you will see a message that says "Your email account has been successfully validated." The invalid account icon will change to a check mark in the "VALID" column as shown:

Email Accounts

Manage the accounts you are using with your BlackBerry device.

Valid Email Account	Edit	Filters	Delete
✔ info@blackberrymadesimple.com	↖️	▼	🗑

Correcting this Invalid Account on the web using your BlackBerry:

Login to your Email Setup icon (usually in the Settings folder).

After logging in, you will see a screen similar to this one.

To correct the "Invalid Account" errors, simply press and click on an email address to get to the Validation screen where you can enter your email account password.

Now, just re-type your password and click OK to Validate the account.

After clicking the "OK" button, you will see a message similar to this:

"Your password has been successfully validated."

Just repeat the process for any other accounts shown as invalid.

More Email Adresses to Add to Your BlackBerry?

Just repeat the process by selecting the "**Add**" button as shown above for up to 10 email addresses.

Need to Edit an Email Address (e.g. Password changed)

Just go back into the Email Setup screens and "Email Accounts" as shown above. You will see a list of email addresses that have been setup. Press and click on "Edit" or "Delete" under the account you want to change or remove.

Need to change the "Sent from (carrier) Wireless" Email Signature?

When you are in the "Edit Email Account" screens as above, you can also change your 'default' email signature directly from your BlackBerry. The box for the email signature is under the other boxes in the Edit Email Account screen.

NOTE: This is the first time you can edit your Email Signature right from your BlackBerry.

TIP!

Press the **SPACE** key to get the "@" and "." Whenever typing any email address: sara@company.com. Type: sara **SPACE** company **SPACE** com

---

You can also change the signature by logging into the carrier's BlackBerry website. Read the sections below showing how to get this done from your wireless carrier's web site.

Setup or Fine-Tune Email Accounts from Your Computer

Your personal email accounts can also be setup from your computer using your wireless carrier's web site. You also might notice that when you send an email from the BlackBerry, the signature is something very basic like "Sent from my Verizon Wireless BlackBerry" or something similar depending on your carrier. You can easily change your email signature from the Carrier Web Site.

Setting up or changing email account settings on the web

Find your way to your carrier's web site in Internet Explorer, Firefox or Opera. Once there, login to your personal account page.

Partial List of Wireless Carrier BlackBerry Email Web Sites

NOTE: These websites change frequently! Some carriers 'imbed' or include the BlackBerry Email setup pages within the main carrier website. Please check with your wireless carrier if the link below is incorrect, or you don't see your carrier listed. You may also want to check for updated sites at the bottom of this web page:
http://na.blackberry.com/eng/support/software/internet.jsp

Alltel (USA) - http://www.alltel.blackberry.com
AT&T/Cingular (USA) - http://www.att.blackberry.com/
Bell Mobility (Canada) - https://bis.na.blackberry.com/html?brand=bell
Cellular South (USA) - https://bis.na.blackberry.com/html?brand=csouth1
Rogers Wireless (Canada) - https://bis.na.blackberry.com/html?brand=rogers
Sprint/Nextel (USA)- https://bis.na.blackberry.com/html?brand=sprint
T-Mobile (USA) - http://www.t-mobile.com/bis/
T-Mobile (Germany) - http://www.instantemail.t-mobile.de/
Verizon Wireless (USA)- https://bis.na.blackberry.com/html?brand=vzw
Vodafone (UK)- https://bis.eu.blackberry.com/html?brand=vodauk
        or http://www.mobileemail.vodafone.net/

NOTE: Below we use Verizon Wireless (USA) as an example. If your carrier is different, then the layout of the web site screens will be different, but some of the names like "Setup BlackBerry Email" and other key links or steps should be similar.

Choose the tab that says something like "Phone & Accessories", "Device", "Handheld" or "Support" from your home page.

If you use Verizon, go to the Verizon Wireless (USA) web page - https://bis.na.blackberry.com/html?brand=vzw. Click "Create New Account." If your account was already set up when you activated your phone, just login with your user name and password.

If you are creating a new account, you will see a screen like the one below – just accept the agreement by clicking on "I agree."

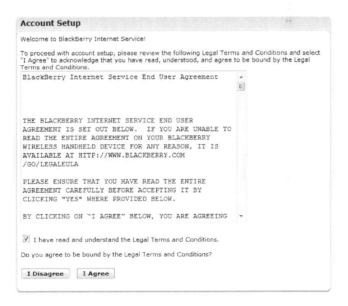

You should now see a screen similar to the one below.

Account Setup

To begin creating your BlackBerry Service account, type your device details below.

Device PIN:

Device ESN/MEID:

[Cancel] [**Continue**]

To find your PIN perform one of the following actions:
- In the BlackBerry device options or settings, click **Status**.
- Look for the PIN and ESN/MEID information on the outside of the box that your BlackBerry device or BlackBerry-enabled device came in.
- Turn the BlackBerry device off and remove the battery. Look for the sticker on the BlackBerry device with the PIN information where the battery is usually located.

Both of the numbers you need are located in your "Options" menu on your BlackBerry. From your Homescreen, press the MENU key to show all your icons and scroll through until you find your "Options" icon – it usually looks like a wrench.

Click on the Options menu and scroll down to "Status." Once there, press and click on "Status" and pay attention to the lines marked **PIN** and **MEID (dec)**.

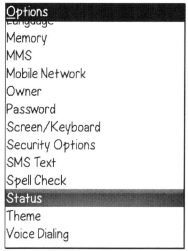

Options
Language
Memory
MMS
Mobile Network
Owner
Password
Screen/Keyboard
Security Options
SMS Text
Spell Check
Status
Theme
Voice Dialing

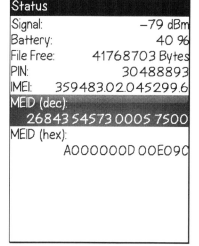

Status
Signal: −79 dBm
Battery: 40 %
File Free: 41768703 Bytes
PIN: 30488893
IMEI: 359483.02.045299.6
MEID (dec):
    26843 54573 0005 7500
MEID (hex):
        A0000000D 00E09C

Type in the PIN and MEID (dec) into the web site screen – but remove any spaces or dots. You should then come to screens that look like those below.

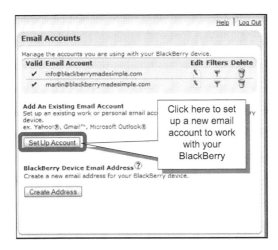

After press and clicking the "Setup Account" button, you will need to input your email address and password on the screen below.

After the email account is successfully set up, you will then receive confirmation email on your BlackBerry usually titled **"Activation."**

Shortly thereafter, your first email will come in on the BlackBerry Repeat this process for each of your email accounts

Once you have all your email accounts configured you will see them listed as shown below. You can then customize ("EDIT"), filter email ("FILTER") or remove them ("DELETE") by selecting the icons on the right side.

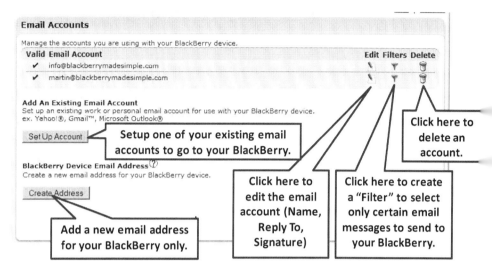

Changing Your Email Auto Signature "Sent from (carrier) name"

TIP: You can also change this Auto Email Signature right on your BlackBerry by going to your Email Setup icon – see page188

On your email accounts page you should see an icon for editing each of your accounts that you have set up. You can then add a unique signature – for every email account that you have set up.

Select the "Edit" icon next to the email account you wish to work with
Make any changes in the fields provided to you
In the signature box, simply type in the new signature you wish to appear at the bottom of that particular email account

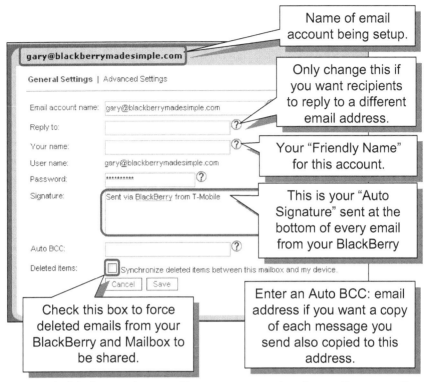

Name of email account being setup.

Only change this if you want recipients to reply to a different email address.

Your "Friendly Name" for this account.

This is your "Auto Signature" sent at the bottom of every email from your BlackBerry

Enter an Auto BCC: email address if you want a copy of each message you send also copied to this address.

Check this box to force deleted emails from your BlackBerry and Mailbox to be shared.

Press and click the save button. Test your new settings by sending an email from your Blackberry to yourself or another email account and verify that the new signature is included.

You can also add a signatures that can be selected "on the fly" from your BlackBerry while typing emails using the "AutoText" feature See page 116.

Advanced Settings Screen: Press and clicking on the "Advanced Settings" link at the top of the email EDIT screen will show you a screen similar to the one below. This will allow you to configure settings like your specific email server, the port number, and whether or not SSL (Secure Socket Layer) encrypted connection is required.

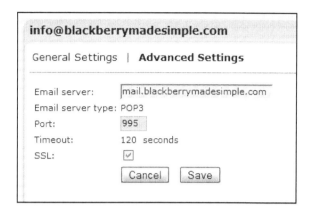

Setting Up Your Corporate Email ("Enterprise Activation")

This process is also known as "**Enterprise Activation**". If your Help Desk or Information Technology department does not do this for you, all you need is your activation password and you can set this up on your own – right from the BlackBerry.

IMPORTANT: If you have not received your "**Activation Password**", then you need to ask your Help Desk or Technology Support department for that password before you may complete this process.

Setup Corporate Email Using the Setup Wizard

Start your "Setup Wizard" icon and select "Email Setup", then choose **"I want to use a work email account with a BlackBerry Enterprise Server"** from the menu.

Verify that you have your Enterprise Activation Password.

Videos are an easy way to Learn: www.MadeSimpleLearning.c

Type in the email address along with the activation password you received from your Help Desk or System Administrator.

Press the Menu key and select **"Activate."**

Then you should see a series of messages that talk about Security, Establishing Connection, Verifying Connection, Loading Contacts, Calendar, etc.

Once completed, and this could take 5 minutes or more, you should see a confirmation screen.

The best way to test is to try to send yourself or your colleague a test email message from your newly connected BlackBerry. Make sure it arrives and you can reply to a new message you have received on your BlackBerry.

TIP: You can also get to your Enterprise Activation screen by going to your Options Icon, selecting "Advanced Options" and then selecting "Enterprise Activation" from the list.

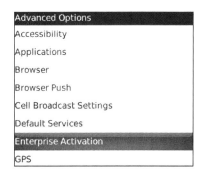

Chapter 2:
Windows™ PC Setup

Have an **Apple Mac™** computer? Please go to page 85.

Unless you work at an organization that provides you access to a BlackBerry Enterprise Server, if you are a Windows™ computer user, you will need to use BlackBerry® Desktop Manager Software to do a number of things:

-   Transfer or "synchronize" your personal information (addresses, calendar, tasks, notes) between your computer and your BlackBerry
-   Backup and restore your BlackBerry data
-   Install or remove application icons
-   Transfer or sync your media to your BlackBerry (songs, videos & pictures)

Do you use both a Windows and Mac computer?
WARNING – DO NOT SYNC YOUR BLACKBERRY WITH BOTH A WINDOWS COMPUTER AND AN APPLE MAC COMPUTER AT THE SAME TIME – YOU COULD END UP CORRUPTING YOUR BLACKBERRY AND/OR COMPUTER DATABASES! ASK GARY, HE LEARNED THE HARD WAY!

Download and Install of Desktop Manager & Free Videos!

Each new version of RIM's Desktop Manager Program has come with more functionality and more versatility than the previous versions. So, it is always a good idea to keep up-to-date with the latest version of the Desktop Manager software.

TIP: Go to the Free Videos > "Desktop Manager" section of www.MadeSimpleLearning.com
To watch videos showing exactly how to download, install and configure Desktop Manager for free!
(You may be redirected to our former web site www.BlackBerryMadeSimple.com, but it has all the same videos!)

The Disk from the BlackBerry Box

It is fairly likely that the disk that arrived with your brand new BlackBerry has a version of Desktop Manager that is already out-of-date. This is because many times, they produced the CDs months ago, and in the mean time a new version has been released. So we recommend grabbing the latest version from the Internet directly from www.blackberry.com.

Check Your Current Version

If you have already installed Desktop Manager, you should check which version you currently have. The easiest was to do that is start up your Desktop Manager program, go to "Help" and then to "About Desktop Manager." You will see right here that the version number of your particular version is shown. If you don't have version 4.7 or higher – it is time to upgrade.

To get the latest version of Desktop Manager:

Do a web search for "**BlackBerry Desktop Software download**" and pick the search results entry that goes to something like:
https://www.blackberry.com/Downloads/entry.do

This should bring you to the BlackBerry web site. Now, from the drop down list, select "BlackBerry Desktop Software v. (highest number shown)" and press and click "Next"

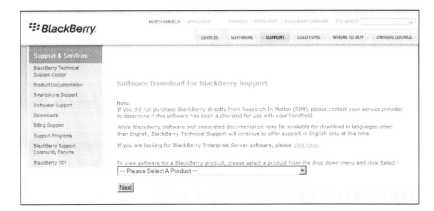

On the next page you will see several versions of the software to download – depending on your language and whether you want the Media Manager component or not.

We would suggest you scroll down until you see BlackBerry Desktop Manager (your language) - With Media Manager - press and click on the **Download** Software link.

Then you'll need to enter your personal information and agree to several legal terms and conditions, then you will be presented with the downloads page that looks something like this – press and click the "Download" and save the file to a place where you will remember it. Now, this is a large file so it may take some time to download.

Overview of BlackBerry Desktop Manager

One of the great things about your BlackBerry is the amount of information, entertainment and fun that you can carry in your pocket at all times. But, what would happen if you lost your BlackBerry or lost some of your information? How would you get it back? What if you wanted to put music from your computer on your BlackBerry? Fortunately, your BlackBerry comes with a program called BlackBerry Desktop Manager which can back up, synchronize, add media and load new applications on your BlackBerry.
To get started, go ahead and press and click on the Desktop Manager icon on our computer – or go to Programs -> Blackberry -> Desktop Manager and press and click.

Make sure your BlackBerry is plugged into the USB cable provided and attached to the computer.

NOTE: Version 4.7 is shown, your version may be higher.

You see the icons here in Desktop Manager – let's take a look at the first row:

The **Application Loader** for installing or removing BlackBerry icons and upgrading your BlackBerry System Software version. (TIP: You can also install new software icons wirelessly right on your BlackBerry, check out page 349)

The **Backup and Restore** icon for making a full backup and then restoring all of it or selected databases at a later time.

The **Device Switch Wizard** is very handy if you want to move your data from an old BlackBerry to a new BlackBerry or an old non-BlackBerry handheld.

Along the second row, we see **Media Manager** for managing songs, videos, pictures and ring tones.

The **Synchronize** icon – which controls the settings for synchronizing your data – your address book, calendar, tasks, memos and more to keep you computer and your BlackBerry up to date with one another.

Synchronizing your BlackBerry Using BlackBerry Desktop Manager

You have probably come to rely on your BlackBerry more and more as you get comfortable using it. Think about how much information you have stored in there. Now ask yourself: "Is all that information safely stored in my computer?" Then ask: "Is all my blackberry information synchronized with the information in my Personal Information Management (PIM) software like Outlook or Lotus Notes?"

This is why synchronizing your BlackBerry with Desktop Manager is so important. Your data will be safe and "backed up" and all your great information will be automatically put into the correct program on your computer – making thing like your calendar, address book, tasks and more be available right where you need them.

FREE VIDEO TUTORIALS

TIP: Check out our Free Desktop Manager Videos! Everything you see in this section and much more detail is available for free at www.MadeSimpleLearning.com *(you may be redirected to www.BlackBerryMadeSimple.com, which is also our web site)* in the Free Videos > Desktop Manager section. Below is an image of one of the free videos showing you the exact step-by-step way to setup your sync. *(We also have many other BlackBerry videos available for a fee.)*

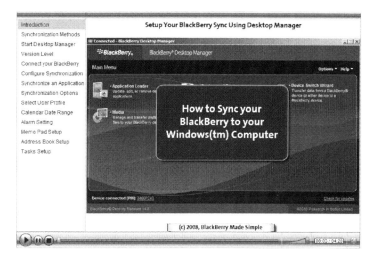

The first thing to do is to open your Desktop Manager Software as you usually do by press and clicking on the Desktop Manager Icon on your Homescreen.

Connect your BlackBerry to your computer using the USB cable and make sure you see your BlackBerry PIN number in the lower left corner instead of the word "**None**" – this shows your BlackBerry is connected

to Desktop Manager.

Then, press and click on the
"Synchronize" Icon.

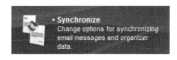

Before you "Sync" for the first time,
press and click on the
"Synchronization" link – right
under where it says **"Configure"** on
the left hand side of the screen.

Press and click on the
"Synchronization" button.

NOTE: If the **Synchronization**
button is grayed out and not-press
and clickable, please make sure
your BlackBerry is connected to
your Computer and your PIN
number is showing in the lower left
corner of Desktop Manager.

Now you will see the main "IntelliSync" Program window shown below.

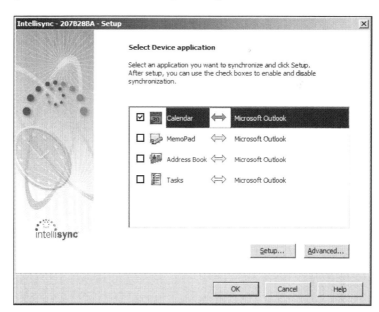

To get started, just check the box next to the Icon you want to sync or on the name of the icon and then press and click the "Setup" button at the bottom. For example, press and clicking "Calendar" and "Setup" will bring you to a few screens with details for how to sync your computer's calendar to your BlackBerry.

First you select your Desktop application and press and click **Next**.

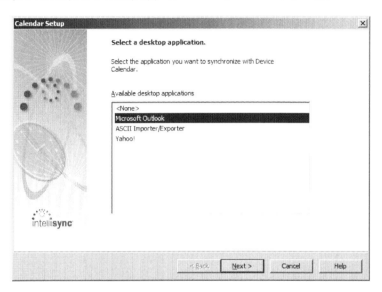

Then determine if you want a One-way or Two-way sync. The "Two way" Sync is where both the BlackBerry and the Desktop get updated (recommended) or if you want one to simply over write the other.

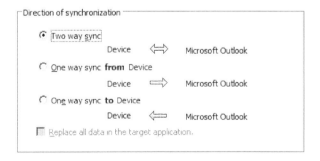

Press and click "Next" to see an advanced screen with more options. This one shows options for the Calendar. Address Book, Tasks and MemoPad may have different options. We recommend settings as shown below to help make sure you never miss out on any data you enter on your BlackBerry if you forget to sync every day. These settings will sync calendar events up to 30 days old from your BlackBerry.

Repeat the procedure for all the applications you want synced.

Once the setup is complete for two-way sync for all four applications, your screen should look similar to the one below.

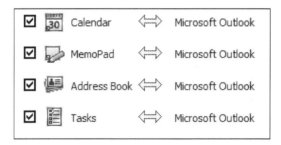

After the Configuration is set, go back to the main "**Synchronization**" screen and put a check mark in the **"Synchronize Automatically"** box if you want the Desktop Manager to Automatically Synchronize as soon as you connect your BlackBerry to your computer. Finally close out all the Sync setup windows to save your changes.

Running the Desktop Manager Sync

To start the sync manually, you need to get to the window shown below by press and clicking the "Synchronize" link in the very left-hand column. Then, press and click the "Synchronize" button in the middle of the window to start your sync.

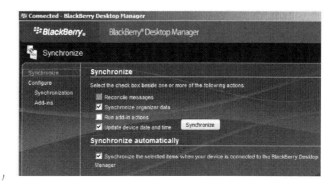

Accepting or Rejecting Sync Changes

To start the sync, close out or "During the sync If there are additions or deletions to be made in either the BlackBerry or the PC application, a dialogue box will show up giving you the option to **"Accept"** or **"Reject"** the changes.

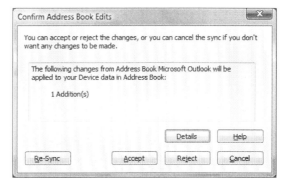

Usually, we recommend to just accept the changes and then the Synchronization process will come to an end and your data will be safely on both your BlackBerry and your computer.

Troubleshooting Your Desktop Manager Sync

Sometimes your Desktop sync will fail due to corrupt or incompatible data.

STEP 1: Try closing down Desktop Manager and re-starting it.

If this doesn't correct the problem then move on to step two or do a search of the **BlackBerry Technical Knowledge Base** (see page 71) or try Step 2.

STEP 2: Try to clear out the 'problem database' on your BlackBerry and re-sync.

Try the sync again after it fails and watch it closely, you should note where it fails – on the Calendar, Address Book, MemoPad, or Tasks – by watching the status screen.

Once you figure out where the sync fails, then you can try one thing to get it running again – clearing out or deleting the 'problem' database from your BlackBerry and starting the sync again.

WARNING: Doing this process will force you to lose any changes you have made on your BlackBerry since your last successful sync.

From the main Desktop Manager window, press and click on "Backup & Restore"
IMPORTANT: First do a "Full Backup" by press and clicking the "Back up" button.

 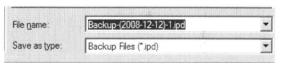

Make a note of the file name and location, you may need to use it later to restore data if this troubleshooting does not work. In the image above the backup file name is "Backup-(2008-12-12)-1.ipd"

Once your full backup is completed, press and click the "Advanced..." button.

Now, locate the 'problem' database in the right hand window and press and click the "Clear" button at the bottom. In the image below, we are getting ready to clear out the "**Address Book**" and "**Address Book – All**" from the BlackBerry.
Both are selected in the right-hand window "Device Databases", then we press and click the "**Clear**" button.

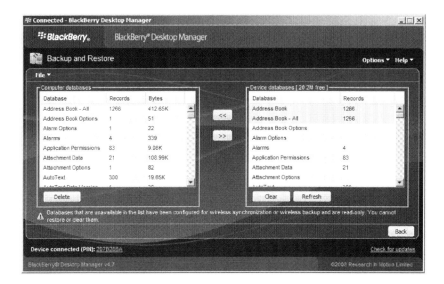

Once they have been cleared out, then press and click the "**Back**" button and then re-try the Sync. Hopefully, this will correct the sync problem.

If the problem has not been corrected, then you can restore the Address Book by going back into the **Advanced** window from **Backup & Restore.** Then you need to **"Open"** the full backup file you just created.

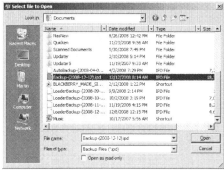

Now you can highlight the correct databases from the Full Backup in the left-hand window and press and click the button in the middle of the screen to individually restore these databases to your BlackBerry.

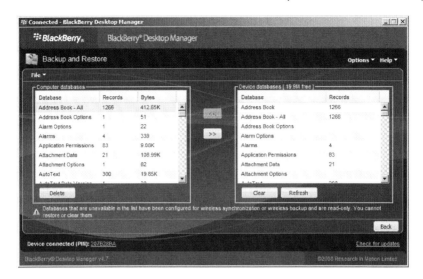

Check out the **Technical Knowledge Base** at BlackBerry.com for more help.

BlackBerry Technical Knowledge Base

Where to go for more help for Desktop Manager and anything to do with your BlackBerry: Do a web search for "BlackBerry Technical Knowledge Base" – one of the top links will usually get you to this page on www.blackberry.com. Just type your question in as few words as possible in the "Search" box in the middle of the screen.

Transferring Music, Pictures & Documents using Desktop Manager

There are at least two ways to load up media (music, videos, pictures) onto your BlackBerry using Desktop Manager:

- Media Manager

-    BlackBerry Media Sync

More options are popping up all the time and will vary depending on who supplied your BlackBerry. (E.g. Verizon's Rhapsody MediaSync)

Use Media Manager When:
1.   You have a non-iTunes media library on your PC
2.   You need to "convert" your music and video for optimum playback on the BlackBerry

Use Media Sync When:
1.   You have iTunes playlists on your PC.
2.   You have non-DRM protected (see page music in your playlists.)

NOTE: If a song is in iTunes and DRM protected, then it is NOT possible to sync it to your BlackBerry.

Your new BlackBerry is not only your personal organizer, address book and memo pad – it is also quite a full-function media player. You can listen to music, watch videos and look at your pictures – all on your BlackBerry handheld.

Having all that functionality is great, but first – you have to get your media onto the BlackBerry. That's where the Media Manager and the Media Sync features in are useful in Desktop Manager.

Before we begin, we strongly recommend that you install a Micro SD memory card into your BlackBerry Handheld. With the price of memory coming way down, you can get a 1 GB, 2 GB or even 4GB Micro SD card for not a lot of money. Obviously, the bigger the card - the more media files you can store on your device. (See page 286 to learn how to add a Media Card)

Using the Media Manager

Remember, you should use BlackBerry Media Sync instead of Media Manager if you want to sync iTunes playlists – see page 77. Go ahead and start your BlackBerry Desktop Manager and plug in your BlackBerry Device with the USB Cable. Press and click on the "**Media**" icon.

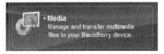

Videos are an easy way to Learn: www.MadeSimpleLearning.c

The first thing you will see is the Media Manager start screen, with the Media Manager on the left and the BlackBerry Media Sync Icon on the right. Look on Page 77 for information on the Media Sync Program.

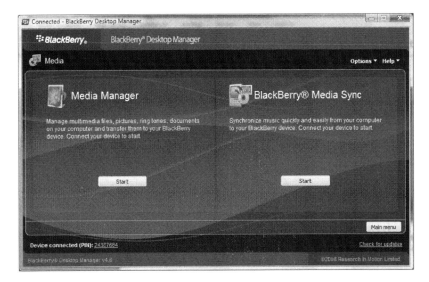

Press and click on the **Media Manager Icon**. The first thing you will have to do is accept the license agreement.

Then once the program loads, you will see icons for your Pictures, Music and Videos. Over here on the right you will see that it says "Devices" and then, if you have a Media Card installed, there will be two lines that start with your BlackBerry Pin – one then says "Media Card" and the other says "Device Memory."

Now, when you start Media Manager for the first time, you can ask it to scan your computer for all music, video and picture files that could be used on your BlackBerry device. This takes a while to do, but it is worthwhile if you have lots of pictures, music and videos scattered over your computer.

After you do this, you can see that the **Media Manager** tells you exactly how many of each kind of file it contains. Under the icon for each type of media you can press and click on **"Manage Media"** to rename, regroup or organize your Media.

What we want to do now is learn how to transfer media, so go ahead and press and click under the **My Devices icon**, in the bottom half of the screen, the line that ends with **"Media Card."** This is your BlackBerry.

This will show us the media files that are on your media card. When you do this, you will see that the Media Manager shows two screens – the top one shows the Media that is on your computer and the bottom one shows what is on your BlackBerry and media card.

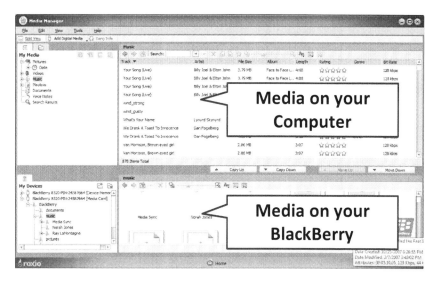

Take a look at the very bottom left corner under where it says **"My Devices."** You should see that your Media Card is highlighted and that there is a little plus sign here which will expand the directory.

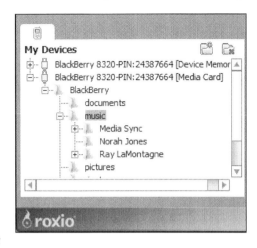

Press and click on the plus sign and then on the plus sign next to the word "**BlackBerry**." You will now see that on your media card, there is a directory tree with folders for Music, pictures, ringtones and videos.

Since we are trying to transfer music, let's go ahead and press and click on the music folder. Now, the music on my BlackBerry is on the bottom screen and the music on my computer is on the top screen.

Transferring music is as easy as highlighting the song you want to copy on the top screen – the song that is on your computer – and then selecting the

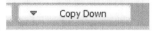

"Copy Down" button in the middle of the screen.

You can search your music on your computer by Genre, artist or album to help you find the song you want to copy.

When you select the song you want to copy, a small window opens asking you if you want the Media Manager program to copy the song and convert it for optimal playback on the BlackBerry – you can select either copy with conversion, without conversion or look at advanced conversion options.

We generally recommend letting the media manager convert your media for optimal playback on your BlackBerry. (Although this may not work with videos, which are much more challenging to convert for your BlackBerry than music.)

Go ahead and select **"OK"** and the song will now be copied onto your Media card. You can check this after the copying is done by looking on the lower window and seeing the song right here on your media card.

You can use the same procedure for copying Pictures. The only difference would be in the media manager screen – in the top window under **"My Media"** just select **"Pictures"** and your pictures will be displayed in the top window. Make sure that down below, you collapse the Music menu and open up your "Pictures" folder on your media card to ensure that your files will be copied to that directory.

Just select your pictures (if you want more than one – just hold down the CTRL key on your keyboard and then press and click each picture you want – they will all highlight. Then, just select **"Copy Down"** and let them be "converted" and they will go right on your media card.

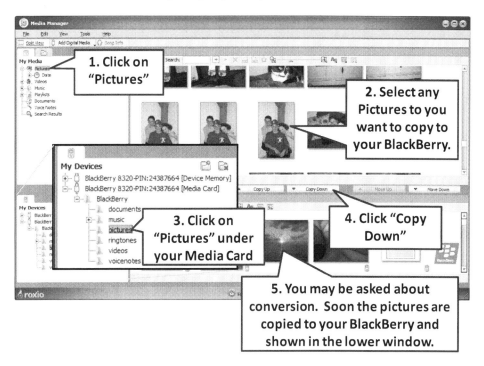

And there you go – your media files are now right on your BlackBerry for you to enjoy as often as you like.

BlackBerry Media Sync

Remember, you should use the BlackBerry Media Manager instead of the Media Sync if you want to sync non-iTunes media and you need to "convert" music and video to be viewable on your BlackBerry – see page 72. Perhaps the easiest way to get music into playlists is using the new BlackBerry Media Sync program. If you are an iTunes user and you have playlists already in your iTunes program, the Media Sync program allows you to transfer those playlists directly to your BlackBerry.

NOTE: If a song is in iTunes and DRM protected (What's this? See page 100), then it is NOT possible to sync it to your BlackBerry.

Start up Desktop manager and press and click on "Media"

On the next screen – press and click "Start" under the Media Sync Logo

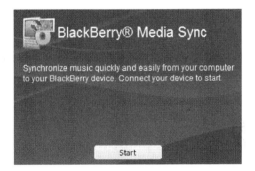

If you just downloaded the Stand alone Media Sync add-on:

One you have the file downloaded, just run the installation program. A window will appear letting you know the application has been installed properly.

To launch the application, just go to Start-> Programs-> BlackBerry MediaSync and press and click on the icon. Make sure that your BlackBerry is connected via the USB cable to your computer – but **don't** have desktop manager running when you do this.

Setting Up Your Media Sync

The Media Sync window will identify your BlackBerry, show your PIN number and then analyze the free space for media on your device and Media Card.

You can see that I don't have any playlists showing yet, since this is my first time running the Media Sync Application.

Press and click on the Options in the upper right

corner to see some of the ways of configuring the Media Sync program

If you want to give your Device a new name – just type a new name next to **"Name your device:"**

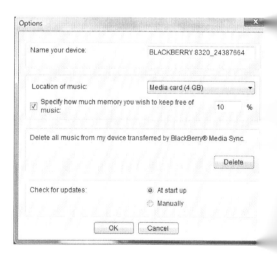

Press and click on the **"Location of Music"** dropdown menu and select where your media will go. Generally, if you have a

media card installed that will be the default location for your music.

You can also specify just how much free memory you want to keep on your media card and specify a percentage right here. If you want to start over and delete your transferred music – just press and click on the Delete button. Close this menu.

Press and click on the "**Show iTunes Playlists**" button at the bottom of the screen – and all of your iTunes playlists will be listed in the menu.

When they are shown, the button changes to "Hide iTunes playlists" as shown.

Syncing your Music

Syncing iTunes playlists is as easy as putting a check mark next to each playlist you want to transfer to the BlackBerry.

We have checked the playlists that we want to use for our bike rides and "classic rock" music.

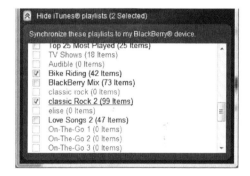

Now, just choose the "Sync" button and press and click and the selected iTunes playlists will be transferred to the BlackBerry and placed in my Media file.

As the Sync progresses, a window shows the progress of the music transfer and will look just like this:

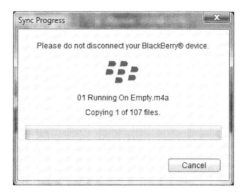

Once the Sync is done, close out the Media Sync window.   Now jump to page 293 to learn how to use Music on your BlackBerry.

Why are some songs not transferred?   DRM Protected

See page 100 explaining "DRM (Digital Rights Management)" for why some music and videos purchased through iTunes cannot be transferred.

Using Windows Media Player to Sync Music

Another option that works to sync music to your BlackBerry is to use the Windows™ Media Player that is included. The screen shots and procedure for this book were taken with Windows Vista™, however it should

NOTE: This assumes you have inserted a Media Card into your BlackBerry to store all your media (music, pictures, videos). See page 286 for help with adding a Media Card.

Start your Windows™ Media Player by press and clicking on the icon or going to your **START** > **All Programs** > **Windows Media Player**. Your Media Player may look slightly different than this picture if you have a different version.

Now, connect your BlackBerry (with the Media Card inserted) to your computer with the USB cable. If you have enabled Bluetooth, you may be able to use the Bluetooth connection, however we prefer USB since it seems more reliable.

Press and click on the SYNC menu command in the upper right corner of the Media Player. If this is the first time you connect your BlackBerry to your computer, then you will be shown a wizard.

Select the option you want. We recommend leaving the default "NO".
CAUTION: If you select "YES" – all your existing media files (music, videos, ring tones, etc.) will be ERASED from your BlackBerry!

On this screen, you can change the name of your BlackBerry device to make it easier to remember for future syncs. Then press and click "Finish" to complete the setup.

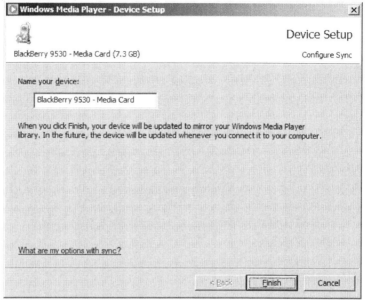

Once you have named and setup the device, you are ready to configure the Sync of your songs and playlists from Windows™ Media Player to your BlackBerry.

To get started, press and click the Sync tab in the upper right corner and make sure your correct device is selected. NOTE: You may see two devices for your BlackBerry – one for the internal (main memory) and one for the Media Card.

Typically, you will see that the Media Card will have much more free memory. To get to the correct device, press and click the "Next Device" link.
This image shows that the media card has 6.9 GB (gigabytes) remaining – plenty to store lots of songs.

Now, to put songs on your BlackBerry, just drag **songs** or **albums** from the left window into the "**Drag items here**" section in the lower right window.

To sync all songs in a "Shuffle" or random mode, then press and click the "Shuffle music" link then, the "Start Sync" button at the bottom.

If you want to sync individual playlists from your computer, then press and click the little pull-down menu below the Sync menu in the upper-right corner and select your device. Then "**Set Up Sync…**" as shown below.

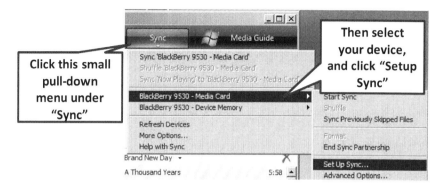

Now you will see the Device Setup screen below, check the box next to "Sync this device automatically" if that is what you want to happen every time you connect your BlackBerry. Then select from your playlists in the left window and "Add" them to the right window (the Sync window). Adjust priority of the playlists in the lower left part of the window and press and click "Finish" when done.

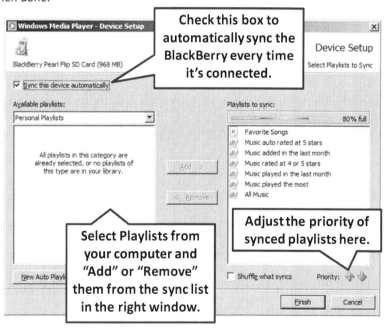

After press and clicking "Finish" you will be back in the main Media Player

window and you'll have to press and click this Start Sync button in the lower left corner to start the sync. After it's done, disconnect your BlackBerry from your computer, go into the Music icon and enjoy. See page 293 to learn all about the Music player on your BlackBerry.

Chapter 3:
Apple® Mac™ Setup

Have a **Microsoft Windows™** computer? Please go to page 60.

For Apple Macintosh Users – PocketMac for BlackBerry™ or Missing Sync for BlackBerry

IMPORTANT: BlackBerry (Research In Motion or "RIM") has decided to license the PocketMac for BlackBerry™ software and make it available for all BlackBerry users for free.

Do you use both a Windows and Mac computer?
WARNING – DO NOT SYNC YOUR BLACKBERRY WITH BOTH A WINDOWS COMPUTER AND AN APPLE MAC COMPUTER <u>AT THE SAME TIME</u> – YOU COULD END UP CORRUPTING YOUR BLACKBERRY AND/OR COMPUTER DATABASES! ASK GARY, HE LEARNED THE HARD WAY!

PocketMac® for BlackBerry® features:
(courtesy www.pocketmac.com and
www.discoverblackberry.com/discover/mac_solutions.jsp as of December 2008)
- ✓ Sync the following applications: Entourage Email, Contacts, Calendar, Tasks and Notes; Daylite; Address Book Contacts; iCal Calendar and Tasks; Lotus Notes Contacts, Calendar and Tasks; Mail.app Email; Meeting Maker Contacts Calendar and Tasks; Now Contact/Now Up-to-Date Contacts, Calendars & Tasks; Stickies Notes and iTunes Music and Movies.
- ✓ Install 3rd Party Applications from Mac to BlackBerry
- ✓ USB/Serial compatibility
- ✓ Password Support
- ✓ USB Charge while connected
- ✓ Requirements: Mac OS 10.4 or higher, 1 USB Port
- ✓ Only specific BlackBerry models are supported – please check their web site to see details
- ✓ *Check out www.pocketmac.com for the latest features and requirements.*

What follows are the steps you need to complete to first load your names, addresses, calendar, tasks and notes (and media – pictures, music and videos) and media (videos, music, pictures) from your personal computer onto your BlackBerry and keep them up-to-date or "synchronized".

Step 1: Download the PocketMac for BlackBerry™ Software
Step 2: Install the Software
Step 3: Setup the Synchronization (Contacts, Tasks, iTunes, iPhoto and more)
Step 4: Perform the Synchronization
Ongoing: How to Automate the Sync

Step 1: Download the PocketMac for BlackBerry Software

On your computer's web browser, go to
http://na.blackberry.com/eng/services/desktop/
Press and click on "BlackBerry for Mac" under "Desktop Software."
Eventually, after filling out your personal information, you will be taken to a web page where you can download the newest version of the Pocket Mac Program.

NOTE: Web site layouts and software versions and screens change frequently, so it is likely that something on the web or in the software will not look exactly like it does in this book. If not, please look for the correct link or correct words in order to continue working through the steps. If you find a mistake and have the time, please email us a correction for our next revision at info@blackberrymadesimple.com, we would greatly appreciate it!

Download the PocketMac© for BlackBerry© Program: Select the highest version of "**PocketMac for BlackBerry**" available and press and click the "**Next**" button. (it is likely that the latest version will be higher than the one shown in the screen shot below) After press and clicking "**Next**", you will see new information appear below the "**Next**" button as shown.

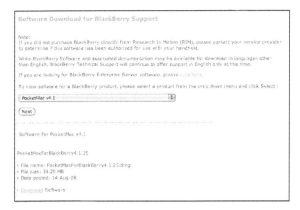

Now you will need to enter your personal information in order to download the software.

Now you will see a legal agreement, you will need to press and click "**Agree**" and "**Next**" to continue to the download page.

Now, verify you have selected the correct software and press and click the "**Download**" button to see the Download popup window below.

NOTE: A **high-speed Internet connection is recommended** because these download files can be 20 or more megabytes ("MB") and would a long time on a slow or dial-up Internet connection, but just a few minutes on a high-speed connection.

When the download is complete, you now have the latest PocketMac for BlackBerry installation file on your computer. Locate it and double-press and click on it to get started with the installation. Then follow the steps below.

NOTE: We recommend that you press and click on the "Manual" before you start the installation process and it contains a great deal of information you may find helpful in using the PocketMac program.

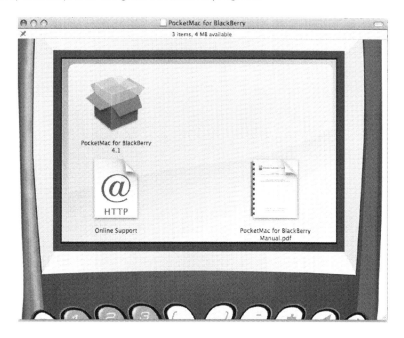

Step 2: Install PocketMac for BlackBerry® Software

After double-press and clicking on the downloaded installation file, you will follow the onscreen installation instructions.

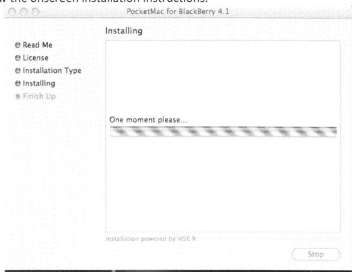

Videos are an easy way to Learn: www.MadeSimpleLearning.

NOTE: Please use the **PocketMac for BlackBerry™ manual** to help guide you through the detailed installation steps.

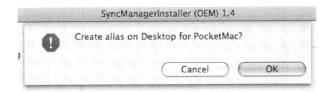

Creating an "Alias" is a good way of keeping an icon for PocketMac right on your Mac Desktop – we recommend press and clicking "OK."

After installation, you may be asked to **re-start your computer**. Please do so if asked.

Step 3: Setup the Synchronization

Now that you've finished installing the software, go ahead and start it up by double press and clicking on the PocketMac for BlackBerry™ desktop alias.

NOTE: Please use the **PocketMac for BlackBerry™ manual** to help guide you through the detailed installation steps.

Setup the synchronization by press and clicking the "**BlackBerry**" icon inside the PocketMac for BlackBerry Sync Manager to see the eleven tabs below the top gray bar like so:

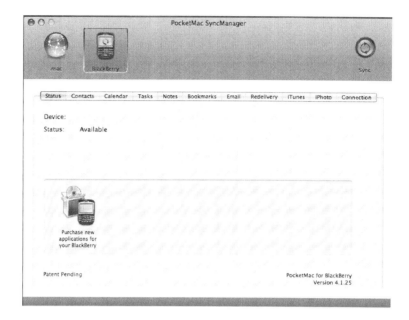

Now, you will need to select the Contacts, Calendar, Tasks, and Notes applications to synchronize to your BlackBerry by press and clicking the tabs near the top of the screen. (#1) Then select the checkbox (#2) if you want to share this application data with your BlackBerry. Select the particular Mac application (#3) that you want to configure. Finally, if you need to configure "Advanced Preferences"- press and click that button (#4).   Advanced preferences allows you to select only certain categories to sync to your BlackBerry or make it one-way synchronization (where your Mac data overwrites the BlackBerry or vice versa).

Shown below is the **"Contacts"** tab.

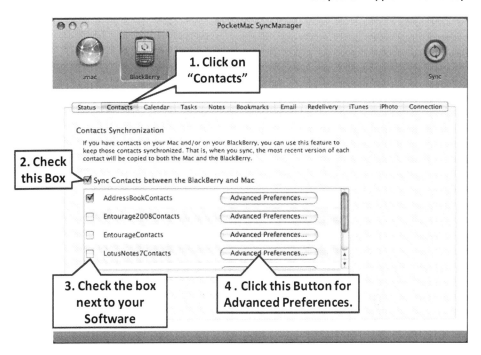

Repeat the above procedure for all the types of information: Calendar, Tasks, Notes, Bookmarks, etc.

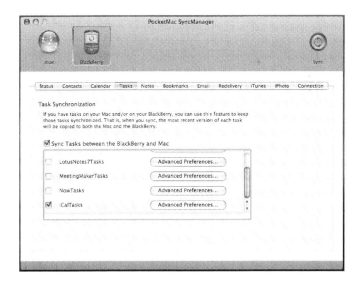

In the "**Advanced Preferences**" window, you can setup to sync all Categories, or only selected Categories (by checking the boxes next to each category listed).

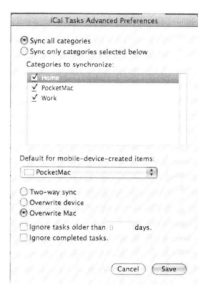

You can also decide whether to keep your BlackBerry in a "Two-way sync" (changes are synced two ways between your BlackBerry and Mac) or "One-Way" where either the BlackBerry "Device" gets overwritten (Mac is in control) or the Mac is "Overwritten" (BlackBerry is in control).

Adjust any other advanced options to meet your needs.

You may choose to also setup Redelivery – this allows all email sent to your Mac (OS X Mail or Entourage v10.1.6 or v11) to be redirected to your BlackBerry. When you reply to this mail then it looks like you are replying from your Mac.

CAUTION: Realize that using the Redelivery option will stop all email delivery as soon as you (1) turn off your Mac or (2) disconnect your Mac from the Internet.

EMAIL SETUP: An alternative option to Redelivery is to use the BlackBerry Internet Service (we highly recommend). This is available to be setup directly on your BlackBerry. Learn about how to setup Email right on your BlackBerry on page 43.)

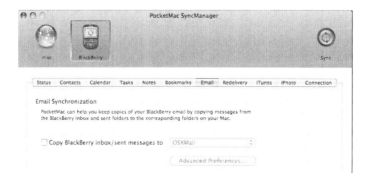

Connect your BlackBerry to your Mac. Make sure you see a status of "Connected and Ready" as shown below.

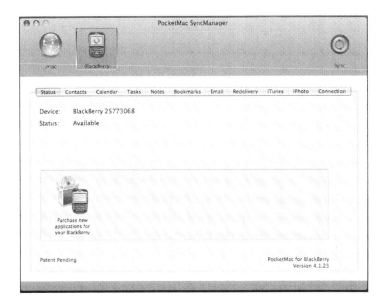

Syncing iTunes and iPhoto to your BlackBerry

One new feature in PocketMac is the ability to sync your iTunes music and movies and iPhoto pictures with your BlackBerry. Just press and click on the "iTunes" tab along the top and then place a check mark in "Music," "Movies," or any of the other categories listed. One you place the check mark, the available files are shown on the right hand pane. Just select the ones you wish to Sync with the BlackBerry.

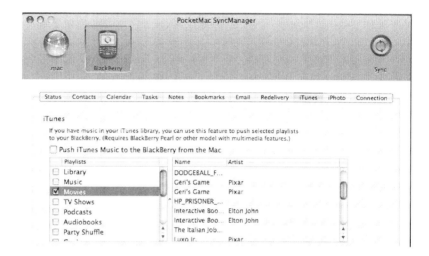

Step 4: Perform the Synchronization

Verify the following before you start your sync:

- ✓ The BlackBerry successfully connected to your Mac
- ✓ You have configured the Sync as shown in Step 3 above and followed detailed instructions from the PocketMac for BlackBerry™ User Guide.

Now, press and click the green sync button in the right side of the PocketMac for BlackBerry Sync Manager window as shown:

Depending on your preferences and whether or not this is your first sync, you will see various pop-up windows with important decisions to make.

Sample popup windows:

- Detected Deletion on Device
- Detected Deletion on Mac
- Sync Alert Message (may ask you to delete all calendars).

WARNING: How you respond to these windows will be critical to protect your data. Please see the detailed instructions about each type of pop-up window in the **PocketMac for BlackBerry™ User Guide**.

How do I know when the Sync is completed?

Unfortunately, you will not see any window saying "Sync Completed." If you have your speakers turned up on your computer, you will hear a little "ding" sound, but other than that there is no notification of the completed sync.

To check that the sync worked, you need to disconnect your Blackberry and verify that changes from your Mac made it to your BlackBerry and vice versa.

Automating Daily Synchronization

In the PocketMac for BlackBerry Scheduling preferences you may set the sync to happen when you first "Login" to your Mac, or run it automatically every so many (you set this) minutes. Please consult **PocketMac for BlackBerry™ User Guide** for details.

Conflict Resolution during Synchronization

Conflicts will be handled by PocketMac and shown to you during the synchronization. We strongly recommend consulting the **PocketMac for BlackBerry™ User Guide** for details.

Once the Sync is Complete

Your data will now be in the associated program which you chose during the synchronization process. Below is a look at my "Address book" on the Mac and what my synced contact information looks like.

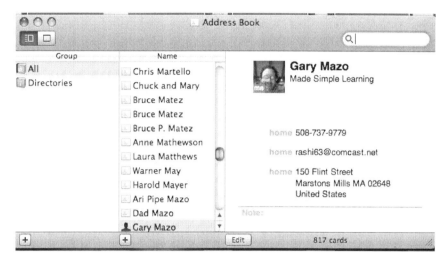

BlackBerry Mac Media Sync

Brand new for Mac users is the new BlackBerry Media Sync program. It is so new, that it is still in Beta format. If you are an iTunes user and you have playlists already in your iTunes program, the Media Sync program allows you to transfer those playlists directly to your BlackBerry. Just go here: https://www.blackberry.com/Downloads/contactFormPreload.do?code=151 7C8664BE296F0D87D9E5FC54FDD60&dl=C554943D3E32E697AF405B9F946F 0689 to download the latest version of Media Sync for the Mac.

> *NOTE: If a song is in iTunes and DRM protected (What's this? See page 100), then it is NOT possible to sync it to your BlackBerry.*
> **WARNING: If you install Media Sync, you will no longer be able to use Pocket Mac or "The Missing Sync" with your BlackBerry until you uninstall the Media Sync Program!**

Download and Installation

Fill out the license agreement and proceed to download the Media Sync for Mac program. "Unpack" the program as you do with other Mac Programs.

Videos are an easy way to Learn: www.MadeSimpleLearning.c

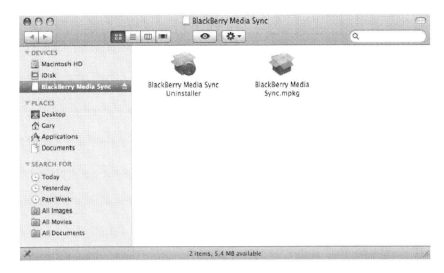

Follow all prompts and agree to have your computer restarted after installation.

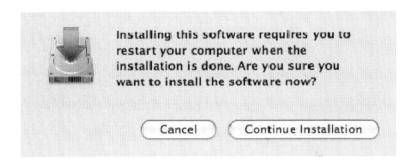

T he Media Sync Icon will now be in your "Applications" folder – just use the "Finder" program to locate it and click on it.

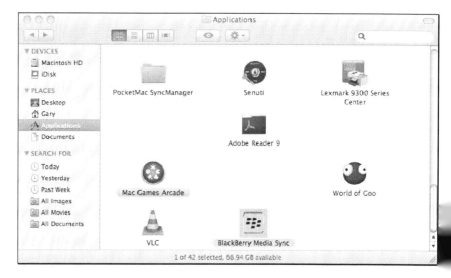

Connect your BlackBerry:

When you see this screen, just plug in your BlackBerry using the USB cable.

Setting Up Your Media Sync

The Media Sync window will identify your BlackBerry, show your PIN number and then analyze the free space for media on your device and Media Card.

I can specify both the location of my music (usually, the media card is chosen) and how much memory to keep free by adjusting the fields in the screen below.

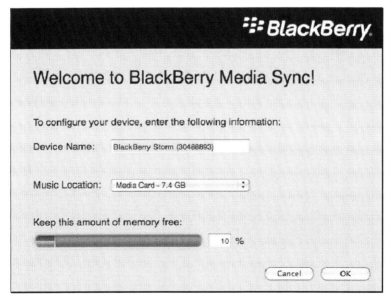

Syncing your Music

Syncing iTunes playlists is as easy as putting a check mark next to each playlist you want to transfer to the BlackBerry.

We have checked the playlists entitled "Genius" and "90's Music" and they will be transferred to the BlackBerry once we choose the "Sync" button.

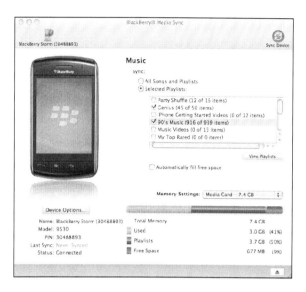

Now, just choose the "Sync" button in the upper right hand corner and the selected iTunes playlists will be transferred to the BlackBerry and placed in my Media file.

DRM Protected – Digital Rights Management

Now, it is important to remember that some music that is purchased on iTunes may contain DRM (Digital Rights Management) restrictions – that means that most iTunes music can only be played on iPods and through iTunes. *NOTE: If a song is in iTunes and DRM protected (What's this? See page 100), then it is NOT possible to sync it to your BlackBerry.*

NOTE: Early in 2009, Apple Computer announced that it will no longer use DRM on songs in iTunes, so this section will become less important.

Any other music you might have put in your iTunes library – like CD's you loaded into your computer or music that does not have DRM restrictions will transfer into the appropriate playlist.

Make sure that you don't disconnect your BlackBerry while the music is transferring.

You can also press and click the link to see a list of songs that were not transferred. Again, if they didn't transfer, it usually means that they had DRM issues and iTunes would not copy them.

Once the Sync is done, close out the Media Sync window. Now jump to page 293 to learn how to use Music on your BlackBerry.

Having Trouble / Need Help?

Visit the **BlackBerry Technical Knowledge Base**. See how to find it on page 71. Or, you can ask your question at one of the BlackBerry user forums like www.crackberry.com or www.pinstack.com.

Chapter 4:
Typing, Spelling & Help

If you have not already done so, please check out our **Quick Reference guide** at the beginning of this book (page 19) for a picture of what every key does on your BlackBerry.

TIP: Multi-Use Buttons – Red Phone Key

Many buttons do more than one thing depending on where you are. **Try pressing the Red Phone key when you're not on a call – it will jump you back to your Home Screen**

Touch Screen Gestures

Please see the list of all the touch screen gestures in our **Quick Reference guide** on page 20.

Icons: What do they all do?

Please see the list of all the icons in our **Quick Reference guide** on page 13.

FOLDERS: Your BlackBerry will have "Folder" icons to organize or group other icon together in sub-groups (sub-menus) such as the "Applications" folder. This folder may contain Tasks, MemoPad, Calculator, Voice Note, BlackBerry Messenger, Password Keeper, Brick Breaker game, Video camera, voice notes, saved messages and the Documents to Go Suite of applications. You may also see folders for "**Setup**," "**Downloads**," and "**Games.**"

Starting and Exiting Icons

See page 18 for a description of each of the keys on your BlackBerry.

You use the touch screen, Menu Key and Escape Key to navigate around your BlackBerry, open folders and select icons. The Escape Key will get you back out one step at a time, the Red Phone key will jump you all the way back to your "Homescreen." You can change the background image (called "Homescreen Image") from your Media player or camera. You can change the look and feel or "Theme" of your BlackBerry by going into the Options icon and selecting Theme (See page 129). You can also move around or hide the icons (page 119).

TIP: Multi-Tasking (Switch Applications) Using the Menu Key and Red Phone Key

You can "**Multi-Task**" using a couple of easy options on your BlackBerry:

Option 1: Press the **Red Phone key** (when not on a call) and you jump right to the Homescreen of icons. Then just start your other icon.

Option 2: Press and hold the Menu Key to see a pop-up window of icons that are running, select any one or the Home to go to your Homescreen.

Say you are writing an email and needed to check the calendar or wanted to schedule a new event.
1. Press the Red Phone key to jump to the Homescreen.
2. Start the calendar to check your schedule.
3. Press the Red Phone key again to return to the Homescreen.
4. Click on the Messages icon to return exactly to where you left off composing your email message.

Three BlackBerry Keyboards

Your BlackBerry comes with not just one, but three keyboards that will allow you to type in just the way you like. Please see our comprehensive keyboards section in our **Quick Reference guide** on page **28.**

Keyboard:	When to use:	More pictures...
SureType™ Keyboard (Portrait Mode)	Short, quick typing tasks, like a quick email or SMS text message.	Page 29
Multitap Keyboard (Portrait Mode)	If you are used to quickly typing on another type of Phone – this will be familiar for you.	Page 30

Full QWERTY Keyboard (Landscape Mode)	If you prefer a single letter per key for ease of entry and accuracy, this is the best keyboard for you.	Page 31

Landscape - Full "QWERTY" Keyboard

Landscape - Full Keyboard Mode

When you tilt your BlackBerry Storm sideways into "Landscape" mode from any program in which you can type, the keyboard will be displayed as a full QWERTY keyboard.

See page 31 for more.

Portrait – SureType™ Keyboard

Portrait - SureType™ Mode

This is an innovative technology from BlackBerry that predicts what you are typing from the keys pressed, even though most keys have two letters on them. You only press each key once and the BlackBerry "guesses" which letter you meant to type based on the context (what you have typed before it) and even what is in your Address Book. It even learns from you!

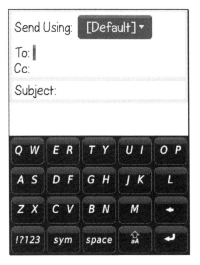

When typing with **SureType** you will see the pop-up window below (or above) what you are typing. The highlighted word is the one currently being "guessed."

If you need to correct it, scroll or just "tap" to highlight or select a different word or group of letters.

Portrait – Multitap Keyboard

Portrait - Multitap Mode

This is the more standard cell phone typing technology, where you press the key once for the first letter on the key and twice for the second letter. For example, with the "ER" key, you would press it once for "E" and twice to get the "R" in Multitap mode. TIP: You will

see the symbol  in the upper right corner whenever you are in Multitap mode.

Switching Between Multitap and SureType™ Keyboards

You can switch back and forth by pressing the Menu key and selecting "**Enable SureType**" or "**Enable Multitap.**"

NOTE: The BlackBerry always switches to **Multitap** mode when you are in a password field.

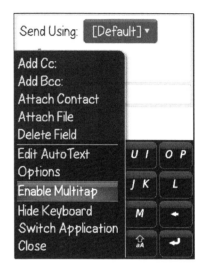

Wait to Select Corrections in SureType Mode

The most important thing to remember in SureType is to WAIT until the end of the word to select a correction. This is because many times, the SureType system will show you the correct word at the 2nd to last or last letter of the word. If you keep adjusting what it guesses after each letter, it will take you all day to type.

Here's an example of the "Fast" and "Slow" ways to type with SureType.

FAST WAY to type 'easy' (4 steps)

1. Press ER,
2. press AS,
3. press AS,
4. then tap "easy" from the pop-up list (or you could have pressed TY and Space key)

SLOW WAY to type 'easy' (8 steps)

1. Press ER
2. Select "e" from correction list
3. Press AS

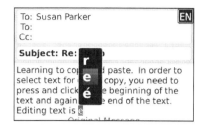

4. Scroll down the correction list once (place your finger on the list and drag down)
5. Scroll down the correction list again
6. Scroll down the correction list again
7. Now you should see the word 'easy'

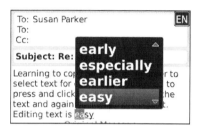

8. Press and lick on the word 'easy.' Alternatively, just highlight the correct word and then "Press" the Space Key.

This scrolling up/down the list of options can be quite time consuming, so we recommend to continue typing letters until you see your word on the list shown on the screen.

Editing Text

Making changes to your text is easy with the BlackBerry.

Deleting characters with the Backspace key

When a cursor is visible, press the **backspace** key 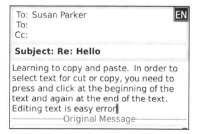 to erase letters to the **left** of the cursor. In the image to the right – the letter erased would be the last 'r' in "error."

In this image, where there is no cursor, but just a highlighted word, pressing the backspace key 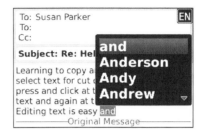 would erase the last highlighted character - the "d" in "and."

Clicking to Move the Cursor Anywhere You Want

Just press and click the screen to put the cursor anywhere in the text. Then you can press Backspace to erase letters or type additional words. When you are done correcting text, just press and click at the end of the text and start typing again.

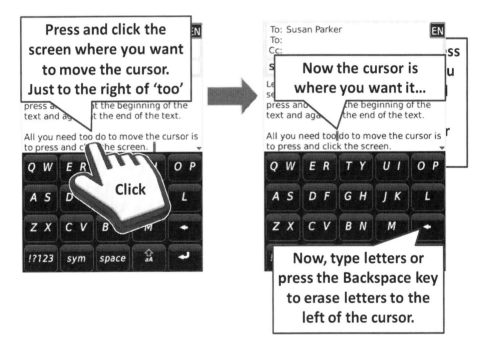

Now, just click at the end of the text where you were last typing to finish typing your message.

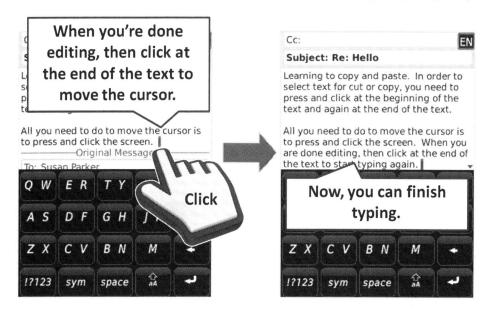

Touch and Slide the cursor around the screen

In order to move the cursor while still seeing where it is when you move it, you need to touch the screen and slide the cursor around.

When you touch the screen and hold (don't press down or click), you will see the solid blue cursor turn into an outline cursor.

While continuing to maintain contact with the screen, just move your finger to move the cursor as shown below.

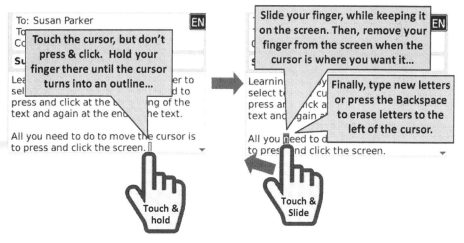

TIP: Switch to Landscape (Full QWERTY Keyboard) mode or Multitap if SureType™ is not working for you.

Just turn your BlackBerry horizontally and the accelerometer (the gadget that detects which way you are holding your BlackBerry – vertical or horizontal) will change the keyboard to a full QWERTY keyboard.

TIP: Switch to Multitap if SureType™ is not working for you.

If the SureType guesses are not working for you, then you can switch to Multitap mode by pressing the **Menu key** and selecting "**Enable Multitap**." (Usually near the bottom of the menu options as shown.)

This will allow you to more precisely type something.

You can switch back by pressing the Menu Key and selecting "**Enable SureType.**"

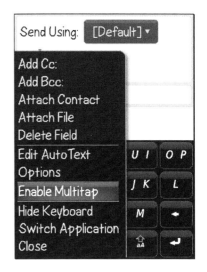

Configure Your Default Portrait (Vertical) Keyboard Layout

Another trick to "set the layout of your keyboard" is to go to the "Screen/Keyboard" option in your "Options" menu.

If you "Press" on the button under "Portrait View Keyboard" you can change the default "Suretype" to "Multitap" if you prefer.

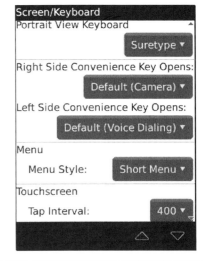

Press & Hold for Automatic Capitalization

One of the easiest tips is to capitalize letters as your typing them.
To do this: just press and hold the letter to capitalize it.

Automatic Period & Cap at End of Sentence

At the end of a sentence, just press the **SPACE** key twice to see an automatic "." (period) and the next letter you type will be automatically capitalized.

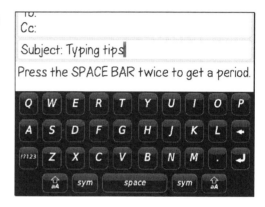

Typing Symbols

Two Types – !?123 and SYM keys
There are two types of symbols you can type on your BlackBerry – numbers

and most punctuation marks can be found by pressing the key.
Parentheses, quotation marks, brackets and most other symbols not shown

on the keyboard which are accessed by pressing the (Symbol) key on the keyboard. Both ways allow you to quickly add symbols to your text. To see images of all the **!?123** and **symbol** keyboards, please see pages 29, 30 and 31.

The Mighty SPACE Key

Like many of the keys on the BlackBerry, the SPACE Key can do some very handy things for you while you are typing.

Using the SPACE Bar while typing an email address

On most handhelds, when you want to put in the "@" or the "." in your email, you need a complicated series of commands – usually a "**!?123**" or "**Symbol**" or something.

On the BlackBerry, you don't need to take those extra steps. While you are typing the email, after the user name (for instance martin) just press the SPACE Bar once and the BlackBerry will automatically insert the "@"
"martin@"
Type in the domain name and then press the Space Bar again and, presto - the BlackBerry automatically puts in the "."
"martin@blackberrymadesimple." No additional keystrokes necessary. Just finish the email address with the "com" and you see
"martin@blackberrymadesimple.com"

Quickly Changing Drop Down Lists

Using the SPACE key to change drop down lists.

Another thing that the SPACE key does is to move you down to the next item in a list. Give it a try. Open up a new calendar event, tap the date to bring it up on the screen. Now gently touch the month to highlight it. Then press the SPACE key – notice you advance to the next month. The same thing happens if you highlight the day, or year. Only the minutes field is different, the SPACE key jumps to the next 15 minute increment (:15, :30, :45, :00)

Now, on the Storm you can always just place your finger on the screen and scroll up or down to do the same thing – but sometimes a keyboard shortcut is faster and more accurate.

Using LETTER keys to change drop down lists or quickly select menu items or other lists

You can even use the letter keys on your keyboard to instantly jump down to the first item matching either letter on the key (if there are two letters), or jumping down to a matching menu item, or jumping down to a matching item in a list (like the long list in the "Options" icon).

Using NUMBER keys to type dates and times in Calendar, Tasks and More

You can even use the number keys on your keyboard to instantly type a new date or time or select an entry in a drop down list with that number. Examples include: typing "40" in the minute field to set the minutes to 40 or typing 9 in the hour field to get to 9 AM or PM. This also works in the fields where drop down list items start with numbers – like in the Reminder field in calendar or tasks. Typing a number "9" would immediately jump you to the "9 Hours" setting.

Using Your Spell Checker

Your BlackBerry comes with a built-in Spell Checker. Normally, your Spell Checker is turned on to check everything you type which you can see with the little dotted underlining while you type things on your BlackBerry. The underlining goes away when the Spell Checker "matches" your words with those in the dictionary showing it is spelled correctly. Normally, you will need to turn it on to have it check your outgoing email messages.

Spelling Checker

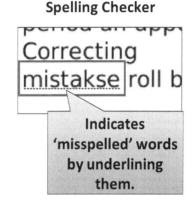

Indicates 'misspelled' words by underlining them.

When your spelling mistakes are not "auto-corrected" with the AutoText feature (see page 116), the other way to quickly correct many typing errors is to use the built-in Spell Checker on your BlackBerry. When your BlackBerry finds what it thinks is a misspelled word, it will underline it as shown below.

To correct one of these words, just press and click on the word with your finger. You will see a list of suggested changes, just scroll to and press and click on the correct word.

Edit or Delete Words from the Spelling Custom Dictionary

Mistakes will happen, and it's fairly easy to press and click the wrong menu item and inadvertently add wrong words to the Custom Dictionary. The authors have done this plenty of times!

Here's how to remove or edit Custom Words

Return to the Spell Checker options screen as shown above. (Messages Icon > Menu key > Options > Spell Check – OR – Options Icon > Spell Check)

Once in the Spell Check screen, press and click on the "Custom Dictionary" button at the bottom.

Now you will see a list of every word in your Custom Dictionary. You can either scroll down and find the word(s) that need to be removed, or start typing a few letters to "Find" the word

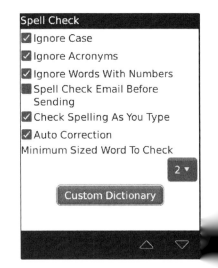

WARNING: Your Spell Checker may not be Turned On for Every Email You Send

By default, many BlackBerry Smartphones will not do a spell check before sending email. You can actually ignore all misspelled (underlined) words and send. Below we show you how to force the Spell Check to be enabled for outgoing email.

Enabling Spell Check for Outbound Email

One of the great features of your new BlackBerry is that you can automatically check the spelling of your emails before you send them out. Many times, this feature must be enabled; it is not turned on when you take your BlackBerry out of the box. Like your spell checker on your computer, you can even create additions to the dictionary for frequently used words. Spell check will save you embarrassing misspellings in your communication, which is especially important with such a small keyboard.

To Enable Spell Check for Email

You can turn on Spell Checking in two areas.
If you are already in the Messages (Email) icon, then it's fastest to press the Menu key and select **"Options"**.

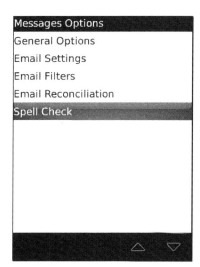
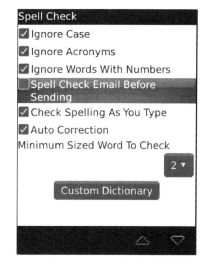

Then scroll down and press and click on "**Spell Check**"

If you are on your Homescreen of icons, press and click on the **Options Icon**.

Then scroll down and press and click on "**Spell Check**" or press the letter "S" a few times to jump down to it.

By default, the first three boxes are "checked" for you, but the fourth box "Spell Check Email Before Sending" is left unchecked, you need to check this box in order to enable spell checking on outbound emails, Press and click on that box to place a check mark inside Press the Menu key or Escape key and Save your changes.

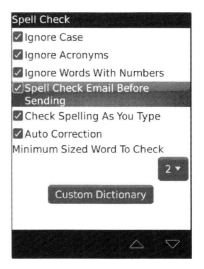

Using BlackBerry Text Based Help (Help Icon)

There might be times when you don't have this book or our video tutorials handy and you need to find out how to do something right away on your BlackBerry.

You can get into the help menu from the Help Icon: and almost every application on the BlackBerry has a built in contextual help menu that can answer some of your basic questions.

Using the "Help" Menus

The Help menu can be accessed from virtually any application. For our purposes, we will take a look at the Help menu built into the Calendar Icon.

Once in the Calendar or most any other program on your BlackBerry, press the Menu key and scroll all the way up to the top and you will see **"Help."** (This is true for most applications.)

Press and click on "**Help**" and options related to the Calendar as shown below.

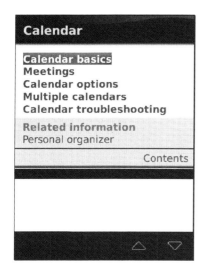

To select any of these options, just scroll and touch to highlight the radio button and press and click or press the screen.

Continue to scroll and press and click on topics you would like to learn about. Press the ESCAPE key to back up one level in the help menus.

Overall Help Index and Finding Help Text

Like pretty much every other feature on the BlackBerry, there are some tips and tricks when using Help.

To jump back to the main Help Index, press the Menu Key and select "**Index**"

If you want to find text on the *currently displayed Help page*, then press the Menu key and select "Find". We are not sure how useful Find feature is, because ideally the Find would search the entire Help database, not just the current screen. *(Maybe this will change with future software releases!)*

Chapter 5:
Personalize your BlackBerry

In this chapter you will learn some great ways to personalize your BlackBerry like moving and hiding icons, organizing with folders, setting your convenience keys, changing your Theme or "look and feel" and adjusting font sizes and types.

TIP: Change Your Homescreen Image "Wallpaper"

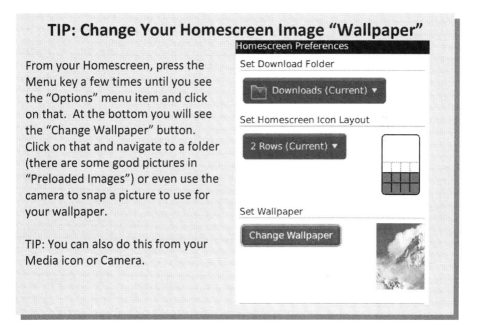

From your Homescreen, press the Menu key a few times until you see the "Options" menu item and click on that. At the bottom you will see the "Change Wallpaper" button. Click on that and navigate to a folder (there are some good pictures in "Preloaded Images") or even use the camera to snap a picture to use for your wallpaper.

TIP: You can also do this from your Media icon or Camera.

Moving Icons, Hiding and Deleting Icons

You may not need to see every single icon on your Homescreen, or you may have your most popular icons and want to move them up to easy access on the top row. Learn how in this section. The way you move and hide varies a little depending on which "Theme" you have on your BlackBerry.

Moving Your Icons Within A Folder

Press the Menu Key to see an array of all your icons. If the icon you want to move is inside a particular folder, like "Downloads" or "Applications" – scroll to and press and click on that folder.

Scroll over and touch it to highlight the icon you want to move -- in this case, we are going to move the "SMS" icon, because it is highlighted.

Press the Menu key (between your Green phone key and Escape key) to bring up the **"Move"** menu item as shown.

Once you select "**Move**," then you see a arrows pointing around the icon (as shown). Just tap the screen in the spot in which you would like to "Move" the icon.

Finally, press and click the screen to "set" the moved icon at the new location.

How do I know when I'm in a Folder?

When you are in a folder you see a little icon at the top of your screen with a folder tab image and the name of the folder. In the image below, you see that you are in the **"Applications"** folder.

Moving Your Icons Between Folders

Sometimes you want to move icons to your Home folder to make them more easily accessible. Or, you might want to move some of the icons you seldom use from your Home folder into another folder to "clean up" your Homescreen.

Let's say we wanted to move our **SMS icon** from Homescreen to the Applications Folder.

First, press the MENU key to show all all your Homescreen icons. Then scroll through and "tap" to highlight the **SMS icon** as shown.

Then, press the **Menu key** and select the "**Move to Folder**" menu item as shown.

Now, we want to move this out of our "Home" folder into the "**Applications**" folder, so we press and click on "**Applications.**"

Now we press the **Escape key** to exit from the Applications folder back to the Home folder to locate our newly moved SMS icon, in this case it is near the bottom of the list of icons.

Setting Your Homescreen Top Icons

Depending on what "Theme" you have selected on your BlackBerry, you may have noticed that only a limited number of icons (usually 8, but you can change this number, see page 126) show up on your main "Homescreen." These happen to be the top icons in the list of icons after you press the Menu key. So, it's simple to get icons on the limited list, just Move them up to the top. Since we will use our SMS Icon quite a bit on the Storm let's move it from the Instant Messaging folder to the top.

Enter the "Instant Messaging" folder by clicking on it.

Then highlight the icon we want to move: **SMS** - and press the Menu key and select **"Move to Folder"** and select "Home".

Next, click on "**Home**" to get the SMS icon on your main "**Home**" list of icons and out of the "Instant Messaging" folder.

Press the Escape key to get back to your Homescreen of icons to see the SMS icon again.

Now, highlight the SMS icon and select "**Move**" this time.

To move the icon just tap the screen at one of the "top" spots in the icons list.   Press and click to set it into place and complete the move.

Now we see "**SMS**" icon on our limited set of icons on the Homescreen:

Working with Folders to Organize Your Icons

On your BlackBerry you can create or delete folders to better organize your Icons. There may already be a few folders created by default. Typically, you will see an "Applications," "Settings," "Downloads," and "Games" folders. You can add your own folders and then move icons into your new folders to better organize them.

Creating a New Folder

Please note that at the time of publication, you could only create folders one level deep – in other words, you can only create New Folders when you are in the Home folder, not when you are already inside another folder. Thi. may change with new software versions.

To create a new folder, first press the Menu key to see all your icons. Then press the Menu key again and select "**Add Folder**"

NOTE: If you don't see the **"Add Folder"** menu item, then press the Escape key to the right of your Menu key once to get back to your home folder.

After you select the "**Add Folder**" menu item, then you will see this screen. Type your Folder Name and then press and click on the folder Icon and scroll left/right to check out all the different folder colors/styles possible.

Once you're done selecting the folder icon style, then press and click on it and scroll down to press and click on the **"Add"** button to finish creating your folder. Then you will see your new folder.

Moving Icons Between Folders

Once you create your new folder, you will want to move icons into it to organize them and so your Homescreen is not too crowded. Please see our instructions on page 121 on how to do this.

Editing a Folder

You can edit a folder by highlighting it, pressing the Menu key and selecting "**Edit Folder**." Then you can change the name and folder icon and save your changes.

Deleting a Folder

Whenever you want to get rid of a folder, just highlight it and select "**Delete**" as shown.

Adding More Rows of Icons to Your Homescreen

The "default" setting on your BlackBerry Storm is to have two rows of four icons on the Homescreen. This can very easily be changed to just one row – if you want fewer icons – or three rows – if you want more.

To change the number of rows, just press the MENU key from the "Homescreen" to bring up the full screen of icons. Next, press the MENU key again and scroll down to "Option" and press and click the screen.

 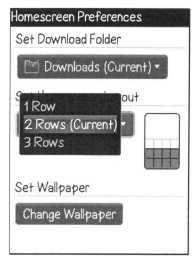

Under **"Set Homescreen Layout"** just press and click and select the number of rows desired. Press the ESCAPE key and save your changes. Press ESCAPE again (or the RED phone key) and your new Homescreen will reflect the new look.

To have your top icons shown on the Zen "Homescreen", follow the instructions to Move icons and Move icons between folder starting on page 119 and make sure your top icons are moved to be across the top row or in the top of the list.

Changing Your Font Size and Type

You can fine-tune the font size and type on your BlackBerry to fit your individual needs.

Do you need to see more on the screen and don't mind small fonts? Then go all the way down to a micro-size 7-point font.

Do you need to see **bigger fonts** for easy readability? Adjust the fonts to a large **14-point font and make it BlackBerry**.

Here's how to adjust your font size and type:

Press and click on the Options icon. ![Options] You may need to press the Menu key and scroll up or down to find it.

Inside the Options icon, press and click on "**Screen/Keyboard**" to get to the screen where you can change your fonts among other things.

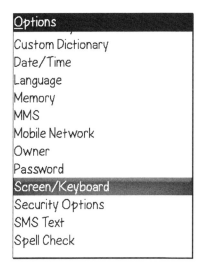

Press and click the screen to select a different font family, size, style or type as shown. You can even see a preview of your currently selected style and size to make sure it will fit your needs.

Selecting New Themes: The "Look & Feel" of Your BlackBerry

You can customize your BlackBerry and make it look truly unique. One way to do this is to change the "Theme" or look and feel of your BlackBerry. Changing Themes usually changes the layout and appearance of your icons and the font type and size you see inside each icon. There may be only one theme pre-installed on your BlackBerry, but soon, there will be literally hundreds more available for download at various web sites.

CARRIER-SPECIFIC THEMES: Depending on your BlackBerry Wireless Carrier (phone company) you may see various customized Themes that are not shown in this book.

MORE STANDARD/GENERIC BLACKBERRY THEMES:
Most of the 'Standard' Themes shown below are on every BlackBerry (or can be downloaded from http://mobile.blackberry.com).

Scroll and press and click on the **Option icon** on your BlackBerry. You may have to press the Menu Key to see all your icons and then locate the Options icon, or you may have to press and click on a "Settings" folder to locate the Options icon. Once in Options, scroll down to "Theme" and press and click.

Then inside the Theme screen, just scroll and press and click on the Theme you want to make "Active". Your currently selected Theme is shown with the word (Active) next to it.

Then press the Escape key to get back to the Homescreen to check out your new theme.

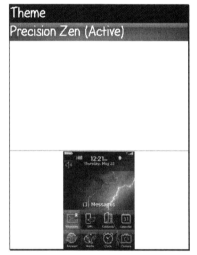

Downloading New Themes:

Note of caution: The authors have downloaded many Themes on their BlackBerry smartphones. Some Themes can cause problems with your BlackBerry. Examples: The BlackBerry may stop working or freeze or you may not be able to see everything on the screen, etc. We recommend only downloading Themes from a web site you know and trust.

To download new Themes for your BlackBerry:

Start your web browser on your BlackBerry. For detailed help and shortcut keys for the Web Browser, please see our section on the Web Browser on page 339.

Move the Cursor into the address bar at the top of the screen (if it isn't already there.)

Type in "**mobile.blackberry.com**" - will read "http://mobile.blackberry.com" – or http://www.mobile.blackberry.com – either is OK. Press and click the ENTER key to go to this site. (NOTE: It will probably look different from what is shown here, as web sites are updated often!)

Go to the "**Fun and Games**" or "**Personalize**" link and press and click the screen.

On the next screen scroll down to the "**Themes**" section and press and click on it. You will notice that there are Wallpapers and Ringtones as well!

 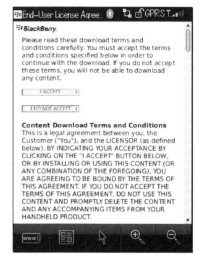

On the Terms & Conditions page, press and click "**I accept**" to continue if you accept these terms.

Try all the different Themes to see what you like best. NOTE: As of publishing time of this book there were no new Themes available, but by the time you read this, there will probably be a few good ones to download!

TIP: Themes, Wallpapers, Ringtones

You can also download themes from some of the BlackBerry community sites such as:
BlackBerry Mobile Site: http://mobile.blackberry.com
CrackBerry.com : www.crackberry.com
BlackBerry Forums: www.blackberryforums.com
Pinstack: www.pinstack.com
BlackBerry Cool: www.blackberrycool.com
Also, try a web search for "BlackBerry Themes, Wallpaper or Ringtones" -- There are probably new sites all the time!

Changing the Homescreen Background Image or "Wallpaper"

Now that you have the font size, type and Theme that you like – you may also want to change the background image or picture on your Homescreen, also called "Wallpaper." You saw above how to download new Themes – you may use the same steps to download new wallpapers.

In addition, since you have a built-in camera, you can simply snap a picture and immediately use it as "Wallpaper." Finally, you may use any image that is stored on your BlackBerry – either in the BlackBerry's main memory or on the Memory Card as Wallpaper. Grab a picture of your favorite person, a beautiful sunset or any landscape for your own personalized BlackBerry background Wallpaper.

Changing Your Wallpaper or Homescreen Image using a Stored Picture:

Press and click on the "**Media**" icon.

Highlight the "**Pictures**" icon and press and click on it.

Once in "**Pictures**," navigate to the location of the picture you wish to use – either in the **All Pictures**, **Picture Folders** or **Sample Pictures**. You may also see an option to select the "Camera" at the top – to take a new picture.

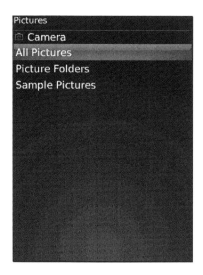 

Highlight (by tapping) the thumbnail of the picture you wish to set as your Wallpaper, and then press the Menu key to select "**Set As Homescreen Image**"

Then press the **Escape** key a few times to check out your new wallpaper on your Homescreen.

Changing Your Convenience Keys to Open Icons or the Keyboard

The two keys on the middle of the sides of your BlackBerry are actually programmable keys called "convenience" keys. This is because each of the two keys can be set to 'conveniently' open any icon on your BlackBerry, even new Third Party icons that you add to your BlackBerry.

To Change your Convenience Keys

Press and click on the "Options" icon (press the Menu key if you don't see it listed.)
Scroll down to **"Screen/Keyboard"** or bring up the keyboard and press the letter "**S**" a few times to jump down to the "**Screen/Keyboard**" item and press and click on it.

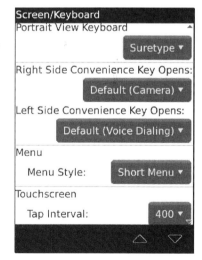

Scroll down the screen until you see **"Right Side Convenience Key Opens:"** and **"Left Side Convenience Key Opens:"**

To change the icon / application these keys open, just press and click on the item to see the entire list. Then scroll and press and click on the icon you want.

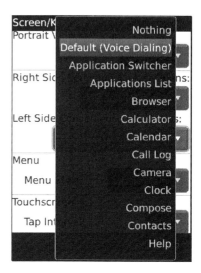

TIP: We recommend setting your left convenience key to open the **"Virtual Keyboard."** It makes is that much easier to just pull up your keyboard when needed.

Then press the MENU key and select "**Save**" to save your changes. Now give you newly set convenience keys a try –

TIP: The Convenience keys **work from anywhere**, not just the Homescreen.

> # TIP: You can set your Convenience Keys to open any Icon, even newly installed ones!
> After you install new icons, you will notice that they show up in the list of available icons to select in the Screen/Keyboard options screen. So if your newly installed stock quote, news reader or game is important, just set it as a convenience key.

Understanding that Blinking Red Light ("Repeat Notification")

One of the features that BlackBerry users love is the little LED that blinks in the upper right hand corner. It is possible to have this light blink different colors:

"Red"   when you receive an incoming message (MMS, SMS or Email) or calendar alarm rings,

"Blue"   when connected to a Bluetooth Device,

"Green" when you have wireless coverage, and,

"Amber"if you need to charge your BlackBerry or it is charging.

To make adjustments to the "Red" Message LED notification:

Start your **Sounds - Profiles Icon.**

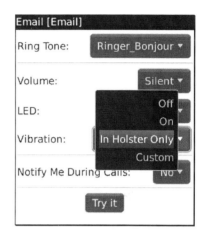

Select **"Set Ring Tones/Alerts** at the bottom of the list of profiles. Press and click and then click on "Messages." You will see each of your email accounts listed as well as Level 1, SMS, Text, etc. Just choose either "yes" or "no" for the LED notification.

To turn on or off the Bluetooth LED notification:

From your Homescreen, press and click on the **Options Icon** (wrench) and then scroll to "**Bluetooth**" and press and click.
Press the Menu key and select "**Options.**"
Go down to "**LED Connection Indicator**" and set to "**On**" or "**Off.**"
Press the MENU or ESCAPE Key and "**Save**" your settings.

To Turn On or Off the "Green" coverage indication LED:

Go into your **Options Icon** and scroll to "**Screen/Keyboard**" and press and click. Scroll down to LED Coverage Indicator and select either "**On**" or "**Off"**

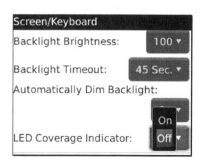

Chapter 6:
Sounds: Ring & Vibrate

Understanding Sound Profiles

Your BlackBerry is highly customizable – everything from Ringtones to vibrations to LED notifications can be adjusted. Traveling on an airplane but sill want to use your calendar or play a game without disturbing others? No problem. In a meeting and don't want the phone to ring – but you do want some sort of notification when an email comes in? No problem.

Virtually any scenario you can imagine can be dealt with preemptively by adjusting the profile settings.

Basic Profile Settings:

By default, the BlackBerry is set to a "Normal" profile – meaning that when a call comes in, the phone rings and when a message comes in, the phone plays a tune.

Changing your Profile:

To set or change the profile settings:

Depending on your selected Theme and BlackBerry carrier (Phone Company), how you get to your profiles icon will be slightly different.

If you don't see this speaker icon on your screen, press the Menu key or tap the middle of your Homescreen to see the entire list of icons, then scroll to the "**Sounds/notifications**" icon and press and click on it.

Six basic 'preset' settings are available from which you can choose: Loud, vibrate, Quiet, Normal, Phone only and Off. Next to one of those options the word "Active" will be displayed.

For most users, "**Normal**" will be the active profile which rings during phone calls and either vibrates or plays a tone when a message arrives.

"**Loud**" increases the volume for all notifications.

"**Vibrate**" enables a short vibration for meetings, movies or other places where cell phone rings are discouraged.

"**Quiet**" will display notifications on the display and via the LED.

"**Phone Only**" will turn off all email and SMS notifications.

"**Off**" will turn off all notifications.

Quickly Change to Vibrate Only (Silence Ringer) or Phone Only

Have you ever needed to put your BlackBerry into your pocket, purse or bag and forget to turn off the ringer in a movie, meeting or restaurant?

Quickly Turn to Vibrate Mode:

Just press and hold the keyboard lock on the upper left (top) of your BlackBerry until you see the "**Owner Information**" displayed indicating the keyboard is locked.

Then, press and hold the "Mute" key

 on the upper right (top) of the BlackBerry. You will feel a vibration and see the profile icon change to indicate "vibration" mode.

Customizing Ring Tones and Alert Tones

There may be some situations where you want a combination of options that one profile alone cannot satisfy. The BlackBerry is highly customizable so that you can adjust your profile options for virtually any potential situation. The easiest way to accomplish this is to choose a profile that is closest to what you need and "Edit" it as shown below.

To enter the Advanced Profile Menu: Press and click on "**Sounds/notifications**" icon as you did above.
Scroll down to "**Set Ring Tones/Alerts**" and press and click.

Each of the profiles can be adjusted by scrolling to the profile you desire to edit, pushing the Menu Key and select "**Expand.**" The Push and Click on the option you want to edit. Or, just Press and Click on the highlighted option to expand it – then press and click again on the option you wish to edit.

Messenger, Browser, Calendar, Level 1 Messages, Email, Messenger (Alert and New Message,) Phone, SMS and tasks can all be adjusted with regards to tone (whether it rings or not), vibration, volume, tune (the ring tone that is played) and LED notification.

For example, choose "**Email**" and notice that you can make adjustments for your BlackBerry both "Out of Holster" and "In Holster". (A "holster" may be supplied with your device or sold separately. This is essentially a carrying case that clips to your belt and uses a magnet to notify your BlackBerry it is "In Holster" and should turn off the screen immediately among other things.)

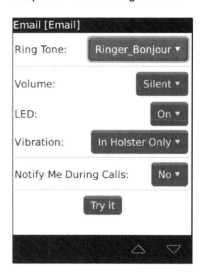

TIP: If you make these profile changes **before** you set up individual Email accounts – you won't need to adjust each one individually.

Changing Your Main Phone Ring Tone

Please see page 297 of our Music chapter to learn how to get this done.

Downloading a New Ring Tone

Sometimes, you may find that your 'stock' ringtones just are not loud enough for you to hear, even when you turn the Volume up to "Loud." Sometimes, you just want a "Fun" Ringtone. We have found that you can download a new ringtone from **mobile.blackberry.com** (among other web sites) to help with this problem.
Open your BlackBerry web browser.

If can't see a place to type a web address, then Menu key and select "**Go To...**"

Type in "**mobile.blackberry.com**" and press the enter key.

Then scroll down and press and click on the link called "**Personalize**." Then, just press and click on **"Ringtones."**

When you press and click, you can "**Open**" (listen/play it) or "**Save**" it on your BlackBerry.

Go ahead and "**Open**" a few to test them out. To get back to the list and try more ringtones, press the Escape key.

If you like the ringtone, then press Menu key after you listened to it and select "**Save**" from the menu.

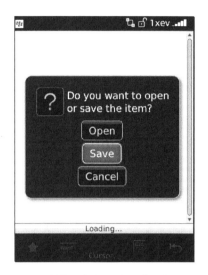

This time, select "**Save**" and scroll down and check the box at the bottom that says **"Set as Ringtone."**
You are done. Next time you receive a phone call the new ringtone should play.

TIP: New Ringtones are available on many BlackBerry user Websites like www.crackberry.com and many are free.

Contact Alerts

The BlackBerry Storm offers many options for "customizing" the ringtone, SMS tone and other alerts for a unique contact. The easiest way to do this is to click on your "Profiles" icon and then scroll down to "**Set Contact Alerts**" and Press and Click.

To set a Contact Alert:

Press and click "**Add Contact Alert**" and select a contact from your Address Book for whom this new profile will apply.

You can choose individual tunes for both the Phone and messages from a particular contact.

Press the **ESCAPE key** and "**Save**" the new profile. In the example below, I want the Phone to ring loud specifically when my friend Martin calls so I don't miss the important call.

To set a Custom Ringtone From "Contacts:"

Start you "Contacts" as you normally would and "Find" the contact you wish to edit. In this case, I will find and edit Martin's contact information to give him a Custom Ring Tone.

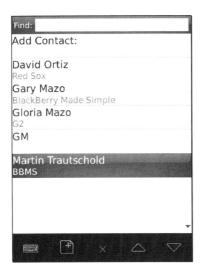

Press the Menu key and scroll down to **"Phone"** or "**Messages.**" Select the tone from the list provided (you will hear the tone play as you move from selection to selection.)

Press the MENU key and select "**Save**" when you are done and save the changes.

Chapter 7:
Phone & Voice Dialing

Call Logs
Press to see the phone call logs.

Contact List
Press to bring up the Contact List / Address Book.

Mute key

Your Phone Number

Dial Pad
Press for the regular dial pad (shown)

Volume Up
Volume Down

Voice Mail
Press & Hold '1'

To dial letters:
Like your old phone, just press the corresponding number key. E.g. to dial "SAM" press "7" "2" "6"

Start Call

End Call

Menu Key
Conf. Call &
More Press & hold to multi-task

Escape Key
Jump to Home

Your BlackBerry Phone and Voice Dialing

We have already covered many of the exciting and powerful features of your BlackBerry in this book. First, and foremost, however, your BlackBerry is your phone – your lifeline for communication. It is a very good and full-featured phone and includes the latest voice dialing capabilities.

The Three Main Phone Screens

When you open the phone the first time, you may notice the three soft keys at the top of the phone screen. These open your Dial Pad (left key and shown by default), Call Logs (middle key) and your Contact List (right key).

Dial Pad	**Call Logs**	**Contact List**
(Default – Dial numbers)	(Calls placed, missed, received)	(Find and call your Contacts)

Adjusting the Volume on Calls

There may be times when you are having trouble hearing a caller. The connection may be bad (*because of their old fashioned phone – e.g. non-BlackBerry*) or you may be using a headset. Adjusting the volume is easy. While on the phone call, simply use the two volume keys on the right hand side of the BlackBerry to adjust the volume up or down.

What's My Phone Number?

You have your phone, and you want to give your number to all your friends – you just need to know where you can get your hands on that important information. There are a couple of ways of doing this:

Press the Green Phone Key and read "My Number" at the top of the screen.

Above your call log is should say "**My Number: nnn-nnn-nnnn**"

TIP: Press the middle soft key at the bottom to dial your voice mail.

Changing Your Ring Tone

To select any **song or pre-loaded ring tone** on your BlackBerry as a new ring tone, please check out the steps in our Media section on page 297.

Placing a Call

The BlackBerry truly excels as a phone – making phone calls is easy and there are many ways to place a call.

Making a Call – Just Dialing a Phone Number

Press the Green Phone key at any time to get into the Phone application.
Your default view should be the number pad – but you can also see your call log or your contacts by pressing the corresponding button along the top.

First, the BlackBerry will try to match the numbers you are typing to Address Book entries. If it cannot find any, then it will just show you the digits you have typed as shown.

Once all the numbers are punched in, just press the **Green Phone key** and the call will be placed.

Answering a Call

Answering a call couldn't be easier. When you call comes in, the number will be displayed on the screen. If you have that particular number already in your **Address Book** the name and/or picture will also be on the screen (if you have entered that information into that particular contact.)

When a call comes in:

Push either the **Green Phone key** or press and click the **"Answer"** soft key to answer the call.

If you are using a Bluetooth Headset, you can usually press and click a button on the headset to answer the call, see page 327.

Calling Voice Mail

The easiest way to call voice mail is to press and hold the number "1" key. This is the default key for voicemail.

If it is not working correctly, then please read below for some troubleshooting help or call your phone company technical support for help in correcting it.

To setup voice mail, just call it and follow the prompts to enter your name, greeting, password and other information.

When Voice Mail Does Not Work

Sometimes, pressing and holding the "1" key will not dial voice mail. This happens if the voicemail access number is incorrect in your BlackBerry. You will need to call your phone company (wireless carrier) and ask them for the local voicemail access number. This sometimes happens if you move to a different area or change cell phones, then restore all your data onto your BlackBerry.

Once you have the new phone number from the carrier, you need to enter it into your BlackBerry.

Start your Phone by pressing the Green Phone Key.

Scroll down to "**Options**" item and press and click to select it.

Now press and click on "**Voice Mail**"

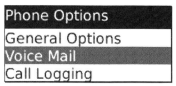

Enter the phone number you received into the "Voice Mail Access Number."

TIP: You can even enter your voicemail password if you like.

Why do I see Names and Numbers in my Call Logs?

You will see both phone numbers and names in your phone call logs. When you see a name instead of a phone number, you know that the person is already entered in your BlackBerry Address Book.

It is easy to add entries to your "Contacts" right from this phone call log screen. Below we show you how.

Quickly Dial from Call Log

You can quickly dial from your contact list by tapping the Green Phone key

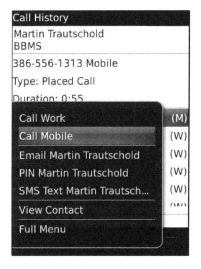

once to get into the "Phone" screen. Then, Press and Click the "Call Log" icon.

Then, once in the call log screen, just scroll to the call log you wish to use. Once there, just press the "Green

Phone Key" and the phone number in that call log will be called.

Add New Addresses from Your Phone Call Logs

If you see just a phone number in your call log screen, then there is a good chance you will want to add that phone number as a new "Contact" entry.

Note: Call log entries are generated whenever you receive, miss, ignore or place a call from your BlackBerry.

Get into the call log screen by tapping the Green Phone key once.

Highlight the phone number you want to add to your Address Book.

Now press the Menu key and select "**Add to Contacts**"

Notice that the phone number is automatically placed in the "Work" phone field but you can also copy the number by selecting the Copy option from the Menu and then past the number into another field – like the Mobile field shown to the right.

Type relevant information, press the MENU key and select **"Save."**

Copy & Paste Text and Phone Numbers

Copy and Paste is a little different with the BlackBerry storm than with other BlackBerry Smartphones. Because the Storm is a "touch screen" device – RIM developed a whole new way to highlight, copy and paste. See page 33 for details on using multi-touch.

Copy and Paste for Phone Numbers

For Underlined Phone Numbers:

With underlined phone number like 313-555-1212, simply press and click on it to see a "Short Menu" and select "Copy" to copy it.

TIP: This trick works on any underlined email address or PIN number as well!

Move to where you want to paste, press the Menu key and select "Paste."

Click

Click on the phone number to see the menu and then click Copy or Cut.

For non-underlined phone numbers and all other text:

Use "Multi-Touch" to highlight the information. Place one finger at the beginning of the phone number you wish to copy and one finger at the end and touch the screen with both fingers. The number should highlight and turn blue.

Press the MENU key and select "**Cut**".

Scroll to the correct phone field, press the Menu key and select "**Paste**"

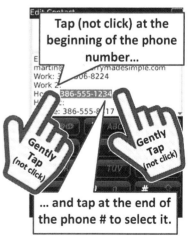

Tap (not click) at the beginning of the phone number...

... and tap at the end of the phone # to select it.

If you need more tips on entering new addresses, please see page 209.

Ignoring and Muting Phone Calls

Sometimes, you can't take a call and you need to make a decision to ignore or perhaps mute the ringing of an incoming call. Both of these options can be achieved quite easily with your BlackBerry.

**Ignoring a Call and
Immediately Stop the Ringing.**

When the phone call comes in, instead of answering by pushing the Green Phone Key, simply press the **Red Phone Key** to ignore. You can also press the "Ignore" virtual button on the screen itself.

Incoming Call

Gary Mazo

508-777-9999 (Mobile)
BlackBerry Made Simple

Answer   Ringer Off   Ignore

 **= Ignore Call,
Send to Voicemail, Stop the Ringer**

TIP: Need to silence the ringer but still want to answer the call?

Just Press and Click the **"Ringer Off"** button on your screen. Also, if the ringing or vibrating had started while your BlackBerry was still in the holster (carrying case), then simply pulling the BlackBerry out of the holster should stop the vibrating and ringing, but still give you time to answer.

Ignoring a call will immediately send the caller to your voice mail.

The "Missed Call" will be displayed on your Homescreen. Press and click on "View" or press the Green Phone Key and select your call log. Press the MENU key   to do various things depending on whether or not this phone number is already in your Address Book. If you see only a phone number, not a name, then this number is not in your address book and you may only "Call or SMS" this number.

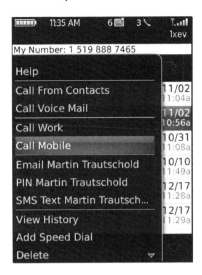

Benefits of Adding People to your Contact List / Address Book

- Call them and any number for this person (that is entered into your address book)
- Send them an email (if this person has an email address entered)
- Send them an SMS text message
- Send them an MMS Message (Multi-Media Message with pictures or other media like songs)
- Send them a PIN message
- View the contact information

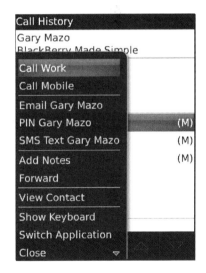

Muting a Call

If you would prefer not send the call immediately to voicemail and simply let it ring a few times on the caller's end, but you don't want to hear the ring (perhaps you are in a movie theatre or a meeting) just tap the MUTE key on the very top right edge of your BlackBerry:

When the call comes in, press the MUTE key on the top right of the BlackBerry. The MUTE key has the small speaker icon with the line through it. All this will do is silence the ring.

You may still pick up the call or let the caller go to voicemail.

Using the Call Log

The Call Log is an especially useful tool if you make and receive many calls during the day. Often, it is hard to remember if you added that individual to your **Address Book** or not – but you definitely remember that they called yesterday. Here is a perfect situation to use your Call Log to access the call, add the number into your Address Book and place a return call.

Checking your Call Log

The easiest way to view your call logs is to just tap the Green Phone key

from anywhere:
Initially, you should see the dial pad. Just choose "Call Log" from the top row of icons to display your call log.

The default setting is to show the most recent calls made and then move sequentially backwards showing calls made and received listed by date and time.

You can either "touch" the screen to highlight a call or press on the call to bring up a more detailed call log.

Placing a Call from the Call Log

Go to the Call Log as you did above and scroll through the list.

Find the number or name you wish to call and press and click the screen. A detailed call log now appears for that call/individual showing the most recent calls to or from that contact. You can press and click on the most recent call or any other call in the list.

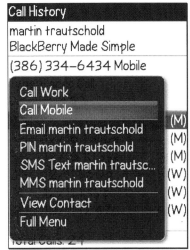

Choose the option from the menu – Call, Email, PIN, SMS or MMS (depending on what numbers or email addresses you have for that individual in your Address Book.)

TIP: If you want to call the number listed – in this case, Susan's Mobile Number (M) – you can skip pressing the screen and press the Green Phone key to immediately start the call.

Press and click on "**Call**" to place the call. If you have more than one number listed – you will be given the option to call "Work," "Mobile" or other numbers you have stored.

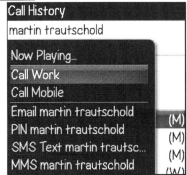

To show your Call Logs in the Messages icon (Inbox)

It might be useful to show calls made, received and missed in your message list for easy accessibility. This allows you to manage both voice and message communication in a single unified inbox.

Press the **Green Phone key** to see your call logs.
Press the **Menu key** and scroll down to "**Options"** and press and click.

Scroll to "**Call Logging**" and press and click.
Under "Show These Call Log Types in Message List" select either:
Missed Calls (see only missed calls)
All Calls (see all placed, missed, received)
None (this is the default, don't see any calls)
Press Menu and select "**Save**."

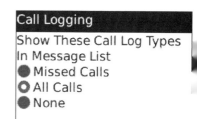

To Add a Note to a Call Log

Press the Green Phone key to get into the phone logs if you are not already there.

Press the **Menu key** and scroll to "**View History**" and press and click.

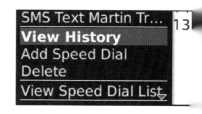

Select the call history item to which you want to add your notes by scrolling up/down.

Once selected, press the Menu key again and press and click "**Add Notes**."

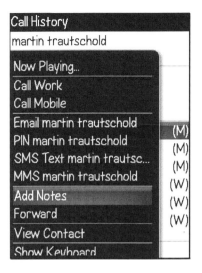

When you are done typing your notes, press the MENU key and select **"Save."**

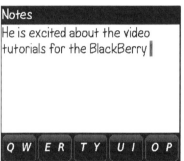

TIP: You can even "**Add Notes**" when you are still talking on the phone.

You may want to use the Speakerphone or your headset so you can hear while typing.

Setting up Speed Dialing

Speed dialing is a great way to call your frequent contacts quickly. Just assign them a one digit number key (or character key) that you hold, and their number is automatically dialed. There are a couple of ways to set up Speed Dialing on your BlackBerry.

> ## TIP: Just Press & Hold Key for Speed Dial
>
> The easiest way to set a speed dial letter on your keyboard is to press and hold it from your Home Screen. You will then be asked if you want to set it as a Speed Dial key. Select "Yes" and select the person from your Address Book to assign. It's very simple.

Option #1: Setting up Speed Dial from the Call Logs

Press the **Green Phone key** and then select "call logs" as you did above.

Highlight the call log entry (either phone number or name) that you want to add to speed dial and press the **Menu key**.

Select "**Add Speed Dial**" and press and click. Confirm that you do want to add this call to Speed dial.

You may be asked to confirm you want to add this speed dial number with a pop-up window looking something like this:

In the Speed Dial list scroll the phone number into a vacant slot or just press and click the screen in a vacant spot.

The number or symbol you selected is now set as the speed dial key for that phone number. If the number gets placed in the wrong spot, just press and click the screen on the number you want to move to a different slot. A "short" menu will pop up and you can then just select "move" from the menu and click any other slot.

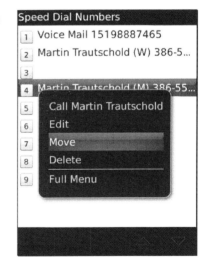

Option #2: Press and hold a key from your Homescreen

If you press and hold **any number key** from the number pad that has not already been assigned to a speed dial number, then you will be asked if you want to assign this key to a speed dial number.

Select "Yes" to assign it. Then you will be shown your Contacts to select an entry or select "[Use Once]" to type in a new phone number that is not in your Address Book.

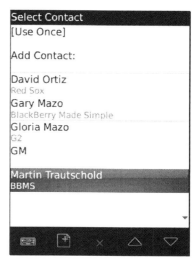

Once you select an entry or **[Use Once]** and type a phone number, you will see the same "**Speed Dial Numbers**" list. Press the **ESCAPE key** to back out. Give your speed dial a try by pressing and holding the same key you just assigned.

Option #3: Setting a Contact Phone Number as Speed Dial

Tap the **Green Phone Key,** choose the **"Contacts"** icon and start entering a contact name or number.

When you see the contact listed, scroll to it and press and click it. You will then see whatever contact information you have for that individual displayed. Just highlight the number you want to assign to speed dial.

Press the **Menu key** and select **"Add Speed Dial"** and follow steps to select the speed dial letter as shown above.

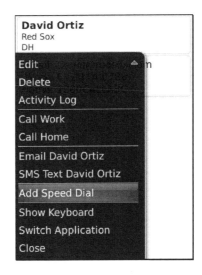

Using Voice Dialing

One of the powerful features of the BlackBerry is the Voice Command program for voice dialing and simple voice commands. Voice dialing provides a safe way to place calls without having to look at the BlackBerry and navigate through menus. Voice Command does not need to be "trained" like on other Smartphones – just speak naturally.

Using Voice Dialing to call a Contact:

The left-hand convenience key is (usually) set for Voice Command simply press this key. If you have set the key for another program, just navigate to your **"Applications"** folder and press and click on **"Voice Command."**

TIP: We show you how to set or change your convenience keys on page 134.

The first time you use this feature, the BlackBerry will take a few seconds to scan your Address Book.

When you hear "**Say a Command**" just speak the name of the contact you wish to call using the syntax "**Call Martin Trautschold**"

You will then be prompted with "Which number." Again, speak clearly and say "Home," "Work" or "Mobile"

Say **"Yes"** to confirm the selection and the BlackBerry will begin to dial the number.

Using Voice Dialing to Call a Number:

Press the Left Hand Convenience Key as you did above. (Assuming your convenience key is set to voice dialing, if it's not, you can change it by reading page 134)

When you hear "**Say a command**" say "**Call**" and the phone number. Example: "**Call 386-506-8224**"

Depending on your settings, you may be asked to confirm the number you just spoke or it will just start dialing.

Chapter 8:
Advanced Phone

Advanced Phone Topics

For many of us, the basic phone topics covered in the previous chapter will cover most of our phone needs with the BlackBerry. For others of us, however, we need to eke out every possible phone feature. This chapter will help you do just that.

Setting the "General Ring Tone"

The BlackBerry supports using many types of audio files as Ringtones. You can set one 'general' ringtone for everyone or set up individual tones for your important callers.

IMPORTANT: Place Ringtones in 'Ringtone' Folders

In some BlackBerry Smartphones, when you are attempting to set a Ringtone for a specific person in the Address Book or in Profiles, you can only browse to the 'Ringtone' folder, not the 'Music' folder. If this is the case, then you must copy your music ringtones to the 'Ringtone' folder using the methods to transfer media found in this book.

Setting the Ring Tone from "Profiles"

Click on the "Profiles" icon, either in the top left of the screen or from your Homescreen. Then scroll down to "**Set Ring Tones/Alerts**" at the bottom and press and click.

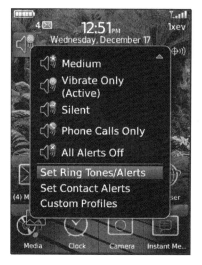 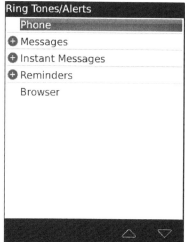

Highlight the top line which should say "Phone" and click the screen once more. The top field lists the current "Ring Tone" for the phone. Just press and click the button and you will see all the available Ring Tones for your phone.

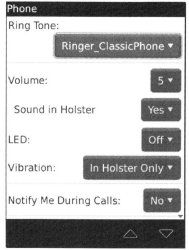 

Just select the new tone (you can even "Try it" and then reject it.) Once you are settled on a new tone – just press the ESCAPE key and **"save"** your changes.

To set one Song (MP3) as your general **"Ring Tone"**

Navigate to your list of music by pressing the "Music" icon (or Media ->Music.)

Find the MP3 file you wish to use as the general "Phone Tune."

Press the Menu key and scroll to "**Set As Ring Tone**" and press and click.

TIP: Unique Ringtones for Callers

Set up unique ringtones for each of your important callers, this way you will know when each of these people is calling without looking at your BlackBerry screen.

Set a Custom Ring Tone for a Single Caller (Set One Song (MP3) as an Individual Person's Ringtone)

Start the **Address Book** icon.

Find the contact you wish to edit by typing a few letters of their first and last name.

After you have the cursor on the correct person, press the **Menu key** and select "edit" and then scroll down to " **Custom Ring Tones/Alerts**" and highlight the word **"Phone."** Press and Click

 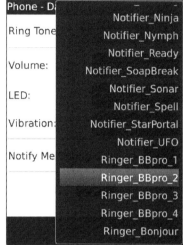

Press and click the button with the current Ring Tone and a list of available Ring Tones is displayed. If you need to navigate a different directory, just select "browse" at the top of the screen and choose the ringtone folder in which you MP3 files are stored. NOTE: You may not be able to browse to your 'Music' folder. (It depends on the version of BlackBerry system software you are running on your handheld).

NOTE: If you have already assigned a custom tune to this person, then it will ask you if you want to overwrite the existing tune.
Find the file you wish to use and press and click on it.
Press the **Menu key** and "**Save**" your changes.

More with Voice Command

Last chapter concluded with an Overview of Voice Command. Voice Command is a powerful tool for enabling not only basic phone calls, but other functions of the BlackBerry without having to push buttons or input text.

Other Commands

You can use the Voice Command Software to perform other functions on the BlackBerry. These are especially useful if you are in a position where you can' look at the screen (while driving) or in an area where coverage seems to fade in and out.

The most common are:
"**Call Extension**" will call a specific extension.

"**Call Martin Home**" will call the contact at their home number.

"**Check Battery**" will check the battery status.

"**Check Signal**" will let you know the strength of your wireless signal and whether or not you have "No Signal", "Low Signal", "High Signal" or "Very High Signal"

"**Turn Off Voice Prompts**" will turn off the "Say a command" voice and replace it with a simple beep.

"**Turn On Voice Prompts**" turns the friendly voice back on.

Changing Your Voice Dialing Options

You can control various features of Voice Dialing by going into your **Options** icon and selecting "**Voice Dialing**"

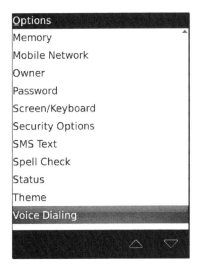 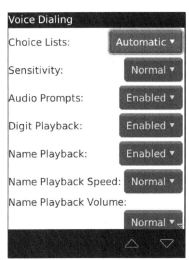

Change the "**Choice Lists**" – if you do not want to be confronted with lots of choices after you say a command. Your options here are "**Automatic**" (default), "**Always On**" or "**Always Off**".

"**Sensitivity**" – you can adjust the acceptance/rejection ratio of voice commands by adjusting the field that initially reads "**Normal**." You can go up to "**3 (Reject More)**" or down to "**-3 (Reject Less)**"

"Audio Prompts" – can be enabled or disabled from this screen or by saying "Turn Prompts On/Off."

"**Digit playback**" which repeats the numbers you say and "**Name playback**" which repeats the name you say, can also be enabled or disabled.

Finally, you can adjust the "**Playback Speed**" and "**Playback Volume**" of the Voice Dialing program.

Voice Dialing / Voice Command Tips and Tricks

There are a few ways to speed up the voice command process. You can also customize the way that Voice Dialing works on the BlackBerry.

To make Voice Dialing calls quicker

When using Voice Command, give more information when you place the call. For example, if you say "**Call Martin Trautschold, Home**," the Voice Dialing program will only ask you to confirm that you are calling him at home. The call will then be placed.

Give your Contacts Nick Names

Make a "Short Cut" entry for a contact – especially one with a long name. In addition to my "**Gary Mazo**" contact, I might also make a contact with the same information, but put "**GM**" as the name.

I would then simply say: "Call GM"

Call Waiting – Calling a 2nd Person

Like most phones these days, the BlackBerry supports call waiting, call forwarding and conference calling – all useful options in the business world and in your busy life.

Using Call Waiting:

Start a phone call with someone. Or receive a phone call from someone.

Now you can receive a call from a second person.
Press the "Answer" button on the screen or the **Green Phone key** while on a call to dial a second phone number or call someone else from your BlackBerry Address Book. This will put the previous caller on "Hold"

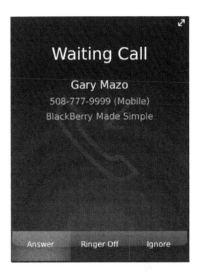

TIP: If a second person calls you while you are speaking to a first caller, just press the "Answer" button or the Green Phone key to answer the second caller – the first caller will still be waiting for you "On Hold".

Press the **Green Phone key** to toggle between calls.

Working with a Second Caller

When you are speaking to a person on the phone and your phone rings again with a second caller you can do a number of things, it just takes a little practice to get "smooth" doing it.

Option 1: Answer and put the 1st caller on hold
This is probably the easiest option – just press the Green Phone key. (This is **"Answer – Hold Current"**)

Then to swap between the callers, just press the Green Phone key again.

With two callers on the phone, pressing the Menu key allows you to do a number of other things including conference calling:

 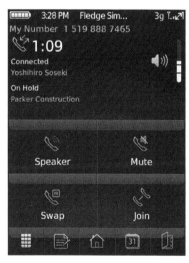

Option 2: Hang up with the 1st Caller and Answer the 2nd Caller

Press and click the "**More**" button in the middle and select "**Answer-Drop Current**" to hang up with the first caller and answer the second caller.

Option 3: Send the 2nd Caller to Voicemail (Ignore them)

Pressing the Red Phone key or just simply doing nothing will send the 2nd caller to voicemail. You are selecting "**Ignore**."

Call Forwarding

Call Forwarding is a useful feature when you are traveling or plan on leaving your BlackBerry at home. With Call Forwarding, you can send your BlackBerry calls to any other phone number you choose.

WARNING: Make sure you know how much your wireless carrier will charge you per Call Forwarding connection, some can be surprisingly expensive. Also, make sure that your SIM card has been set up by your service provider for this feature.

NOTE: Not all BlackBerry phone companies (service provider) offer this feature.

To Forward Calls Received by Your BlackBerry:
Press the **Green Phone key** and then press the **Menu key**.
Scroll to "**Options**" and press and click and then scroll to "**Call Forwarding**" and press and click.

Your screen may look a little different from the one below, but the functionality will be very similar. If your screen just lists "All Calls, Busy, No Answer, Unreachable," then you need to press and click on these items and select whether or not you want to forward each instance.

If your screen looks similar to the one below, then you have two options: "**Forward All Calls**" or "**Forward Unanswered Calls**."

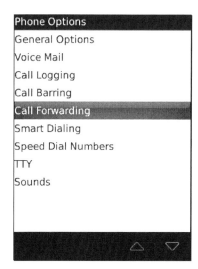
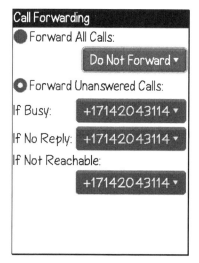

If you press and clicked "**Forward All Calls**," change the field to the Number you wish forwarded calls to be sent by pressing the Menu key and press and clicking **New Number**. This will forward every call received to the number you specify.

In the "**If Busy**," field press and click and edit the numbers (Just like you did above) for Call Forwarding in the **"If No Reply"** and "**If Not Reachable**" NOTE: the default set up is to send these calls to your voicemail – that is the phone number that is most likely already in these fields.
To Delete a Call Forwarding number, repeat steps 1-4 and press and click "Delete" after you have press and clicked "Edit Numbers."
Press the **Menu Key** and select "save."

Call Barring

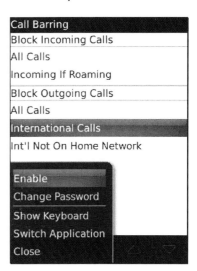

You would use Call Barring mostly when you travel to avoid surprisingly large phone bills (roaming or international calls can sometimes cost $1.00 / minute or more!)

You can select to block incoming calls, outgoing calls or both.

Press the **Green Phone Key**
Choose to block Outgoing Calls, All Calls or International Calls
Press and click on the MENU key and select **"Enable."**

Conference Calling

Conference Calling is a very useful option so that you can talk with more than one person at a time.

> **TIP**
> In your Calendar, you can pre-load conference call dial-in information so you don't have to dial it every time. This works great if you use the same conference call service regularly. See page 232 for details.

Take the recent scenario of one of the author's, where conferencing together two parties was faster (and safer) way to transfer needed information.
The author was leasing a new car and the car dealer left a voicemail to call the insurance company to "Approve" the proof of insurance being faxed to the dealer.
The author called the insurance company, expecting they already had received the dealer's fax number.

Unfortunately, the insurance company did not have the fax number.
Instead of hanging up and calling the dealer, asking for the fax number and calling the insurance company back, the author used the **BlackBerry conference call feature**.

Once the conference call between the dealer and insurance company completed, the dealer's fax number was immediately relayed along with any special instructions.

To Set Up a Conference Call
Place a call as you normally would.

While on the call, press the **Green Phone**

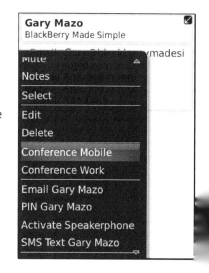

key  (press the "Conference Call" button on the screen) and either choose a contact from your Contact List or type in a phone number and place the call.

Choose which number (if the contact had more than one) that you wish to "Conference."

Gary Mazo
BlackBerry Made Simple

ymadesi

Mute
Notes
Select
Edit
Delete
Conference Mobile
Conference Work
Email Gary Mazo
PIN Gary Mazo
Activate Speakerphone
SMS Text Gary Mazo

1:54
My Number
1 519 888 7465
Conference
Martin Trautschold
David Ortiz

New Call
Susan Joh... (M)   9:05a
Martin Tra... (W)   12/04

If you add more than two callers to the conference call, just repeat the process starting with another "**New Call**" (press the **Green Phone key**). "**Join**" the calls as you did above. Repeat as needed.

To speak with only one of the callers on a Conference Call
Press the **Menu key** while on the Conference Call, select "**Split Call**." You will then be able to speak privately with that one caller.

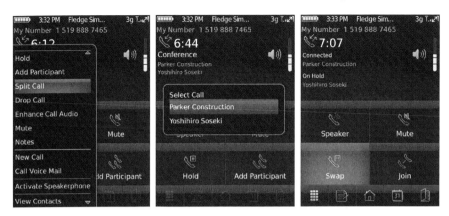

To End or Leave a Conference Call

To hang up on everyone and end the conference call for all, press the Red Phone key or press the Menu key and select **"Drop Call"**

How can I see missed calls on my Homescreen?

Many of the Themes will show you your missed calls with an icon with a phone and an "X" next to it as shown to the right.   Here is an image with one missed call showing on the Homescreen.

Dialing Letters while on a Phone Call ("Dial by Name Directory")

Sometimes you call a company with a "Dial by Name" directory that will ask you to "Dial a few letters of the person's last name to look them up."

If you have done this in the past with a regular phone or cell phone, you already know how to do it. *(If you are used to dialing letters while holding the ALT key on your old BlackBerry devices, think again!)*

To dial a name, you first have to hit the keyboard button in the lower left corner to see the dial keyboard.
.

Then you can dial as you would normally on any other phone. Example to dial "MAZO" you would press these keys:

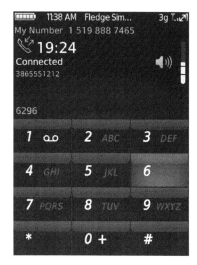

6 (for M)
2 (for A)
9 (for Z)
6 (for O)

Dialing Letters in Phone Numbers in your Contact List

Typing phone numbers with letters in your Address Book or in the phone: Use the same technique. If you had to enter **1-800-CALLABC** into your address book, you would type in 1 800 then press the ABC key and hold it until it locks. Then type "**CALLABC**" using the "Multi-Tap" method.

Adding Pauses and Waits in Phone Numbers (Voicemail Access, etc.)

Sometimes you want to type a phone number that has preset pauses and waits.

PAUSE = 2 second pause, then dialing continues. If you need more than 2 seconds, just put more than one pause in the phone number. Press and hold the '*' key.

WAIT = waits for you to press the screen before continuing dialing. Press and hold the '#' key.

If you have the need for a variable amount of time to wait, then you should use a WAIT instead of a PAUSE.

TIP: This is a great way to enter a voice mail access number to quickly check voice mail on a work or home number.
Here is an example of an address book entry with the VM access number, 2 waits, your phone number, 2 waits, then your VM password. 1800-555-1234 ww 386-506-8224 xx 13234

Just add a new Address Book entry with this phone number and then setup a speed dial number for this new entry. (See page 160 for help on Speed Dial)

More Phone Tips and Tricks

Like most features on the BlackBerry, there is always more you can do with your Phone. These tips and tricks will make things go even quicker for you.

To view and dial a name from your **Address Book**, press and hold the **Green Phone key**.

To insert a "**plus**" sign when typing a phone number, hold the number zero "0."

To add an extension to a phone number, press the "X" key and then type the extension number. It should look like this: **8005551212 x 1234.**

To check your voice mail, press and hold the number "1."

To view the last phone number that you dialed, scroll to the top of the Phone screen, then press the **ENTER key**. Press the **Send** key to dial the number.

Chapter 9:
Social Networking

BlackBerry smartphones aren't just for business executives anymore – but, you already know that. Your BlackBerry can keep you in touch in many ways beyond the messaging features shown earlier in this chapter.

Some of the most popular places on the "Web" these days are those sites that are often called "social networking" sites – places that allow you to create your own page and connect with friends and family to see what is going in their lives. Some of the most popular websites for "social networking" are facebook, MySpace and Flickr. Another popular site is Youtube for watching short videos on just about everything.

Fortunately, for BlackBerry users, each of these popular sites is now in "mobile format" for the BlackBerry.

Downloading applications for facebook®, MySpace® and Flickr®

Some BlackBerry smartphones may come with a link for the facebook application already installed – usually in the "Downloads" folder on the Homescreen.

The easiest way to get these applications is to go to the **mobile.blackberry.com** home page in your web browser (as we showed you on page 284) and press and click on the "IM & Social Networking" icon.

Facebook®

If you have the Facebook icon on your BlackBerry already, it will look like this:

Just press and click on the Facebook icon and you will be taken to the download page. Otherwise, go to the **"IM & Social Networking"** icon off the BlackBerry mobile Home Page and find the Facebook download.

Your wireless carrier may have a special download page for Facebook as well.

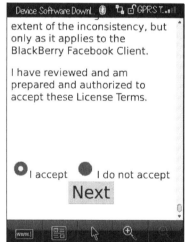

Accept all license agreements and proceed to download as per the instructions. Just press and click on "Download" and the program will begin to install.

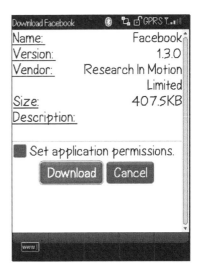

Once Facebook is successfully downloaded, the icon in your **"Download Folder"** should look something like this:

There is a lot to like about having Facebook on your Blackberry. All of your messages will be "pushed" to your device, just like your email, so you can always stay in touch. You also navigate the site in a very similar way to that on your computer. Just log in (usually with your email address and password) and you are ready to go.

MySpace®

Just like you did with Facebook, go to the mobile BlackBerry home page and download the MySpace client under the **"Staying in Touch"** category.

Accept all license agreements and download just as you did previously and you will then find a new MySpace icon in your download directory.

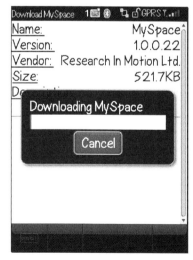

There will be one more license agreement to accept after you press and click on the icon. Then, just log in as you do on your PC and your MySpace page will be loaded for you. Like Facebook, all your MySpace messages will be pushed right to your BlackBerry.

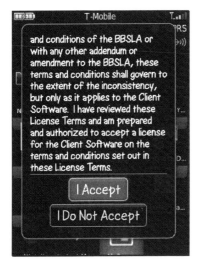 

Flickr®

Flickr is a social networking site that puts a heavy emphasis on the uploading of pictures. You can manage your Flickr page and upload pictures right from your BlackBerry.

Just navigate to the **"Staying in Touch"** section of the BlackBerry mobile home page as you did above and download the Flickr application the same way you did the other applications.

You will find a new Flickr icon in your **"Downloads"** folder. Just press and click and log in as you do on the computer to access your Flickr page. You can also press the MENU key and upload pictures right away.

TIP: See page 310 to see how to enable Geotagging of your pictures. This allows your GPS location to be tagged to each picture you take so Flikr and other software can show you a map of where every picture was snapped.

YouTube®

One of the most fun sites to visit on the computer is YouTube for viewing short video clips on just about everything. Your new BlackBerry is able to view YouTube videos without doing anything special.

Just navigate to the YouTube website (www.youtube.com) and then set a bookmark to remind you to go back there. Go to page 341 to learn how to set bookmarks and it will detect that you are on a mobile device. Search just like you do on your computer for any video you might want to watch. The video will load in your media player and you can control it just like you do any other video.

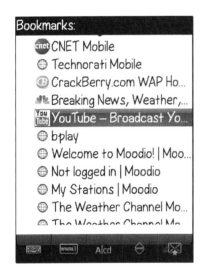
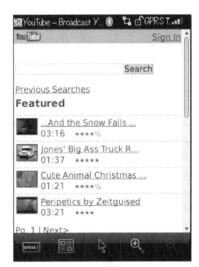

Chapter 10:
Email Like a Pro

Getting Started with Email

The BlackBerry, even though 'small and stylish,' is a BlackBerry to the core – a powerful email tool. This chapter will get your up and running with your email. In minutes, you will be an emailing pro!

Composing Email

The BlackBerry, like all BlackBerry Smartphones, gives you the freedom to email on the go. With the cellular network, you are no longer tied to a Wi-Fi hotspot or your desktop or notebook; email is available to you at all times almost anywhere in the world.

Emailing from the "Messages" icon

This first option is perhaps easiest for learning how to initially send an email.

Select your "Messages" icon on the Homescreen and press and click.

Just press the **Menu key** and scroll down to "**Compose Email**" and press and click.

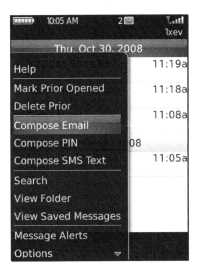

Type in the recipient's email address in the "To" field, if your BlackBerry finds a match between what you are typing and any Address Book entries, those are shown in a selectable drop-down list. Then you may just select the correct name by pressing and clicking on it.

TIP
Press the SPACE bar for the "@" and "." in the email address. EXAMPLE: To type susan@bbms.com, you would type "susan" **SPACE** "bbms" **SPACE** "com"

Repeat this to add additional "To:" and "Cc:" addressees.

If you need to add a Blind Carbon Copy ("Bcc:"), then press the Menu key and select "Add Bcc:"

 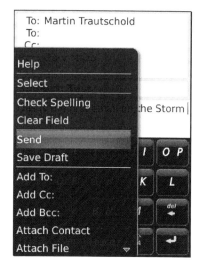

Then type the Subject and Body of your email message, when you are done, just press the MENU key and press and click "send." That's all there is to it.

If you have several email addresses integrated with your BlackBerry, you can select which one to send your email from the "**Sent From**" or "**Send Using**" address. Just scroll and press and click the field next to "Send Using" at the top of the Email composition screen. Press and click the "Send Using" button and select which Email Account to use.

Sending Email from your Address Book

After you have entered or synced your names and addresses to your BlackBerry, you may send emails directly from your Address Book. (See page 60 for help on sync setup for Windows™ PC users or page 85 for Apple Mac™ users.)

Navigate to your **Contacts** icon (Address Book) and press and click.

Begin to type a few letters from your person's first and last name to "**Find**:" them.

Once you see the name you want, then press the **Menu key** and select "**Email (name)**". The only time you will not see the option to "**Email**" someone is if you do not have an email address stored for that contact.

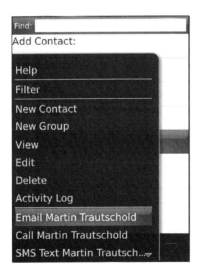

Tip: Hover or press "Q" To Quickly See a Person's Email Address

When you receive email on your BlackBerry, many times you will see the person's real name: "Margaret Johnson" and not their email address in the "From" field.

Sometimes you want to quickly see their true email address, many times it can tell you exactly where they work. The trick to do this is to scroll up and highlight their email address and press the "Q" (or "QW" if you are in SureType mode) key on your keyboard. Their name will switch to the email address and if you press "Q" again, it switches back.

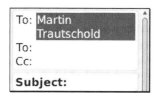 

Alternatively, you can just hover your finger over the person's name and see their email address in a little pop-up window as shown.

Replying To Messages

Once you get the hang of emailing on your BlackBerry, you will quickly find yourself checking your email and wanting to respond quickly to your emails. Replying to messages is very easy on the BlackBerry.

Open your email inbox by press and clicking on the **Messages** icon.

Notice the bottom row of icons on the screen. Just gently touch the screen on the icon at the bottom left (it has a green arrow and an envelope.)

Keep your finger there and "hover" over the icon and you will see the word "Reply" show up. Just press and click the "reply" button to reply to the email.

The recipient is now shown in the "**To**" field.

Type in your message, and press the MENU key when you are done and choose "**Send**" and your email is sent.

Email "Soft Keys"

We just used the "Soft Key" to reply to an Email message. There are a series of "Soft Keys" that you can use while in the Email program.
To use a "Soft Key" – just "hover" and you will see the function of the key. Simply press and click to activate that function.

The Soft Keys are:

 "Reply" – press and click to reply to an Email

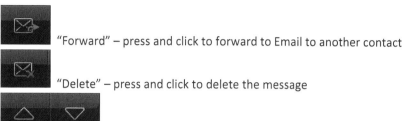

"Forward" – press and click to forward to Email to another contact

"Delete" – press and click to delete the message

"Scroll Up/Down" – press the Up/Down arrow to scroll up and down in the email

TIP: Press and hold the Scroll Up button to jump to the top of your Messages inbox.
TIP: Press and hold the Scroll Down button to jump to the bottom.

Attaching a "Contact" Entry (Address Book Entry) to Email

At times, you might need to send someone an address that is contained in your BlackBerry Contacts.

Start composing an email by selecting "Compose Email" from the Menu in Messages Icon.
Press the **Menu key** and scroll to "**Attach Contact.**"

Either scroll your contacts and then press the screen, or use the Keyboard to type in the first few letters of the desired contact and then press and click the highlighted name.

You will now see the attached contact shown as a little address book icon at the bottom the main body field of the email.

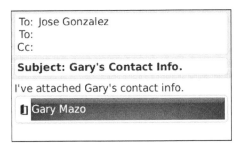

Viewing Pictures in Email Messages you Receive

On some email messages, you may see blank spaces where images should be. If you see this, then press the Menu key and select "Get Image" to retrieve just one image, or "Get Images" to retrieve them all. You may see a warning message about exposing your email address; you need to press and click "OK" or "YES" in order to get the image.

Attaching a File to Email

The BlackBerry is a powerful business tool. As such, there are times that you might need to attach a file (much like you would do on your computer) to the email you send from the BlackBerry.

NOTE: Depending on the version of your BlackBerry software, this "Attach File" menu option may not be available for you.

Start composing an email message and press the Menu key.

Select "**Attach file**" from the menu. Next, you need to locate the directory in which the file is stored. Your two initial options are "**Device Memory**" or "**Media Card**."

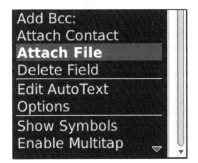

Navigate to the folder where the file is stored. Once you find the file, simply press and click on it and it will appear in the body of the email.

Setting the "Importance" of the Email:

Sometimes, you want your email to be noticed and responded to immediately. The BlackBerry lets you set that importance so that your recipient can better respond.

Begin composing a new email message then press the **Menu key**. Select the "**Options**" menu item. (Shortcut tip: Pressing the letter key that matches the first letter of the menu item -- the "O" key a couple of times will jump you down to that item.)

In the Options screen, you will see a line that says "Importance" and the default "Normal" at the end of the line. Press and click on the word "**Normal**" and you see the options "**High**" or "**Low**."

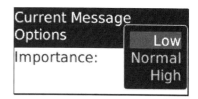

Just press and click on the appropriate option. Press the Menu key and "**Save**" your choice to return to the email message. Then press the Menu key and "**Send**" the message.

Finally, you will see high importance and low importance messages marked with special icons in your messages list (Inbox):

High = Exclamation point,

Normal = Nothing,

Low = Arrow pointing down.

Spell Checking Your Email Messages

Please see page 113 to learn how to enable spell checking on email messages you type and send. The spell checker may not be turned on when you take your BlackBerry out of the box the first time.

Opening Email Attachments & Supported Formats

One of the things that makes your BlackBerry more than just "another pretty Smartphone" is its serious business capabilities. Often, emails arrive with attachments of important documents; Microsoft Word™ files, Excel™ Spreadsheets or PowerPoint™ Presentations. Fortunately, the BlackBerry lets you open and view these attachments and other common formats wherever you might be.

Supported Email Attachment Formats:

- Microsoft® Word (DOC)
- Microsoft Excel® (XLS)
- Microsoft PowerPoint® (PPT)
- Corel® WordPerfect® (WPD)
- Adobe® Acrobat® PDF (PDF)
- ASCII text (TXT)
- Rich Text Format files (RTF)
- HTML
- Zip archive (ZIP)
- (Password protected ZIP files are not supported)
- MP3 – Voice Mail Playback (up to 500Kb file size)
- Image Files of the following types: JPG, BMP, GIF, PNG, TIFF (Note: Multi-page TIFF files are not supported)

  NOTE: Additional file types may be supported in newer versions of the system software running on your BlackBerry.

Features available in attachment viewing:
- Images: Pan, Zoom or Rotate.

- Save images to view later on your BlackBerry.
- Show or hide tracked changes (e.g. in Microsoft Word)
- Jump to another part of the file instead of paging through it
- Show images as thumbnails at the bottom of the email message.

Documents to Go™

Your BlackBerry also comes with the Documents to Go™ program from DataViz. This is an incredibly comprehensive program that allows you to not only view, but also edit Word, PowerPoint and Excel Documents and it preserves the native formatting. That means that the documents can open on your BlackBerry and look just like they do on your Computer.

How do you know if you have an email attachment?

You will see an envelope with a paperclip as shown.

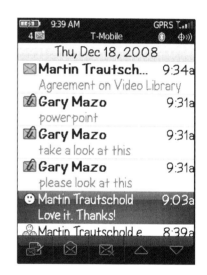

= Has Attachment

= No Attachment
(or it has an attachment that cannot be opened by the BlackBerry)

To Open an attached file:

Navigate to your message with the attachment icon showing (paperclip on envelope) and press and click on it.

At the very top of the email, in parenthesis, you will see **[1 Attachment.]** or **[2 Attachments]**, depending on number of attachments.

Press and click on the Attachment shown and select "**Open Attachment**"

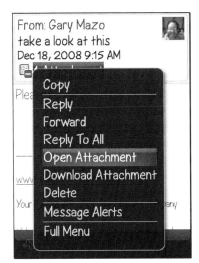

If the document is a Microsoft Office™ document format, then will then be presented with the option of **"View"** or
"Edit with Documents to Go."

For a quick view without true Word formatting – select **"View."**

To really see the document the way it was meant to be seen, we suggest you select **"Edit with Documents to Go."**
Press and click on the option you desire and the document will be retrieved into your BlackBerry.

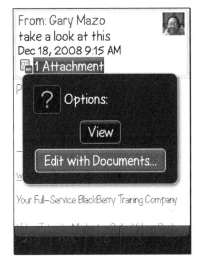

If you get an error message such as "**Document Conversion Failed**" you it is very likely that the attachment is not a format that is viewable by the BlackBerry Attachment Viewer. Check out the list of supported attachment types on page 197.

Editing with Documents to Go:

Once you select "**Edit with Documents to Go**" the document will open on your screen. You can scroll through just like you were reading a Word Document on your computer.

 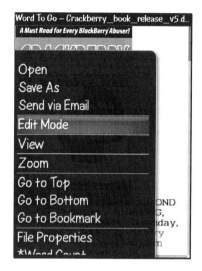

If you want to "Edit" and make changes to the document, just press the MENU key and select **"Edit Mode"** from the menu.

If you want to adjust the "Formatting" of the document, just press the MENU key and select **"Format."**

 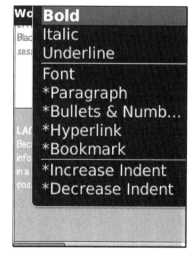

You will then see the Formatting options available to you:

Using the Standard Document Viewer

You may decide you don't want to use the Documents to Go Program. In that case, just select the "View" option when you go to open the attachment.

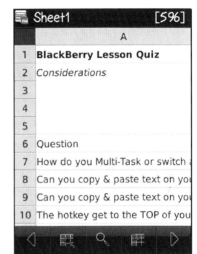

The document won't have the same look, but you will be able to navigate through it quickly.

To open a Presentation file or Spreadsheet

Follow the same steps you did earlier when you opened the word processing document.

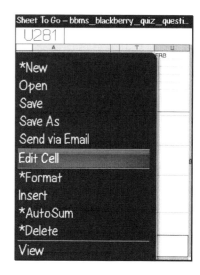

To Open a Picture

Open a message with pictures attached.

Press and click on the **[1 Attachment]** or **[2 Attachments]**, etc. at the top of the email message.

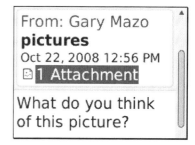

Select "Open Attachment" or "Download Attachment" (to save it on your BlackBerry). Then press and click on the image file names to open them.

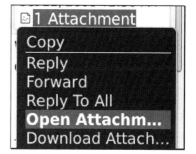

TIP: Once you have opened the pictures, then the next time you view that email, you will see the thumbnails of all the pictures attached to that email at the bottom of the message. You can then just scroll down to them and press and click on them to open them.

To save the picture, press the Menu key and press and click on "**Save Image**." The picture will be saved where you specify, either on your 'Media Card' or the main 'Device Memory'.

Other menu options include "**Zoom" (to expand the image)** or "**Rotate,**" (which will rotate the image) or "**Send as Email**" (Email as an attachment) or "**Send as MMS**" (Multi-Media Message = imbed image as part of email message).

To save it as a "Caller ID" picture in contacts, select "**Set as Caller ID**" from the Menu and then begin to type in the contact name. Navigate to the correct contact and save as prompted.

earching for Messages (Email, SMS, MMS)

You might find that you use your messaging so often, since it is so easy and fun, that your messages start to really collect on your BlackBerry.

Sometimes, you need to find a message quickly, rather than scroll through all the messages in your in box. There are three primary ways to search through your messages; searching the entire message through any field, searching the sender and searching the subject.

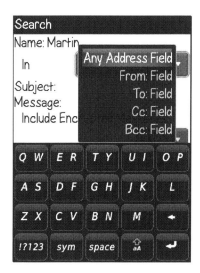 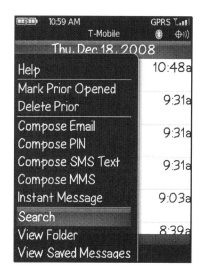

The General Messages Search Command

This is the easiest way to search for a message if you are not sure of the subject or date.

Press and click on your **Messages icon** and press the **Menu key**.
Scroll down to "**Search**" and press and click.
Enter in information in any of the fields available to you. When you are done, press and click the screen.
The corresponding messages are then displayed on the screen.

Using the "Hover" Technique to Search Messages & Call Logs (Activity Log)

One of the coolest ways to "Search" for all messages and call logs ("Activity Log") from a particular person is to simply "Hover" (just gently touch the screen from the messages list) over a particular message.

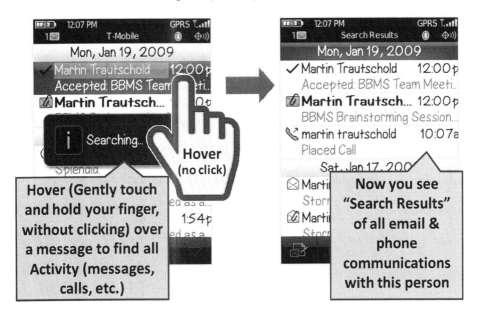

Hover (no click)

Hover (Gently touch and hold your finger, without clicking) over a message to find all Activity (messages, calls, etc.)

Now you see "Search Results" of all email & phone communications with this person

Your BlackBerry will display a "Searching" indicator and then will simply show you all communication with that particular Contact.

TIP: You can also find this Activity Log from the MENU in your Contacts icon.

Using the "Search Sender" or "Search Recipient" Command

> **TIP**
>
> The "**Search**", "**Search Sender**", "**Search Recipient**" and "**Search Subject**" work on SMS messages, Email, MMS – anything in your Messages Inbox!

Sometimes, you have many messages from one particular sender and you only want to see the list of your communication with that particular individual.

From the messages list, scroll to any message from the person you wish to search and press the Menu key - (Say that you want to find a specific message from Martin and you have 50 messages from Martin on your device – just highlight one of the messages and then press the Menu key.)

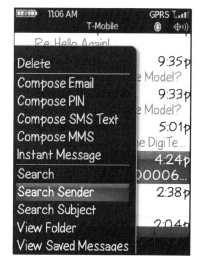

Only the list of messages sent by that particular person (in this case, Martin) is now displayed. Just scroll and find the particular message you are looking for.

Using the "Search Subject" Command

You might be having an SMS conversation with several people about a particular subject and now you want to see all the messages about those subject that are on your device.

Navigate to any message which has the subject displayed that you are searching for. The subject is displayed right under or next to the sender's name.

Press the Menu key and scroll to "Search Subject" and press and click.

All the corresponding messages are now displayed – just navigate to the one you wish to read.

Chapter 11:
Your Contact List

The "Heart" of Your BlackBerry

Your Address Book is really the "heart" of your BlackBerry. Once you have your names and addresses in it, you can instantly call, email, send text ("SMS") messages, PIN-to-PIN BlackBerry Messages or even pictures or Multi-Media Messages ("MMS"). Since your BlackBerry came with a camera, you may even add pictures to anyone in your address book so when they call, their picture shows up as "Picture Caller ID."

Picture Caller ID

How to get contacts from my SIM card onto my Contact List

If you are using your SIM (Subscriber Identity Module) card from another phone in your BlackBerry and have stored names and phone numbers on that SIM card, it's easy to transfer your contacts into your Contact list.

Start your Setup Wizard Icon; it may be in the Setup Folder.

Complete the screens in order to get to the **"Import SIM Card Contacts"** item as shown.

Then you will see a screen that says "Contacts Imported" or "No Contacts are saved on your SIM Card."

TIP: Your SIM Card only contains the bare minimum - Name and Phone. You should review your imported contacts and add in email addresses, mobile/work phone numbers, home/work addresses to make your BlackBerry more useful.

Setup Wizard
Date and Time
Navigation and Typing Tutorials
Email Setup
Set up Bluetooth®
Import SIM Card Contacts
Font
Language
Learn about the touch screen
Help

How do I get my Addresses on my BlackBerry?

You can manually add contact addresses one-at-a-time, see page 209. You can also sync your computer's contacts with your BlackBerry.

If your BlackBerry is tied to a BlackBerry Enterprise Server the synchronization is wireless and automatic. Otherwise, you will use either a USB cable or Bluetooth wireless to connect your BlackBerry to your computer to keep it up to date. For Windows™ PC users, see page 60 or an Apple Mac™ computer users, see page 85.

If you use Gmail (Google Mail), you can use the Google Sync program to wirelessly update your Contacts on your BlackBerry with your Address Book from Gmail for free! See page 240.

When is your "Contact List" Most Useful?

Your "Contacts" program is most useful when two things are true:

1. You have **many names** and addresses in it.
2. You can **easily find** what you need.

Our Recommendations:

We recommend keeping two "Rules" in mind to help make your "Contacts" most useful.

Rule 1: Add anything and everything to your "Contacts."

You never know when you might need that obscure restaurant name/number, or that plumber's number, etc.

Rule 2: As you add entries, make sure you think about ways to easily find them in the future.

We have many tips and tricks in this chapter to help you enter names so that they can be instantly located when you need them.

How to <u>Easily</u> Add New Addresses

On your BlackBerry, since your Address Book is closely tied to all the other icons (Messages/Email, Phone and Web Browser) you have many methods to easily add new addresses:

Choice 1: Add a new address inside the Contacts Icon.
Choice 2: Add an address from an email message in Messages.
Choice 3: Add an address from a phone call log in the Phone.
Choice 4: Add a new address from an underlined email address or phone number anywhere (Web Browser, Email, Tasks, MemoPad, etc.)

Choice 1: Add an Address into "Contacts."

Press and click on the **"Contacts" Icon.**

OR

Press the **Menu key** and select **"New Contact"** or just scroll to the top and press and click on **"Add Contact:"** at the top of the Contact List.

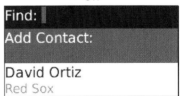

Add as much information as you know because the more you add, the more useful your BlackBerry will be!

TIP: Press the **SPACE key** instead of typing the "@" and "." in the email address.

TIP: If you add their work or home address, you can easily **MAP their address** and get directions right on your BlackBerry.

Need to put in several email addresses for a person?

While you are adding or editing their Contact entry, Just press the Menu key and select "**Add Email Address**"

Be sure to SAVE your changes by pressing the Menu key and selecting "Save"

Need to enter a phone number that has letters?

Some business phone numbers have letters, like "**1 800-REDSOX1**". These are easier than you might think to add to your BlackBerry address book (or type while on the phone).

The trick is to hold down your ABC key until you see the little lock sign. Then use the Multi tap method for putting in letters instead of numbers.

TIP: Need to enter a phone number with pre-set **pauses** or **waits** – like the pause before entering a voice mail password. See page 179 for more information.

Videos are an easy way to Learn: www.MadeSimpleLearning

Choice 2: Add an Address from an Email Message

Another easy way to update your address book is to simply add the contact information from emails that are sent to you.

Navigate to your message list and scroll to an email message in your inbox.

Press and click on the email message and press the Menu key.
Scroll to "**Add to Contacts**" and press and click.
Add the information in the appropriate fields, Push the ESCAPE key and **"Save."**

Choice 3: Add an Address from a Phone Call Log

Sometimes you will remember that someone called you a while back, and you want to add their information into your address book.

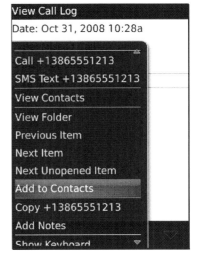

Press the Green Phone button to bring up your call logs.

Scroll to the number you want to add to your address book.

Press the Menu key and select "**Add to Contacts**"

Add the address information, press the Menu key and select **"Save"**.

Choice 4: Add an Address from an <u>underlined email address</u> or <u>phone number</u> Anywhere (Web Browser, Email, Tasks, MemoPad, etc.)

One of the very powerful features of the BlackBerry is that you can really add your contacts from just about anywhere. While the next steps show on the MemoPad, they can be applied to Tasks, Emails (email addresses in the To:, From:, and CC: fields and in the body of the email), and Web pages. Let's say you wrote down a contact's name and phone number in a memo, but never added it to your address book;

Navigate to your Applications folder and then click on the **MemoPad** icon.

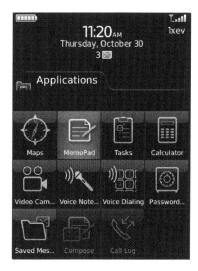

Scroll to the memo in which the contact information is stored and press and click.

Press and click on the phone number to bring up the "Short Menu" shown.

Click on the **"Add to contacts"** option and follow the steps above.

Why Can I Not See All My Names & Addresses?

If you are only seeing no names, a few names, or if you just added a new name and do not see it on the list, it is very likely your Contact List is filtered. This means it is showing you only those names that are assigned to a particular Category.   The tip-off that it's filtered is the BLACK bar (or other color) at the top with the category name – in the case of the image to the right; the category applied for the filter is "Business".

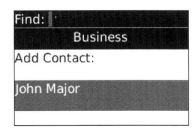

See page 220 to learn how to 'un-filter' or see all your names again.

How to Easily "Find:" Names & Addresses

Option 1: Use the "Find" feature in "Contacts"

The "Contacts" has a great "Find:" feature at the top that will search for entries that match the letters you type in one of three fields:
✓   First Name,
✓   Last Name, or,
✓   Company Name

Inside Contacts, just type a few letters of a person's first name, last name and/or company name (separated by spaces) to instantly find that person.

Press the letter "M" to see only entries where the **first name**, **last name** or **company name** start with the pressed letter:

"Martin Trautschold" – Match on first name

"John Major" – Match on last name

"Maritz company" – Match on company name.

Then press the Space key and type another letter like "T" to further narrow the list to people with an "M" and a "T" starting their first, last or company name. In this case, there is only one match: "Martin Trautschold"

Option 2: To Find & Call Someone

Sometimes, you just want to make a phone call to someone in your Contacts. Just press and hold the **Green Phone key** will start your phone with the Dial pad showing. Press the **"Contacts"** button and you can begin to search your Contacts.

 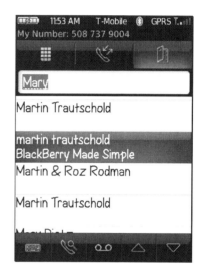

Type a few letters of someone's first name, last name or company name and the BlackBerry immediately starts searching for matching entries from your Contacts.

Press the screen on the "Contact" and the complete contact information is displayed. To place a call, just press and click on the number desired (if there is more than one) or press the MENU key and select the number to call.

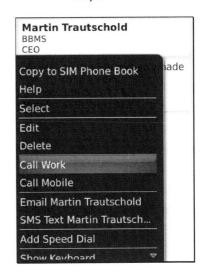

Press the **Green Phone key** to immediately call this contact.

Or, you may press and click the screen to place the call.

Managing your Contacts

Sometimes, your contact information can get a little unwieldy. Multiple entries for the same individual, business contacts mixed in with personal ones, etc. There are some very powerful tools within the **"Contacts"** application that can easily help you get organized.

Basic Contact Menu Commands

One of the first things to do is to make sure that all the correct information is included in your contacts. To do this, you will follow the steps to select and edit your contact information.

Select the Contacts icon and press and click on it.

Type in a few letters of the first, last or company name to "Find:" the contact or just scroll through the list.

Highlight the contact you want to manage by "touching" the screen.

Press the Menu key and choose "**Edit**" to access the detailed contact screen and add any information missing in the fields.

Adding a Picture to the Contact for Caller ID

Sometimes it is nice to attach a face with the name. If you have loaded pictures onto your Media Card or have them stored in memory, you can add them to the appropriate contact in your "Contacts." Since you have a BlackBerry with a camera, you can simply take the picture and add it as "**Picture Caller ID**" right from your camera.

Select the contact to edit as you did above.

Scroll down to the Picture or picture icon and press and click the screen.

Choose "**Add or Replace Picture**" from the short menu.

You have the choice of finding a picture already stored on your BlackBerry or taking a new one with the camera.

If you want to use a stored picture, then navigate to the folder in which your pictures are stored by scrolling the screen up/down and pressing and clicking on the correct folder.

Once you have located the correct picture, press and click on it and you will be prompted to "**crop**" the picture and save it. Just press and click.

You can use the camera instead to take a picture right now. To do this, press and click on the camera and take the picture. Move the box to center the face, press and click and select "**Crop and Save**"

The picture will now appear in that contact whenever you speak to them on the phone.

Changing the way Contacts are Sorted

You can sort your contacts by **First Name**, **Last Name** or **Company Name**.

Press and click on your "Contacts" – but don't press and click on any particular contact.

Press the **Menu key** and scroll down to "**Options**" and press and click. Then, press and click on **"General Options."**

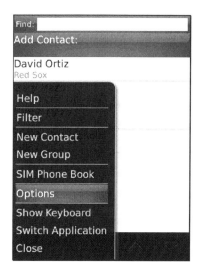 

In the "**Sort By**" field press and click on the "First Name" selection (It may say "Last Name" or "Company" if you have changed it) and choose the way you wish for your contacts to be sorted. You may also select whether to allow duplicate names and whether to confirm the deleting of contacts from this menu.

Using Categories

Sometimes, organizing similar contacts into **"Categories"** can be a very useful way of helping to quickly find people. What is even better is that the Categories you add, change or edit on your BlackBerry are kept fully in sync with those on your computer software.

Find the Contact you want to assign to a Category, press and click to view the contact, then press and click it again and select "**Edit**" from the short menu.

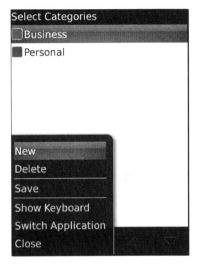

Press and click the Menu key and select "**Categories**."
Now you will see the available categories. (The defaults are **Business** and **Personal**.)

If you need an additional category, just press the Menu key and choose "**New**."

Type in the name of the new category and it will now be available for all your contacts.
Scroll to the category in which you wish to add this contact and press and click.

TIP: Unlimited Categories

You can assign a contact to as many categories as you want!

Filtering your Contacts by Category

Now that you have your contacts assigned to categories, you can filter the names on the screen by their Categories. So, let's say that you wanted to quickly find everyone who you have assigned to the "business" category.

Press and click on your Contacts.

Press the Menu key, scroll up and select "**Filter**"

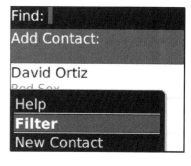

The available categories are listed. Just press and click (or press the **SPACE key**) on the category you wish to use as your filter. Once you do, only the contacts in that category are available to scroll through.

How do you know when your Contact list is "Filtered"?

You will see a black bar at the top of your Contact list with the name of the category –in this case you see the category is "**Business**"

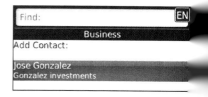

Un-Filtering your Contacts by Category

Unlike the "Find" feature, you cannot just press the ESCAPE key to un-filter your categories. You need to reverse the "Filter" procedure.

Inside your "Contacts," press the Menu key. Select "**Filter**" and scroll down to the checked category and uncheck it by press and clicking on it or pressing the **SPACE key** when it is highlighted.

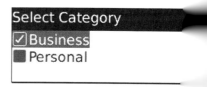

Use Groups as Mailing Lists

Sometimes, you need even more "Organizing Power" from your BlackBerry. Depending on your needs, grouping contacts into mailing lists might be useful so that you can send "Mass Mailings" from your BlackBerry.

Examples:
Put all your team in a group to instantly notify them of project updates. You're about to have a baby – put everyone in the "notify" list into a "New Baby" group – then you can snap a picture with your BlackBerry and instantly send it from the hospital!

Creating and Using a Group Mailing List

Start the Contact List (Address Book) by pressing and clicking on the "Contacts" icon.

Press the Menu key and Scroll to "**New Group**" and press and click.

Type in a name for your new group.

Press the Menu key again and press and click "**Add Member.**"

TIP: Make sure each member has a **valid email address**, otherwise you will not be able to send them email from the group.

Scroll to the contact you want to add to that group and press and click. Their name is now under the name of the Group.

Continue to add contacts to that group or make lots of groups and fill them using the steps above.

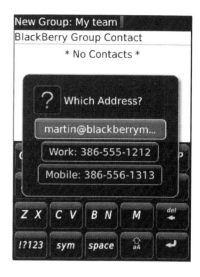

TIP: You can add either a mobile phone number (for SMS groups) or email address for Email groups – We recommend keeping the two types of groups separate. In other words, have an SMS-only group and an email-only group. Otherwise, if you mix and match, you will always receive a warning message that some group members cannot receive the message.

Sending an Email to the Group

Just use the Group Name as you would any other name in your address book. If your group name was "My Team" then you would compose an email and address it to "My Team." Notice, that after the email is sent, there is a separate **"To:"** for each person you have added to the group.

Chapter 12:
Manage Your Calendar

Organizing You Life with Your Calendar

For many of us, our calendar is our life line. Where do I need to be? With whom am I meeting? When do the kids need to be picked up? When is Martin's birthday? The calendar can tell you all these things and more.

The Calendar on the BlackBerry is really simple to use, but it also contains some very sophisticated options for the power user.

How do I get my Calendar from my Computer to my BlackBerry?

You can also sync your computer's calendar with your BlackBerry calendar.

If your BlackBerry is tied to a BlackBerry Enterprise Server the synchronization is wireless and automatic. Otherwise, you will use either a USB cable or Bluetooth wireless to connect your BlackBerry to your computer to keep it up to date. For Windows™ PC users, see page 60 or an Apple Mac™ computer users, see page 85.

If you use **Google Calendar**, you can receive wireless and automatic updates to your BlackBerry calendar! Learn how on page 240.

Switching Views and Days in the Calendar

The calendar is where you look to see how your life will unfold over the next few hours, day or week. It is quite easy to change the view if you need to see more or less time in the Calendar screen.

Day View   Week View

Month View

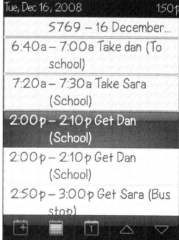

Agenda View

Videos are an easy way to Learn: www.MadeSimpleLearning.

Swipe to Move Between Days

Navigate to your Calendar icon and press and click. The default view is the "Day" view which lists all appointments for the current calendar day.
Swipe your finger left or right to a previous day or an upcoming day.
Notice the date changes in the upper left hand corner.

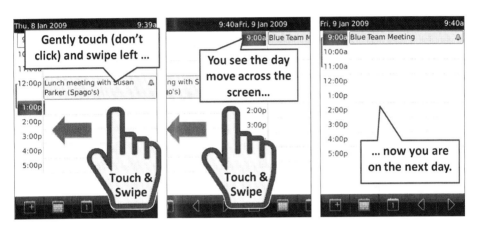

Using the Soft Keys to Change Views, Schedule or Navigate

Like many programs on the Storm, the Calendar has some "soft" keys at the bottom (or the top) of the screen. In the Day View screen, you will see keys for scheduling a "New" Appointment, "Viewing the Month", looking at "Today" or moving to the "Previous or Next Day. Just "hover" to see the function of the soft key revealed and then press and click.

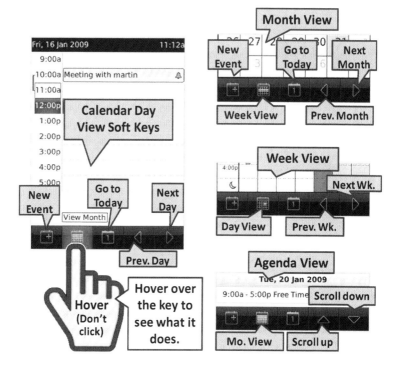

Scheduling Appointments

Putting your busy life into your BlackBerry is quite easy. Once you start to schedule your appointments or meetings, you will begin to expect reminder alarms to tell you where to go and when. You will wonder how you lived without your BlackBerry for so long!

Quick Scheduling (Use for simple meetings)

It is amazingly simple to add basic appointments (or reminders) to your calendar. In Day view, scroll to the correct day and time, press the **MENU** key to bring up your keyboard and just begin tying.

When you're done, press the ENTER key.

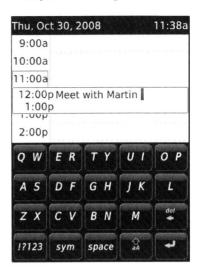

TIP

Quick Scheduling is so fast you can even use your calendar for reminders like:
"Pick up the dry cleaning"
"Pick up Chinese food"
"Pick up dog food"

Detailed Scheduling (Use when you need advanced options)

Press and click on the Calendar icon.

If you are in Day view you can simply press and click the hour closest to when your appointment starts.

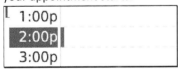

Or, in any view or press the Menu key and select "**New**" to get into the "New Appointment" Screen.

Type the Subject and optional Location. Press and click "All Day Event" if it will last all day, like an all day conference.

Press and click on the field you need to change and then just swipe your finger up or down to change the field. Press and click the screen again and the new value will be set.

TIP: Press and hold the "!?123" key to lock the number keyboard. Then you can use your **number keys (1, 2, 3**...) to enter specific dates, years and times. Example type in "23" to change the minutes to "23".

Alternatively, you can skip changing the end time of the appointment, and instead just change the length of the appointment by scrolling to "Duration" and putting in the correct amount of time.

Set a reminder alarm by press and clicking on "Reminder" and setting the reminder time for the alarm from five minutes prior to nine hours prior. TIP: The default reminder time is usually 15 minutes, but you can change this by going into your Calendar Options screen. (See page 231)

If this is a recurring appointment, press and click on Recurrence and select "Daily," Weekly," "Monthly" or "Yearly".

Mark your appointment as **"Private"** by press and clicking on the radio box.

If you would like to include notes with the appointment, simply input them at the bottom of the screen.

Press the Menu key and select **"Save."**

Customizing Your Calendar with Options

You can change a number of things to make your Calendar work exactly the way you need.

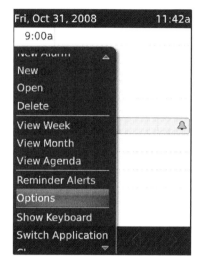
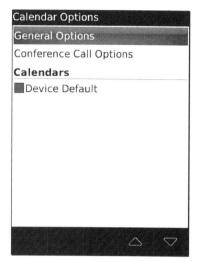

Before you can make any of the changes below, get into your Calendar Options screen. To get there, first open the calendar, press the Menu key and select "**Options**" from the menu.

Next, press and click on **"General Options"** at the top of the screen.

Change your Initial View (Day, Week, Month, Agenda or Last)

If you prefer the Agenda view, week view or month views instead of the default Day view when you open your Calendar, you can set that in the options screen. Press and click the drop down list next to **"Initial View"** to set these.

Change your Start and End of Day Time on Day View

If you are someone that has early morning or evening appointments, the default 9a – 5p calendar will not work well. You will need to adjust the 'Start of Day' and 'End of Day' hours in the options screen. These options are up at the top of the screen, under **"Formatting."**

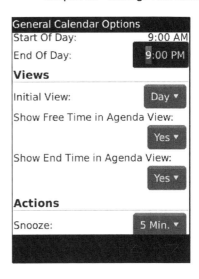

TIP: If you "Show Keyboard" from the Menu, then you may also use the number keys on your keypad to type in the correct hours (e.g. type 7 for 7:00 and 10 for 10:00).

Changing the Default Reminder (Alarm) and Snooze Times

If you need a little more advanced warning than the default 15 minutes, or a little more snooze time than the default 5 minutes, you can change those also in the options screen.

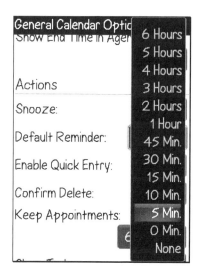

Scheduling Conference Calls on your BlackBerry

The BlackBerry has some very useful features built-in for scheduling and joining conference calls. You can actually pre-load the Conference call Participant or Moderator dial in and access code numbers so when the alarm rings as shown – you can simply click on the "Join Now" button.

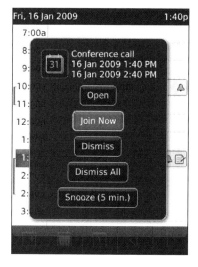

Videos are an easy way to Learn: www.MadeSimpleLearning

How do you make this happen?

It's easy – in the "Appointment Details" screen when you schedule a new appointment, you press and click to check the box next to "Conference Call." Then you can type in the access numbers as shown.

TIP: You might want to set the reminder at "**0 Min.**" so you are reminded to dial-in right on time, instead of 15 minutes early (the default reminder).

TIP: If you use the same Conference Call Dial-In service regularly, then you should pre-load the information in your Calendar Options screen.

From the Calendar, press the Menu key and select "Options."

Then click on "Conference Call Options"

Then, type in the Moderator and Participant basic information. This is used to pre-load the conference call numbers on all scheduled appointments. If it changes, then you can alter the individual appointment.

Copying and Pasting Information into Your Calendar or Anything

The beauty of the Blackberry is how simple it is to use. Let's say that you wanted to copy part of a text in your email and paste it into your calendar. A few good examples are:

- Conference Call information via email
- Driving directions via email

- Travel details (flights, rental cars, hotel) via email

First, scroll to or compose an email from which you want to copy and open it.

Method #1:

Press the MENU key and choose **"Select"** – then highlight (by touching the screen) the text you wish to copy. Once it is highlighted, press the MENU key again and choose **"Copy."**

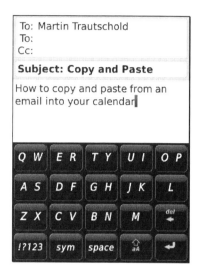

Method #2: Use Multi-Touch Method

Multi-touch allows you to touch the screen at two points and then highlight the text in between. It takes a little practice, but once you master it you will be copying like a pro!

We recommend placing your thumb at one end of the line you wish to copy and your forefinger at the other.

Videos are an easy way to Learn: www.MadeSimpleLearning

Notice below that when text is highlighted in an email, there are two highlighted "soft" keys at the bottom – one for "Copy" and one for "cancel selection." Just press the "copy" key to copy the selection.

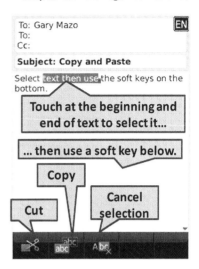

Press the **Red Phone key** to "jump" back to your Homescreen and leave this email open in the background.

Scroll to and press and click on the  "**Calendar**" icon to open it.

Schedule a new appointment by press and clicking on a time slot in day view.

Move the cursor to the field in which you want to insert the text that is on the clipboard. Then, press and click the "Paste" icon at the bottom of the screen or press the Menu key and select "Paste." Finally you will see your information pasted into the calendar appointment:

TIP: See page 232 to learn how to enter dial in information to your calendar for scheduled calls.

Press the **ESCAPE key** (between the Menu key and Red Phone key) and select "**Save**" when prompted. Now your text is in your calendar. Now it's available exactly when you need it. Gone are the days of hunting for the conference call numbers, driving directions or asking yourself "What rental car company did I book?"

Dialing a scheduled Phone Call from a Ringing Calendar Alarm

What is really great is that if you put a phone number into a calendar item (like shown above in copy/paste), you can actually dial the phone right from the ringing calendar alarm!

All you need to do is "**OPEN**" the event and then press and click the underlined phone number.

TIP: This is a great way to instantly call someone at a specified time without ever having to hunt around for their phone number!

TIP: You can also set a calendar event as a conference call so that you get a "Join Now" menu item. See page 232.

Alarms and Recurring Appointments

Some appointments are ones that occur every week, month or year. Others are easy to forget, so setting an alarm is helpful to remind us where to be or where to go.

To Schedule an Alarm:

Navigate to the Calendar icon and press and click.

Begin the process of scheduling an appointment as detailed above.

In the New Appointment screen, scroll down to "**Reminder**."

The default reminder is 15 minutes – press and click on the highlighted field and change the reminder to any of the options listed.

Press the **ESCAPE** key or the Menu key and select "**Save**".

To Change the Calendar Alarm to Ring, Vibrate or Mute:

Scroll to the upper left hand corner and press and click on the "**Profile**" icon or scroll through your applications and select "**Profiles**" and press and click. If you only see a listing of "**Loud**", "**Vibrate**", "**Quiet**", etc. as shown below, then you need to scroll down to the bottom of the list and press and click on "**Set Ring Tones/Alerts**"

Press and Click on the "Calendar" bar that should be highlighted in blue. You will be able to set a unique "Ring Tone" for Calendar reminders (and you can use any Ring Tone or MP3 Music track that is on your BlackBerry.

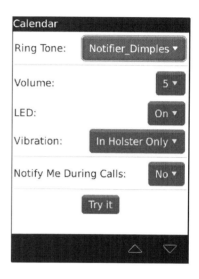

You can also set the vibration to occur either in a "holster" or all of the time or none of the time. You can adjust the LED to flash or not flash for calendar reminders. In short, virtually every aspect of notification can be customized from this screen.

Press the **ESCAPE** key or the Menu key and select "**Save**".

To Set a Recurring (Daily, Weekly, Monthly or Yearly) Appointment

Press and click on your Calendar icon.

Press and click on an empty slot in day view to bring up the appointment scheduling screen.

Scroll down to "**Recurrence**" and press and click in the highlighted field.

Select either "**None**," "**Daily**," "**Weekly**," "**Monthly**" or "**Yearly**."

Press the **ESCAPE** key or the Menu key and select "**Save**".

TIP: If your meeting is every 2 weeks, and ends on 12/31/2008, then your settings should look like this.

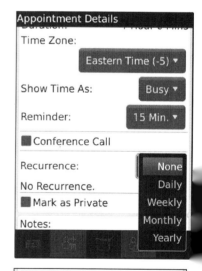

To Snooze a Ringing Calendar or Task Alarm

When a calendar or task alarm rings, you can "Open" it, "Dismiss" it or "Snooze" it.

To make sure you have the "Snooze" option active:
Open the Calendar Application
Push the **MENU** button and scroll down to "Options."
Press and click on "General Options"
Look under the **ACTIONS** sub heading and press and click in the field next to "Snooze."

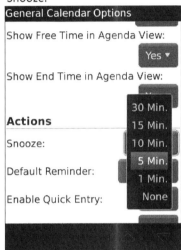

If you don't see a "**Snooze**" option, then you need to change your setting in your Calendar or Task options screen from "None" to some other value.

Press and clicking on the "**Snooze**" option does just that – it will snooze 5 minutes, 10 minutes, or whatever you have set in the Calendar or Task options screen.

But what if your 'pre-set' snooze time is not going to work for you?

In this case you should select "**Open**" and scroll down to the scheduled time and change that. Bring up the keyboard and use the **number keys** to **change the date or time**. For example, typing "55" in the minutes field would change the time to ":55."

You can also simply Press and Click on the number you wish to change and then just swipe up or down with your finger anywhere on the screen. When you are done, just click the Screen to "set" the change.

Google Sync for Calendar & Contacts to Your BlackBerry

The great thing about using Google Sync for BlackBerry is that it provides you a full two-way wireless synchronization of your BlackBerry Calendar & Contacts with and your Google Calendar and Address Book. What this means is anything you type in on your Google Calendar/Addresses "magically" (wirelessly and automatically) appears on your BlackBerry Calendar/Contacts in minutes! The same thing goes for Contacts or Calendar events you add or change on your BlackBerry – they are transmitted wirelessly and automatically to show up on your Google Calendar and Address Book.

NOTE: The only exceptions are those calendar events you have added on your BlackBerry prior to installing the Google Sync application – those 'old' events don't get synced. Contacts on your BlackBerry prior to

This wireless calendar update function has previously only been available with an expensive BlackBerry Enterprise Server (whether in-house or hosted)

Getting Started with Gmail and Google Calendar on your Computer
First, if you don't already have one, you must sign up for a free Google Mail ("Gmail") account at www.gmail.com.

Then, follow the great help and instructions on Google to start adding address book entries and creating calendar events on Gmail and Google Calendar on your computer.

Installing the Google Sync Program on Your BlackBerry

Click on your Browser Icon to start it.

Type in this address to the address bar on the top: http://m.google.com/sync

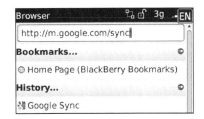

Then click on the "**Install Now**" link on this page.

NOTE: This page may look slightly different when you see it.

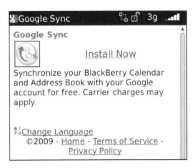

And click on the "Download" button here.

Note: The version numbers and size will probably be different when you see this page.

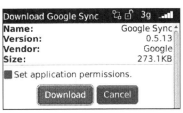

After you "Download" and install it, you can "Run" it or just click "OK". If you clicked "OK" and exited the Browser, you may need to check in your "Downloads" folder for the new Google Sync icon.

After you successfully login, you will see a page similar to this one describing what Google Sync will sync to and from your BlackBerry.

Welcome to Google Sync for mobile.

To get started, click the **Sync Now** button below and Google Sync will start synchronizing your handheld's calendar and contacts with Google automatically.

To access settings or initiate a manual synchronization, click on the **Google Sync** entry in the menu of your handheld's Calendar.

The first time Google Sync runs, it may take quite a while to complete the synchronization. If you have many Contacts, your Blackberry may also feel a little unresponsive for a short period, while Google Sync adds them to your Address Book.

Notice at the bottom of this screen, you will see details on which fields (or pieces of information) from your BlackBerry will be shared or "synchronized" with your Google Address book.

Finally, click "Sync Now" at the bottom of this page.

Google Sync can synchronize the following fields with your handheld: Title, First, Last, Job Title, Company, Email, Work, Work 2, Home, Home 2, Mobile, Pager, Fax, Other, Work Address, Home Address, and Notes. Other fields will not be synchronized with your Google Contacts.

You will see some sync status screens...

Then, finally, you will see a screen like this. Click "**Summary**" to see the details of what was synced.

Last Successful Sync

Calendar 20 Jan 2009 20:48:51
New Events   3
Deleted events   0
Updated events   0

Contacts 20 Jan 2009 20:49:25
New contacts   6
Deleted contacts 0
Updated contacts 6

Data Usage

Transfered since 1 Jan **22 KB**

From this point forward, the Google Sync program should run automatically in the background. It will sync every time you make changes on your BlackBerry or at a minimum every two hours. From both the BlackBerry Calendar and Contacts icons, you will see a new "**Google Sync**" menu item. Select that to see the status of the most recent sync. You can also press the Menu key from the Sync status screen to "**Sync Now**" or go into "**Options**" for the sync. If you are having trouble with the sync, check out our "Fixing Problems" section on page 376 or view Google's extensive online help.

Looking at the Results of a Successful Google Sync (Calendar & Contacts)

Google Calendar on the Computer: BlackBerry Calendar:

Notice the calendar events from Google Calendar are now on your BlackBerry. Anything you add or change on your BlackBerry or Google calendar will be shared both ways going forward. Automatically!

Google Address Book on your Computer: BlackBerry Contact List:

Notice all contacts from your BlackBerry Contact List are now in your Gmail Address Book. Also, all contacts from your Gmail Address Book are now in your BlackBerry.

Chapter 13:
Get Tasks Done

The Task Icon

Like your Contacts, Calendar and Memo Pad, your Task list becomes more powerful when you share or synchronize it with your computer. Since the BlackBerry is so easy to carry around, you can update, check-off, and even create new tasks anytime, anywhere they come to mind. Gone are the days of writing down a task on a sticky note and hoping to find it later when you need it.

How do I get my Tasks from my Computer to my BlackBerry?

You can 'mass load' or sync up your computer's task list with your BlackBerry Task icon.

If your BlackBerry is tied to a BlackBerry Enterprise Server the synchronization is wireless and automatic. Otherwise, you will use either a USB cable or Bluetooth wireless to connect your BlackBerry to your computer to keep it up to date. For Windows™ PC users, see page 60 or an Apple Mac™ computer users, see page 85.

Viewing Tasks On Your BlackBerry

To view your tasks, locate and press and click on the "**Tasks**" icon. Push the MENU button to bring up all your applications on the BlackBerry Homescreen.
You may need to press and click on the "Applications" FOLDER.

Then, find the icon that says "**Tasks**" when you scroll over it. You may need to press the Menu key (between the Green Phone key and Escape key) to see all your icons.

The first time you start tasks on your BlackBerry, you may see an empty task list if you have not yet synchronized with your computer.

Adding A New Task

Press the Menu key and select "**New**." Then you can enter information for your new task. TIP: Keep in mind the way the "**Find**" feature works as you name your task. For example, all tasks for a particular "Project Red" should have "Red" in the name for easy retrieval.

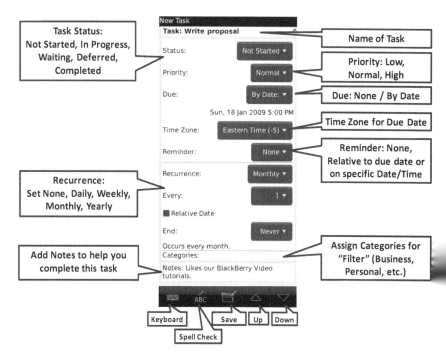

Task Status:
Not Started, In Progress,
Waiting, Deferred,
Completed

Name of Task

Priority: Low,
Normal, High

Due: None / By Date

Time Zone for Due Date

Reminder: None,
Relative to due date or
on specific Date/Time

Recurrence:
Set None, Daily, Weekly,
Monthly, Yearly

Assign Categories for
"Filter" (Business,
Personal, etc.)

Add Notes to help you
complete this task

Keyboard   Save   Up   Down

Spell Check

Categorizing Your Tasks

Like Address Book entries, you can group your tasks into Categories. And you can also share or synchronize these categories with your computer.

To assign a task to a category:

Highlight the task, press and click the screen and "**Open**" it.

You can set the "Status" of your task, as well as set the priority and the "Due" date from this screen.

To categorize, press the Menu key and select "**Categories**"

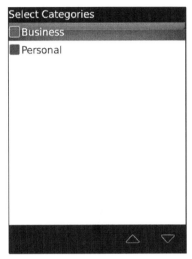

Select as many categories as you would like by checking them by clicking the screen or pressing the **SPACE key**.
You may even add new categories by pressing the **Menu key** and selecting "**New**"
Once you're done, press the **Menu key** and select "**Save**" to save your Category settings.
Press the **Menu key** and select "**Save**" again to save your Task.

Finding Tasks

Once you have a few tasks in your task list, you will want to know how to quickly locate them. One of the fastest ways is with the "**Find**" feature. The same "**Find**" feature from the Address Book works in Tasks. Just start typing a few letters to view only those that contain those letters.

In the example below, if we wanted to quickly find all tasks with "GO" in the name, then we type the letter "g" to quickly see them.

Managing or "Checking-Off" Your Tasks

Scroll down to a task and "touch it" to highlight it. (Don't press and click on it, unless you want to open it and make changes.)

Once a task is highlighted, you can use the soft keys at the bottom to manage the task:

- Mark it done - "Completed"
- Mark it in-progress
- Or even delete it.

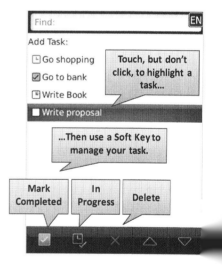

Sorting Your Tasks & Task Options

You may sort your tasks by the following methods in your Task Options screen: **Subject (default)**, **Priority**, **Due Date** or **Status**. You may also change "**Confirm Delete**" to "**No**" (default is "**Yes**"). You may also change the default Snooze from "**None**" to "**30 Min**."

Chapter 14:
MemoPad: Sticky Notes

One of the simplest and most useful programs on your BlackBerry is the included MemoPad. Its uses are truly limitless. There is nothing flashy about this program – just type your memo or your notes and keep them with you at all times.

Using the MemoPad is very easy and very intuitive. The following steps guide you through the basic process of inputting a memo and saving it on your BlackBerry. There are two basic ways of setting up Memos on the BlackBerry, either compose the note on your computer organizer application and then synchronize (or transfer) that note to the BlackBerry or compose the Memo on the BlackBerry itself.

How do I get my MemoPad items from my Computer to my BlackBerry?

You can also sync your computer's MemoPad notes list with your BlackBerry MemoPad icon.

If your BlackBerry is tied to a BlackBerry Enterprise Server the synchronization is wireless and automatic. Otherwise, you will use either a USB cable or Bluetooth wireless to connect your BlackBerry to your computer to keep it up to date. For Windows™ PC users, see page 60 or an Apple Mac™ computer users, see page 85

The sync works both ways, which extends the power of your desktop computer to your BlackBerry – add or edit notes anywhere and anytime on your BlackBerry – and rest assured they will be back on your computer (and backed up) after the next sync.

1,001 Uses for the MemoPad (Notes) Feature

OK, maybe we won't list 1,001 uses here, but we could. Anything that occupies space on a sticky note on your desk, in your calendar or on your refrigerator could be written neatly and organized simply using the MemoPad feature.

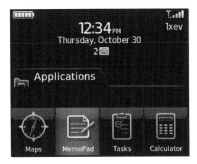

Common Uses for the MemoPad:

o Grocery list
o Hardware Store list
o Any Store list for shopping
o Meeting Agenda
o Packing list
o BlackBerry Made Simple Videos you want to watch
o Movies you want to rent next time at the video store.
o Your parking space at the airport, mall or theme park.

Adding or Editing Memos on the BlackBerry

To locate the **MemoPad** icon (your icon may look different, but look for "MemoPad" to be shown when you highlight it). NOTE: You may

need to first press and click on the "Applications" Folder to find it.

To add new memos to the list, simply press and click on "**Add Memo**:" at the top of the list.

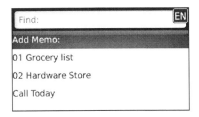

To open an existing memo, just scroll to it and press and click on it.

When typing a new memo, you will want to enter a title that will be easy to "**Find**" later by typing a few matching letters.

Type your memo below in the 'body' section. Press the **ENTER key** to go down to the next line.

When you're done, press the MENU key and select **"Save."**

Notice, if you have copied something from another icon, like Email, you could "**Paste**" it into the memo. (See page 233 for details on copy & paste.)

Quickly Locating or 'Finding' Memos

The memo pad has a "**Find**" feature to help you locate memos quickly by typing the first few letters of words that match the title of your Memos. Example, typing "**gr**" would immediately show you only memos matching those three letters in the first part of any word like "**grocery.**"

Ordering Frequently Used Memos

For frequently used memos, type numbers (01, 02, 03, etc.) at the beginning of the title to force those memos to be listed in order at the very top of the list. (The reason we started with zero is to keep memos in order after the #10):

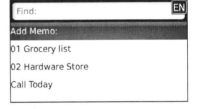

Viewing Your Memos

Scroll down by gently touching the screen and scrolling to a memo or press and click in the "**Find**" field at the top to type a few letters to find the memo you want to view.

Press and click on the highlighted memo to instantly view its contents.

TIP

Typing "**ld**" (stands for 'Long Date') and pressing the SPACE key will insert the date "Tue, 28 Aug 2007" and "**lt**" ('Long Time') will enter the time: "8:51:40 PM" (will be in the local date/time format you have set on your BlackBerry)

Organizing your Memos with Categories

> **TIP**
>
> **Categories** are shared between your Address Book, Task List and MemoPad. They are even synchronized or shared with your desktop computer.

Similar to your Address Book and Task list, the MemoPad application allows you to organize and filter memos using Categories.

First, you must assign your memos to categories before they can be "**Filtered**"
One way to be extra organized with your MemoPad application is to utilize Categories so all your Memos are "filed" neatly away.

The two default categories are **"Personal"** and **"Business"** but you can easily change or add to these.

To File a Memo in a New or Existing Category:

Start the **MemoPad** icon by press and clicking on it.
Locate the memo you want to file to one or more categories by scrolling and press and clicking on it or by typing a few letters and using the "Find" feature at the top.
Press the Menu key again and select **"Categories"**.

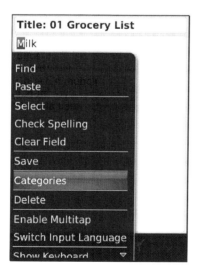
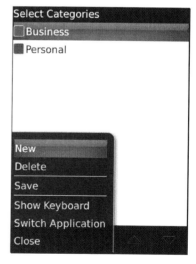

Now you will see a screen similar to the one below. Scroll to a category and press and click to check/uncheck it. You can also bring up the keyboard and use the "Space" key as well. You can add a new category by pressing the MENU key and selecting **"New"**

Then **"Save"** your category settings, and "Save" the memo.

To Filter memos using Categories / To only see memos in a specific Category Start the MemoPad by press and clicking on it.

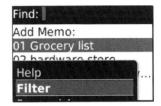

Press the Menu key and select **"Filter"**

Now scroll to and press and click (or press SPACE) on the Category you would like to use to filter the list of memos.
Filtered List: Category shown in black line at top under **"Find"**

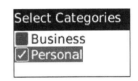

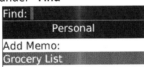

To 'Un-Filter' (Turn Off the Filter) on Your MemoPad:

You probably noticed that pressing the ESCAPE key (which clears out the 'Find:' characters typed) will do nothing for the Filter – it just exits the MemoPad. When you re-enter, you still see the filtered list. To 'un-filter' or turn off the filter, you need to:

Press the **Menu key**.
Select "**Filter**"
Scroll to and uncheck the checked category by **press and clicking the screen** or by pressing the **SPACE key**.

Switch Application / Multi-Tasking

From almost every icon on your BlackBerry, the MemoPad included, pressing the Menu key and selecting "**Switch Application**" allows you to "**Multi-task**" and leave whatever your current icon open and jump to any other icon on your BlackBerry. This is especially useful when you want to copy and paste information between icons.

TIP: Press and hold the MENU key to Multi-Task

Instead of using the "Switch Application" menu item, try
pressing & holding the **MENU key**. It's a good short cut!

Here's how you jump or "switch" applications:
Press the **Menu key** and select "**Switch Application**"

You will now see the "**Switch Applications**" pop-up window which shows you
every icon that is currently running.
If you see the icon you want to switch to, just press and click on it.

If you don't see the icon you want, then press and click on the "**Home
Screen**" icon. Then you can locate and press and click on the right icon.

You can then jump back to the MemoPad or application you just left by
selecting the "**Switch Application**" menu item from the icon you jumped to.

Press & hold the Menu key to jump back:

Forward Memos via Email, SMS, or BlackBerry Messenger

You might want to send a memo item via email, BlackBerry PIN message or
SMS text message to others. If so, you can use the "**Forward As**" command
from the menu. Alternatively, if the keyboard is hidden, you will see the

"Forward As" soft key on the bottom of the screen:
Highlight the memo you want to send and press the **Menu key**.
Select "**Forward As**", then select if you want **Email**, **PIN** or **SMS**.

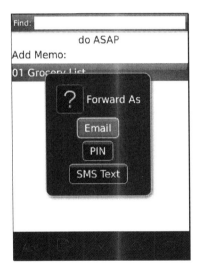

Finally finish composing your message, press the MENU key and select
"**Send**"

Other Memo Menu Commands

There may be a few other things you want to do with your memos, these can
be found in the more advanced menu commands.

Start the **MemoPad** icon.
Some of these advanced menu items can only be seen when you are either
writing a "**New**" memo or "**Editing**" an existing one.
So you either select "**New**" and begin working on a new Memo or select
"**Edit**" and edit an existing Memo.

From the Editing screen, press the Menu key and the following options become available to you:

Find – If you are in a memo item, then this will allow you to find any text inside the memo.

Paste – Suppose you have copied text from another program and want to paste it into a Memo. Select and copy the text (from the calendar, address book or another application) and select "Paste" from this menu. The text is now in your Memo.

Select – Allows you to do just the reverse – press and click here and select text from the Memo, then press the Menu key again and select "Copy." Now, use the "Switch Applications" menu item to navigate to another application and press the Menu key and select "Paste" to put the text in that application.

Check Spelling – Will run the BlackBerry spell checker on the currently open memo item.

Clear field – Clears all contents of the entire memo item – **USE WITH CAUTION!**

Save – Saves the changes in the Memo.

Categories – Allows you to file this Memo into either the "Business" or "Personal" categories. After selecting "Categories" you can press the Menu key again and select "New" to create yet another category for this Memo. (Learn more on page 254)

Delete – Deletes the current Memo.

Enable Multitap – Use if you want to change from SureType

Hide Keyboard – Use to see more of the screen and temporarily hide the keyboard

Switch Application – this is explained on page 255.

Close – similar to pressing the ESCAPE key.

Memo Tips and Tricks

There are a couple of tricks you can use to make your filing and locating of memos even easier.

Add separate items for each store in which you need to shop

- This can help eliminate the forgetting of one particular item you were supposed to get at the hardware or grocery store (and save you time and gas money!).

Put numbers at the beginning of your Memo names.

- This will then order them numerically on your BlackBerry. This is a great way to prioritize your memos and keep the most important ones always at the top of the list.

Chapter 15:
SMS Text & MMS

Text & Multi-Media Messaging

As you may be aware, a key strength of all BlackBerry devices is their Messaging abilities. We have covered Email extensively and now turn to SMS and MMS Messaging. SMS stands for "**Short Messaging Service**" (text messaging) and MMS stands for "**Multi-Media Messaging**" Service. MMS is a short way to say that you have included pictures, sounds, video or some other form of media right inside your email (not to be confused with regular email when media is an attachment to an email message.) BlackBerry is beautifully equipped to use both of these services – learning them will make you more productive and make your BlackBerry that much more fun to use.

TIP: SMS / MMS Usually Costs Extra!

Watch out! Most phone companies charge extra for SMS Text Messaging and MMS Multi-Media Messaging, even if you have an "unlimited" BlackBerry data plan. Typical charges can be $0.10 to $0.25 per message. This adds up quickly!

The Solution: Check with your carrier about bundled SMS/MMS plans. For just $5 / month or $10 / month you might receive several hundred or thousand or even 'unlimited' monthly SMS/MMS text messages.

SMS Text Messaging on your BlackBerry

Text messaging has become one of the most popular services on cell phones today. While it is still used more extensively in Europe and Asia, it is growing in popularity in North America.

The concept is very simple; instead of placing a phone call – send a short message to someone's handset. It is much less disruptive than a phone call and you may have friends, colleagues or co-workers who do not own a BlackBerry – so email is not an option.

One of the authors uses text messaging with his children all the time – this is how their generation communicates. "R u coming home 4 dinner?" "Yup." There you have it – meaningful dialogue with a seventeen year old – short, instant and easy.

Composing SMS Text Messages

Composing an SMS message is much like sending an email. The beauty of an SMS message is that it arrives on virtually any handset and is so easy to respond to.

Option #1: Sending an SMS message from the message list

Press and click on your "Messages" icon.

Now, press the Compose soft key at the bottom right of the screen.

Select **"SMS"**

Begin typing in a contact name or simply type someone's mobile phone number.

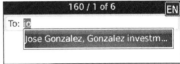

If you are typing a name, when you see the contact appear, press and click on it.

If the contact has multiple phone numbers, the BlackBerry will ask you to choose which number – select the Mobile number you desire and press and click.

In the main body (where the cursor is) just type your message like you were sending an email. Remember: SMS messages are **limited to 160 characters** by most carriers. If you go over that in the BlackBerry, two separate text messages will be sent. When you are done typing, just press and click the MENU key and choose "**Send**." That's all there is to it.

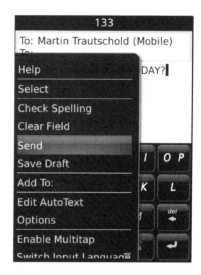

Option #2: Sending SMS message from the Contact List

Press and click on your Address Book icon (it may say Contacts, instead). Type a few letters to "Find" the person to whom you want to send your SMS message.

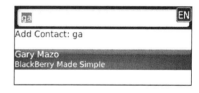

With the contact highlighted from the list, press the Menu key and you will see one of your menu options is "**SMS**" followed by the contact name.

Basic SMS Menu Commands

As with the Email feature, there are many options via the menu commands in SMS messaging.

Menu Commands from Main SMS screen

The BlackBerry adds an SMS Icon to the Homescreen for the first time on a BlackBerry. One way to initiate SMS messaging is to just press and click on the icon:

On the "Compose SMS Text" screen, when you are typing your text message, press the Menu key. The following options are available to you:

Help – Gives you contextual help with SMS messaging (See page 116 for more tips on this Help feature)

Save Draft – Keeps a copy of SMS for later referencing

Add To: Adds a second line for putting in a Contact

Choose Address – Allows you to send SMS to a Contact in your BlackBerry

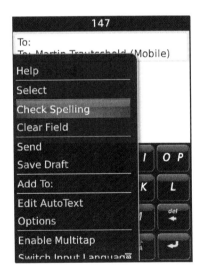

Edit AutoText – Takes you to AutoText Menu

Options – Brings up the SMS option menus

Switch Input Language – Allows you to send SMS in another language

Switch Application – Jump over to another icon so you can Multi-Task (learn more about this on page 255)

Close – The same as pressing the **ESCAPE key** – this closes your SMS text window and asks if you want to save changes.

Once you actually start typing your SMS message and press the MENU key, a new option appears: "Check Spelling" giving you the power of BlackBerry Spell Check in your SMS messages.

Opening and Replying to SMS Messages

Opening your SMS messages couldn't be easier – the BlackBerry makes it simple to quickly keep in touch and respond to your messages.

Navigate to your waiting messages from either the message icon on the Homescreen or your messages screen and press and click on the new SMS message.
If you are in the midst of a dialogue with someone, your messages will appear in a "threaded" message format which looks like a running discussion.
Press the **MENU key** and select "**Reply**."
The cursor appears in a blank field – type your reply, press and click the **MENU key** and select "**Send**."

Need to find an SMS or MMS message?

Go to page 203 to learn how to search for messages.

MMS Messaging on your BlackBerry

MMS stands for Multi-Media Messaging which includes Pictures, Video and Audio. **NOTE**: Not all BlackBerry devices or carriers support MMS messaging, so it is a good idea to make sure that your recipient can receive these messages before you send them.

Sending MMS from the Message List

Perhaps the easiest way to send an MMS message is to start the process just like you started the SMS process earlier:

Press and click on the **Messages icon** and press the **Menu key.**
Scroll down to "**Compose MMS**" and press and click.

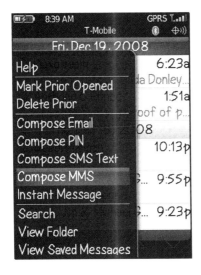
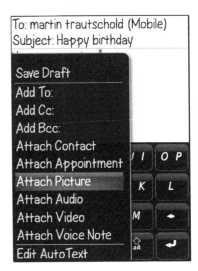

Depending on the phone company that supplied your BlackBerry, you may be prompted to find the MMS file you desire to send (these are often stored in your "templates" file)

Some BlackBerry devices have a pre-loaded "Birthday.mms" in this folder. Press and click on the Birthday MMS, if you have it.

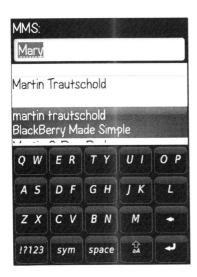

Then type in the recipient in the "To:" field and scroll to the appropriate contact and press and click.

You can add a subject and text in the body of the MMS. When finished, just press the Menu key and click on "Send."

There are lots of template MMS files you can download on the web and put into this folder to be selected in the future.

Sending a Media file as an MMS from the Media Icon

This might be the more common and easier way for you to send Media files as MMS messages.

Scroll on the screen to locate the **Media** icon and press and click. You will be brought to the Media screen.

Press and click on "**Pictures**" and find the picture either on your device or Media Card that you wish to send.

Just highlight the picture (no need to press and click on it) and press the Menu key.

Scroll down to "**Send as MMS**" and press and click. You will then be directed to choose the recipient from your contacts. Find the contact you desire and press and click.

TIP AND CAUTION: If you do not have an MMS or SMS Text Messaging service plan from your phone company, you can usually "**Send as Email**" for no additional cost. The only other thing to be aware of is whether or not you have an 'unlimited BlackBerry data plan.' If you don't have this 'unlimited data plan' then you will want to send pictures only very rarely because they can eat up your data much faster than a plain-text email.

Type in a subject and any text in the message, press the Menu key and "Send."

Basic MMS Menu Commands

You can personalize your MMS message even more through the MMS menu.

When you are composing the MMS message, press the **Menu key**.

Scroll through the menu to see your options; you can easily add more recipients "**To:**" "**Cc:**" "**Bcc:**"

You can also attach addresses from your Address Book. To add an Address – just press and click "**Attach Address**" and find the appropriate address on the next screen.

If you had scheduled a Birthday Dinner together, then you might want add an appointment from your BlackBerry Calendar ("Dinner at the Fancy French Restaurant for Two"), press and click the "**Add Appointment**" option.

To add an audio file to accompany the picture, choose "**Attach Audio**" and then navigate to the folder that contains the audio file.

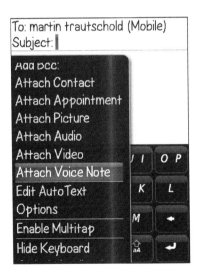 

You can also attach another picture by choosing the appropriate option from the menu.

Advanced MMS Commands:

While you are composing your MMS message, press the **Menu key** and scroll down to "**Options**."

In the **"Current Message Options"** Screen you will see the estimated size of the MMS – which is important, because if the file is too big, your recipient may not be able to download it onto their device.

You can also set the importance of this MMS as well as set delivery confirmation options.

For additional Advanced MMS commands, navigate from the Homescreen to "Options" and press and click. Scroll to "MMS" and press and click.
From this screen you can set your phone to always receive multimedia files by setting the first line to say "**Always**."
You can also set your automatic retrieval to occur "**Always**" or "**Never**".
You can check each checkbox to set your notification and message filtering options as well.

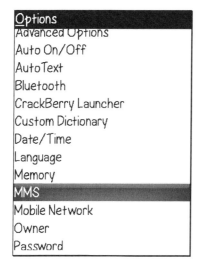

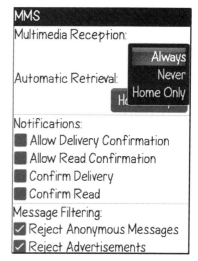

"**Allow Delivery Confirmation**" means to allow you to send delivery confirmation messages when you receive MMS messages from others.

"**Allow Read Confirmation**" means to allow your BlackBerry to send a confirmation message when you have opened an MMS message you received.

"**Confirm Delivery**" means to request a delivery confirmation from people to whom you send MMS messages.

"**Confirm Read**" means to request a 'read receipt' message when your MMS recipient opens the MMS message you sent them.

We recommend leaving the filtering options checked as they are by default.

MMS and SMS Text Troubleshooting – Host Routing Table "Register Now"

These troubleshooting steps will work for MMS, SMS, Email, Web Browsing – anything that requires a wireless radio connection. Please see page 376 for our entire chapter with more detailed steps on troubleshooting your wireless signal.

HOST ROUTING TABLE – REGISTER NOW: From your Homescreen, press and click on the **Options** icon.

Press and click on "**Advanced Options**" and then scroll to "**Host Routing Table**".

Press the **Menu key** and then press and click on "**Register Now.**"

NOTE: This image shows "Verizon" – you will see your own wireless carrier name on the screen.

While the BlackBerry is still on, do a "**Battery Pull**" – take off the back of the casing and remove the battery, wait 30 seconds and then re-install it. Once the BlackBerry reboots, you should be all set for SMS Text and MMS messaging.

Chapter 16:
Even More Messaging

PIN Messaging and Sending Your PIN with the "Mypin" Shortcut

BlackBerry handhelds have a unique feature called PIN-to-PIN, also known as "PIN Messaging" or "Peer-to-Peer" Messaging. This allows one BlackBerry user to communicate directly with another BlackBerry user as long as you know that user's BlackBerry PIN number. We'll show you an easy way to find your PIN, send an Email to your colleague and a few good tips and tricks.

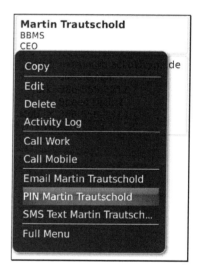

Compose an email to your colleague. In the body type of the email type the code letters "**mypin**" and hit the SPACE key – you will then see your pin number in the following format "pin:2005xx11" where the 2005xx11 is replaced by your actual PIN. Press the MENU key and select "**Send**".

Just press the MENU key and select **"Send"** to deliver the email with your PIN number.

You can also hide the keyboard and use the **"Send"** soft key at the bottom of the screen.

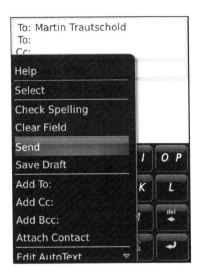

Replying to a PIN Message

Once you receive your PIN message, you will see that it is highlighted in RED text in your Inbox.

To reply to a PIN message, simply press and click on the message to open it, then press and click the Menu key and select **"Reply,"** just like with email and other messaging.

Adding Someone's PIN to your Address Book

Once you receive an email containing a PIN number from your colleague or family member, then you should put this PIN number into your Contact list.

If you don't already have this person in your contact list, then press and click on the PIN number to see a "Short Menu." Select "Add to Contacts" from the menu and then enter the person's information. Be sure to "SAVE" you new entry.

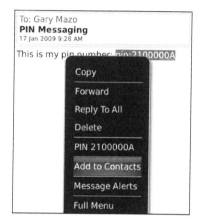

If you already have this person in your Contact List, then you should select "Copy" from the menu and Paste the PIN into their contact record.

Then press and hold the Menu key until you see the **"Switch Application"** pop-up window.
Select "Contacts" if you see it.
Select "Home Screen" if you don't see "Contacts" – then click on Contacts

 to start it from the Home Screen.

Type a few letters of the person's first, last or company name to "FIND" them and then press the Menu key and select "Edit"

Scroll down to put the cursor in the **PIN** field, press the Menu key and select "**Paste**."

Press the Menu key and select **"Save"**

Now, next time you search through your "Contacts" you will have the new option of sending a PIN message in addition to the other email, SMS, MMS and phone options.

BlackBerry Messenger

So far, we have covered email, SMS text, MMS and BlackBerry PIN-to-PIN messaging. If you still need other ways of communicating with friends, family and colleagues you can try BlackBerry Messenger or any one of the most popular Instant Messaging programs like AIM® (AOL Instant Messenger), Yahoo® or GoogleTalk® instant messengers. The BlackBerry is really the ultimate communication tool.

TIP: Don't see the BlackBerry Messenger Icon?

First, look in your "Messaging" folder or "Applications" folder. If you don't see it then download and install the BlackBerry Messenger icon. Go to "**mobile.blackberry.com**" from your BlackBerry Web Browser and follow the directions.

Many users have IM programs on their PC, or even their Mobile Phone. BlackBerry Includes a Messaging program just for fellow BlackBerry users called BlackBerry Messenger. You will find the BlackBerry Messenger icon in your applications menu.

Setting up BlackBerry Messenger

BlackBerry Messenger offers you a little more "secure" way of keeping in touch quickly with fellow BlackBerry users. Setup is very easy.

If you don't see the Blackberry Messenger icon, then press the Menu key and look for the "Instant Messenger" folder, click on it.

Press and click on the **BlackBerry Messenger** icon. You will be prompted to set your User Name.

Type in your **"Display" Name** - this is the name that others will see - and press and click OK. You will then be asked to set a BlackBerry Messenger password. Type in your password and confirm, then press and click OK.

Add Contacts to your BlackBerry Messenger Group

Once your User Name is setup, you need to add contacts to your BlackBerry Messenger Group. In BlackBerry Messenger, your contacts are fellow BlackBerry users who have the BlackBerry Messenger program installed on their handhelds.

Navigate to the main BlackBerry Messenger screen and press the Menu key. Scroll to "**Add a Contact**" and press and click.

Begin typing the name of the desired contact. When the desired contact appears, press and click on contact. Choose whether to invite the contact by PIN or email.

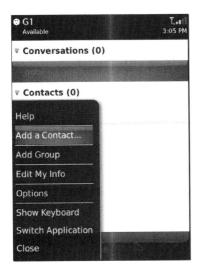 

The BlackBerry generates a message stating: "(Name) would like to add you to his/her BlackBerry Messenger. Press and click OK and the message is sent to this person."

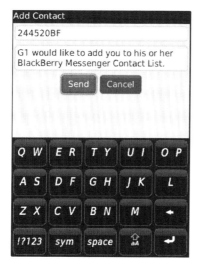 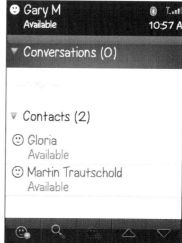

The Message request shows up in your Pending group, under Contacts.

The contact will be listed under "**Pending**" until the recipient responds to your invitation.

If you do not get a response, then press and click on their name and use another communications method (e.g. Phone, Email, SMS Text) to ask your

colleague to "hurry up."

Joining a Fellow User's BlackBerry Messenger Group

You may be invited to join another BlackBerry user's Messaging group. You can either **Accept** or **Decline** this invitation.

You will receive your invitations via email or you can see them directly in BlackBerry Messenger.

Press and click on your BlackBerry Messenger icon.

Scroll to your "**Requests**" group and highlight the invitation and press and click.

A menu pops up with three options: Accept, Decline, or Remove.

Press and click on "**Accept**" and you will now be part of the Messaging group. Press and click "**Decline**" to deny the invitation or "**Remove**" to no longer show the invitation on your BlackBerry.

BlackBerry Messenger Menu Commands

Open BlackBerry Messenger, get to your main screen and press the Menu key.

The following options are available to you:

"**Add a Contact**" – Use this to add people to your conversations and groups.

"**Expand**" – simply expands the dialogue screen – if screen is already open. The menu command reads "**Collapse**." (TIP: Press and clicking on the main conversation screen does the same thing.)

"**Collapse All**" – Hides all group members.

"**Add Group**" – Press and click to add a new messaging group such as "Work", "Family" or "Friends."

"**Edit Group**" – Use this to rename your messaging groups.

"**My Status**" – Press and click to make yourself "Available" or "**Unavailable**" to your Messaging Buddies

"**Edit My Info**" – Change your Name and/or Password

"**Options**" – Press and click to bring up your Options screen (see below for details)

"**Switch Application**" – Press this to "multi-task" or jump to another application while leaving the messenger application running.

"**Close**" – Exit the Messenger application.

BlackBerry Messenger Options Screen

If you wanted even more control of your Messenger, you would press the Menu key and select **"Options."** On the Messenger Options screen, you can set the following:

Whether or not your BlackBerry will vibrate when someone "**PING**s" you (the default is **"Yes"**).

Have the BlackBerry force you to enter your password every time you send a "new contact" request – would be a good security measure if your BlackBerry was lost.

Set whether or not your requests can be forwarded by other people – the default is **"yes."**

Finally, you may choose to display your Messenger conversations in your Messages (Email Inbox) – the default is **"Yes"** If you change it to **"No"** then none of your Messenger conversations will show up in your email inbox.

Starting or Continuing Conversations and Emoticons

While Messaging is a lot like Text Messaging, you actually have more options for personal expression and the ability to see a complete conversation with the Messaging program.

Your Conversation List is in your Main Screen. Just highlight the individual with whom you are conversing and press and click on them. The conversation screen opens.

Just type in the new message and press and click the MENU and select "**Send**".

To add an Emoticon to your message, press the **"Emoticon"** soft key button 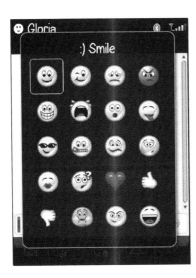 and swipe your finger to the emoticon you wish to use.

Just press and click on the desired emoticon and it will appear in the message. TIP: You can also type the characters shown to get the emoticon you want: e.g. ":)" = Smile and "<3<3" = Love Struck as shown below.

Sending Files to a Message Buddy

In the midst of your conversation, you can send a file very easily (At the time of publishing of this book, you were limited to sending only files that are images, photos or sound files – ringtones and music).

Press and click on the contact in your conversation screen and open the dialogue with that individual.

Press the Menu key and select "**Send a File**." Choose whether you wish to send an image or an audio file.

Using the touch screen, navigate to where the image or audio file is stored on your BlackBerry and press and click on it.

Selecting the file will automatically send it to your message buddy.

NOTE: Some BlackBerry providers (phone companies) may limit the size of file you can send via Bluetooth to a small size, such as 15 kilobytes (kb). Most pictures maybe 300kb or more and full songs might be 500kb or more.

PING a Contact

Let's say that you wanted to reach a BlackBerry Messenger contact quickly. One option available to you is to "**PING**" that contact. When you Ping a BlackBerry user, their device will vibrate once to let them know that they are wanted/needed immediately. (TIP: You can set your BlackBerry to vibrate or not vibrate when you receive a "PING" in your BlackBerry Messenger Options screen.)

Open up a conversation with a contact from the contact screen.

Press the Menu key and scroll down to "**Ping Contact**"

The dialogue screen will reflect the Ping by showing "PING!!!" in capital red letters. The Ping recipient will notice that their BlackBerry vibrates and indicates that you have "pinged" them.

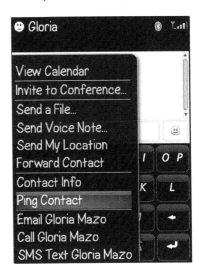

Using the "My Status" Options (Your Availability to Others)

Sometimes, you might now want to be disrupted with Instant Messages. You can change your status to **"Unavailable"** and you won't be disturbed. Conversely, one of your contacts might be "Offline" so to speak and you want to know when they become **"Available."** You can even set an alert to notify you of their availability.

Navigate to your main Messaging screen and press the Menu key.

Scroll to "**Edit My Info**" and press and click.

Choose either "**Available**" or "**Unavailable**."

To set an alert, just highlight an "**Unavailable**" contact from your Contact List screen and press the Menu key.

Scroll to "**Set Alert**" and you will be notified as soon as he/she becomes available.

Conferencing with BlackBerry Messenger

One very cool new feature on BlackBerry Messenger is the ability to have a "**Conference**" chat with two or more of your Messenger Contacts. Just start up a conversation as you did before. Here you can see that I am in a conversation with my Friend Martin:

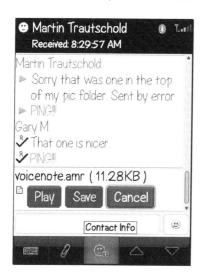

Now, let's say I wanted to invite my wife Gloria to join the conversation; I would press the **MENU** button and click on *"Invite to Conference."*

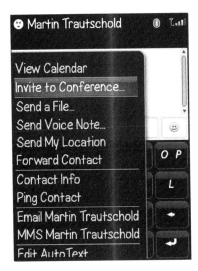

I then just find the Contact from my Messenger list I want to invite, in this case – Gloria.

An invitation is sent for her to join us. When she accepts, it will be noted on the Messenger screen and all three of us can have our conversation.

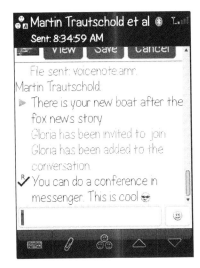
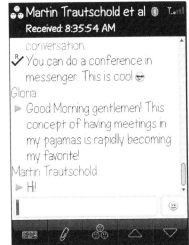

Using AIM™, Yahoo™ and Google Talk™ Messaging

After you get used to BlackBerry Messenger you will begin to see that it is a powerful way of quickly keeping in touch with friends, family and colleagues. Realizing that many are still not in the "BlackBerry" world, you can also access and use popular IM programs like AOL Instant Messenger ("AIM"), Yahoo

Messenger and Google™ Talk™ Messenger right out of the box on the BlackBerry. Individual carriers do have some restrictions, however, and you will need to check your carrier web sites to see which services are supported.

To Install More Instant Messenger Applications on the BlackBerry

First see if your carrier has placed an "**IM**" or "**Instant Messaging**" folder icon in your applications directory – this may already have the icons installed that you want to use. Navigate to "Applications" and scroll for an icon that simply is called "IM."

If you have an IM folder icon, press and click and follow the on screen prompts.

If there is no IM icon, start your **Web Browser** on the BlackBerry. Press the **Menu key** and select "**Go To...**" then type in www.mobile.blackberry.com or "**mobile.blackberry.com**" to get to the BlackBerry "Home" page which may look something like the image below.

(Please forgive us if this web page looks very different by the time you see it – web sites can change very frequently!)

Locate the "**IM & Social Networking**" group, you need to scroll down a bit, then press and click on the Instant Messenger application you want to download and install.

At publishing time, this was the list of currently available **Instant Messaging** and **Social Networking** applications from mobile.blackberry.com.

Almost certainly this list will be different by the time you are reading this book.

Facebook® for BlackBerry

Flickr

Windows Live™ Messenger

AOL Instant Messenger™

ICQ®

Yahoo! Messenger™

Google Talk™

BlackBerry Messenger

ShoZu

For more help to download and install Third Party software, please check out our chapter devoted to adding and removing software starting on page 349.

Chapter 17:
Add Memory & Media

How to Boost Your Memory with a Media Card

Your BlackBerry comes with 128 MB (Megabytes) of flash memory and 1 GB of "on board" memory, but all that won't all be available to you. Operating system and installed software takes up some of that room and so will all your personal information. (The image of the SanDisk MicroSD card and the SanDisk logo are copyrights owned by SanDisk Corporation)

Since your BlackBerry is also a very capable Media device, you will probably want more room to store things like Music files, Videos, Ringtones and pictures.

That's where the "MicroSD" memory card comes in. Some wireless carriers are pre-installed an 8GB memory card in the BlackBerry – but you can expand that to 16GB if you like.

Installing your Memory Card / Media Card

The BlackBerry actually has the MicroSD card slot inside the back cover, near the battery.

Just press the release buttons and take off the back battery cover.

Hold the Memory card with the metal contacts facing downwards.

The small "notch" on the card should be on the right hand side.

Battery

SIM Card slot.

Media Card slot.
Slide card up with notch to right and metal contacts facing down.

Just slide the card into the slot until it stops – don't force it!

To remove the card, we recommend using the eraser tip of a pencil to help "move" it out of the slot.

You don't even need to power off the BlackBerry; you can insert the card with the BlackBerry on.
When the card is correctly inserted you should see "Media Card Inserted" appear on the screen.

Verify the Media Card Installation and Free Memory

Once installed, it is a good idea to double check that the card is installed correctly and how much free space is available.

Press the MENU key and scroll to the **"Options"** icon and press and click on it. Scroll down and select **"Memory"** and press and click.

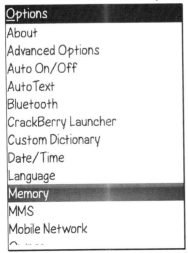

TIP: Pressing the first letter of an entry in the Options screen (or in menus) will jump to the first entry in the list starting with that letter. So pressing "M" will jump to the first entry starting with "M", pressing it a second time will jump to the next "M" entry.

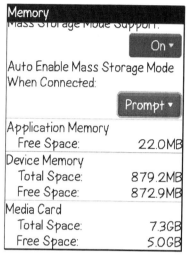

Look at the total space figure at the bottom of the screen. An 8.0 GB card will read about 7.3GB (1GB equals about 1,000 MB). If you see that, all is good.

This image shows a Media Card with 5.0 GB of free space.

How to transfer Pictures, Songs and Videos onto your Media Card - Using "Mass Storage Mode" (Both Mac™ and Windows™ users)

This works whether you have a Windows or a Mac computer. We will show images for the Windows computer process, and it will be fairly similar for your Mac. This transfer method assumes you have stored your media on a MicroSD media card in your BlackBerry.

To get to this screen, go into your **Options** icon, then scroll down and press and click on "**Memory.**"

Make sure your Media Card "**Mass Storage**" mode support is "**On**" and other settings are as shown.

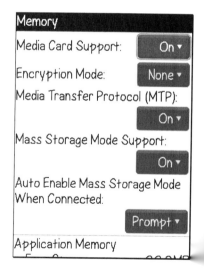

Now, connect your BlackBerry to your computer with the USB cable. If you selected **"Prompt"** above, you will see a

"Turn on Mass Storage Mode?" question.

Answer **"Yes"** (You should probably check the box that says **"Don't Ask Me Again"**). When you answer "Yes", then your Media Card looks just like another hard disk to your computer (similar to a USB Flash Drive).

TIP: If you set the **"Auto Enable Mass Storage Mode"** setting to "Yes" – then you won't be asked this question, the media card on the BlackBerry will automatically look like a "Mass Storage" device.

IMPORTANT

For the newest version of BlackBerry Desktop Manager (v4.7 at publishing time) you need to have **"Mass Storage Mode"** enabled or turned **ON**, otherwise you cannot see the files on your BlackBerry media card using BlackBerry Desktop Manager's Media Manager. *NOTE: This was not the case with some previous versions of Desktop Manager.*

After your BlackBerry is connected and in "Mass Storage" mode, just open up your computer's file management software. On your Windows™, press the Windows key + "E" to open Windows Explorer or on your Mac™ start your Finder. Look for another hard disk or "BlackBerry (model number)" that has been added.

You may see two separate disks: "BLACKBERRY1" and "Removable Disk" – this is your Media card

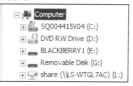

Or, you might see your BlackBerry, and then under it the "Device Memory" and "Media Card"

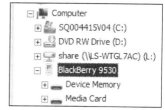

In the image below you see "**Removable Disk (G:)**" – that is the BlackBerry media card. Then navigate to the media type you want (movies, pictures, etc.) and just drag and drop or copy the pictures between your BlackBerry and you computer as you normally do with other files on your computer.

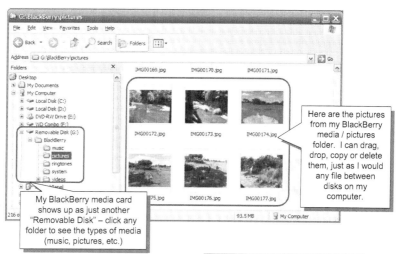

When you plug your BlackBerry into your Mac, it will identify the Main Memory and the contents of the Micro SD card as two separate drives and place them right on your desktop for easy navigation.

To copy pictures from your BlackBerry, select the files from the "**BlackBerry / pictures**" folder. Then draw a box around the pictures, or press and click on one and press "**Ctrl+A**" or "**Command+A**" (Mac™) to select them all. Or hold the **Ctrl key** (Windows™) or **Command key** (Mac™) down and press and click on individual pictures to select them. Once selected – right-press and click (Windows™) or right press and click on the Mac or press Control+Press and click (Mac™) on one of the selected pictures and select "**Cut**" (to move) or "**Copy**" (to copy).

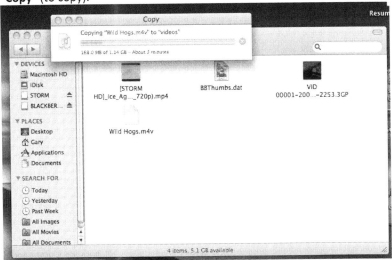

Then press and click on any other disk/folder – like "My Documents" and navigate to where you want to move / copy the files. Once there, right press and click again in the right window where all the files are listed and select "**Paste**"

On your Mac, click on the "Finder" icon in the lower left hand corner of the Dock.

You will see your "Devices" (including both BlackBerry drives) on the top and your "Places" (where you can copy and paste media) on the bottom.

You can also delete all the pictures / media / songs from your BlackBerry in a similar manner. Navigate to the BlackBerry / (media type) folder like "BlackBerry / videos" – Press the key combination shown above on your computer keyboard to select all the files then press the Delete key on your keyboard to delete all the files.

You can also copy files from your computer to your BlackBerry using a similar method. Just go to the files you want to copy, select (highlight them). Then right-press and click "Copy" and paste them into the correct "BlackBerry / (media type)" folder.

IMPORTANT: Not all media (videos), pictures (images), or songs will be playable or viewable on your BlackBerry – if you use desktop software such as Desktop Manager (for Windows™, see page 60) or PocketMac™ for BlackBerry™ (for Mac™, see page 85) to transfer the files, most files will be automatically converted for you.

Chapter 18:
Your Music Player

Listening to Your Music

One of the things that sets your BlackBerry apart from many of the earlier BlackBerry smartphones is the inclusion of Multi-Media capabilities and the ability to expand memory with the use of a media card. While some of the most popular formats of digital media are supported, you may have to take some steps to get all your music and videos working on the BlackBerry.

With a good sized media card, the media capabilities of the BlackBerry, one might even suggest: **Why do I need an iPhone or iPod? --- I've got a BlackBerry!**

Getting Your Music & Playlists On your BlackBerry

The BlackBerry comes with internal memory but the operating system ("OS") and other pre-loaded programs take up some of that space, what's left over is usually not enough to store all your music.

STEP 1: Buy and Insert a Media Card (**if** you don't already have one) to boost the memory available to store your favorite music – see page 286 for help.

Note: Some BlackBerry smartphones com pre-installed with media cards – see page 314

STEP 2: Transfer your Music from your Computer
If you are Windows™ user, please refer to page 71.
If you are an Apple™ Mac™ user, please refer to the information found on page 93 and page 288.

Playing your Music

Once your music is in the right place, you are ready to start enjoying the benefit of having your music on your BlackBerry – with you at all times.

The fastest way to get to your music is by press and clicking on the **Music** icon

. However, you can also get to the same place by press and clicking on

your **Media** icon then selecting **Music** from the options .

You are now presented with various preset options to find and play your favorite music.

All Songs: Shows you every song on your BlackBerry.

Artists: Shows you all artists, then you can press and click on an artist to see all their songs.

Albums: Shows list of all albums.

Genres: Shows list of all Genres on your BlackBerry (Pop, Rock, Jazz, etc.)

Playlists: Shows all playlists, or allows you to create new ones.

Sample Songs: Shows one or more sample songs preloaded on your device.

Shuffle Songs: Plays all your music a shuffle mode or random order.

Finding and Playing an Individual Song

If you know the name of the song, then just type a few letters of any word in the song's name in the "Find" field at the top to instantly locate all matching songs.

In this case, we type "Back" and see all matching songs.

TIP: To narrow the list, press the SPACE key and type a few more letters of another word:

Then just press and click on the song to bring up the media player and the song starts playing.

Once you press and click on a song, the Music Player will open and your song will begin to play.

Just "Touch" the screen and the "Control Bar" will pop up allowing you to press on the "Pause," "Stop," "Next Track," "Previous Track" or adjust the "Volume" slider control. TIP: Pressing the **MUTE key** will also pause or resume playback.

The volume keys on the side of the BlackBerry also control the song volume.

Setting a New Song or Ring Tone as Your Phone Ring Tone

Navigate to and play the song you want to use as a ring tone as described above.

Press the Menu Key and select "**Set as Ring Tone.**"

Now, the next time you receive a call, your favorite song will be played.

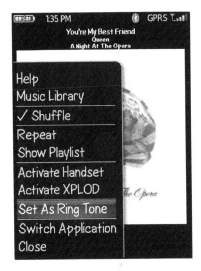

If you wanted to use a pre-loaded ringtone, then instead of going to "**Songs**" in your Media icon, you would select "**Ring tones**"

Then select "**All Ring Tones**" "**My Ringtones**" or "**Preloaded Ring Tones**"

Then press the Menu key and select Set **As Ring Tone**

Playing All your Music

Navigate to your music as above and highlight the first song you wish to play. If you have not set up individual playlists, just highlight the first song – then press the **Menu key**.

Scroll down to either "**Play**" or "**Shuffle**" and the music player will begin to play all the songs listed.

If you "**Shuffle**," then all the songs listed will be played in a random order.

Finding your Music when you use a Memory Card

Assuming you have followed the steps above, your music is now on your Micro SD media card. Now, you want to play your music – so what do you do?

From your Homescreen of icons, you have two ways to view and listen to music.

Option 1: Press and click on the "**Music**" icon
Option 2: Press and click on the **"Media"** icon, then press and click on the Music icon.

The available music folders are now displayed.

Press and click on the appropriate folder (if your music is on a Media Card, press and click that folder) and all of your music will now be displayed.

Press and click on any song to start playing it.

aying one of Your Using Playlists

To see the playlists on the BlackBerry, just scroll over to the Media Player icon and press and click on it. Find the **"Music"** icon and press and click on that. Or, just press and click on the Music icon from the home page.

Then scroll down to press and click on **"Playlists."**

You can see that the two playlists synced from iTunes are now listed right on the BlackBerry. Simply press and click on the **"Bike Riding"** playlist to begin to playing the songs.

To see the list of songs in a playlist, press the Menu key and select **"Show Playlist."**

Many MP3 players utilize playlists to organize music and allow for a unique "mix" of songs.

What types of music are supported on the BlackBerry? See page 303.

To Create Playlists from your Computer

Use the supported computer software on your Computer to create playlists and sync them to your computer.
Windows™ users, If you are Windows™ user, please refer to page 71.
If you are an Apple™ Mac™ user, please refer to page 288.

To Create Playlists on your BlackBerry

Press and click on your Music icon or your **Media** icon then press and click on Music.

Press and click on **"Playlists"** to get into the Playlists section as shown.

Either press and click on "[**New Playlist**]" at the top or press the Menu key and select "New Playlist" from the menu.

Now, you need to select **"Standard Playlist** or **Automatic Playlist"**

Select **"Standard Playlist"** to select and add any songs already stored on your BlackBerry.

Then type your Playlist name next to "Name" at the top and press the **Menu key** and select **"Add Songs"** to add new songs.

TIP: To find your songs, you can just scroll up down the list or type a few letters you know are in the title of the song like "love" and instantly see all matching songs.

When you find the song you want, just press and click on it to add it to your Playlist.

TIP: You can remove songs from the Playlist by selecting the song, pressing the Menu key and selecting "**Remove**."

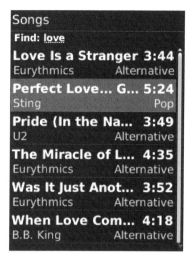

TIP: The "**Automatic Playlist**" feature allows you to create some general parameters for your playlists based on Artists, songs or Genres.

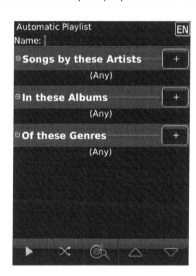

You can also add music to playslists by using the "soft keys" at the bottom of the screen. This works when you are in the "Add Song" mode or even when you just have a song playing and decide to add it to one of your existing playlists.

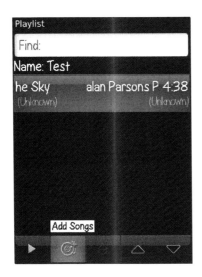

Supported Music Types

The BlackBerry will play most types of music files. If you are an iPod user, all music except the music that you purchased on iTunes should be able to play on the BlackBerry. HOWEVER, if you burn your iTunes tracks to a CD (make a new playlist in iTunes, copy your iTunes tracks, then burn that playlist) Roxio Media Manager can "Convert" these tracks to play on the BlackBerry.

The most common audio/music formats supported are:

ACC - audio compression formats AAC,
AAC+, and EAAC+ AMR - Adaptive Multi Rate-Narrow Band (AMR-NB) speech coder standard
MIDI - Polyphonic MIDI
MP3 - encoded using MPEG
WAV - supports sample rates of 8 kHz, 16 kHz, 22.05 kHz, 32 kHz, 44.1 kHz, and 48 kHz with 8-bit and 16-bit depths in mono or stereo.

Note: Some WAV file formats may not be supported by your BlackBerry.

TIP: MUTE Key for Pause & Resume

You can pause (and instantly silence) any song or video playing on your BlackBerry by pressing the **MUTE key** on the top of your BlackBerry. Press **MUTE** again to resume playback.

Music Player Tips and Tricks

To Pause a Song or Video, press the **MUTE key**.

To Resume playing, press the **MUTE key** again.

To move to the next item, press the "Next" arrow at the bottom of the screen

To move to a previous item (in your playlist or Video library,) press the "Previous" arrow at the bottom left of the screen.

Chapter 19:
Snapping Pictures

Using the Camera

Your BlackBerry includes a feature-rich 2.0 mega pixel camera. This gives you the option to just "snap" a picture anywhere you are. You can then send the picture to friends and family and share the moment.

Camera Features and Buttons

You can get as involved as you want in your picture taking with your BlackBerry. Every feature of your photo is configurable. Before we do that, however, let's get familiar with the main buttons and features.

Starting the Camera Application
The Camera can be started in one of two ways:

Option #1: The right side convenience key
Unless you have re-programmed your convenience key (See page 134 for details), then pressing the right side key will start your camera – the one directly below the volume control buttons. Push this button once, and the Camera should be started.

Start the Camera with this Right Convenience key (unless it has been re-programmed.)

Option #2: The Camera Icon
Navigate to your "Applications" Menu and press and click. Scroll to the **"Camera"** Icon and press and click.

Camera

305

Icons in the Camera Screen

Usually, when you open the Camera application either the last picture you took is in the window or the Camera is active. Underneath the picture window are five icons.

 The "Take a Picture" icon

Press and click on this to take another picture.

 The Delete Key

Sometimes, the picture you take might not be what you want. Simply scroll to the "Red X" and press and click. The last picture taken will then be deleted.

 The "Save" / Folder Icon

With the picture you desire to sav on the screen, press and click on the folder to specify a new locatic or name. We recommend using t Media Card if you have one installed.

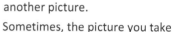 **Save a Wallpaper or Home Screen Image - The "Set as" or "Crop" Icon**

You can use the picture in the m: window as a picture caller ID for one of your people in your Addre Book by selecting the **"Set as Ca ID"** button.

"Set as Home Screen Image."

You can also set that picture as a background image for your Homescreen (Like "desktop background image" on your computer)

Just open a picture from "My Pictures" Press the MENU key and select **"Set as Homescreen Image"** and press and click.

Sending Pictures with the "Email" Envelope Icon

There are several ways to send your pictures via email. The Camera application contains this handy Icon which lets you email the picture on your screen quickly to one of your contacts.

Press and click the "Envelope" Icon which brings up the email dialogue box.

Press and click one of the six options:
Send as MMS – Multi Media Message (as body of email) – Learn all about MMS on page 264
Send to Messenger Contact (This option may not be available if you have not yet setup BlackBerry Messenger – see page 273 for details)
Send as Email (Attached to an email as an image file)

You can also send your picture to your **Flickr, MySpace** or **Facebook** accounts by just pressing the appropriate button.

Setting the Flash Mode

One of the nice features of the BlackBerry Camera is the inclusion of a Flash. Just like with most digital cameras, you can adjust the properties of the Flash.

Changing Flash Mode for current Picture

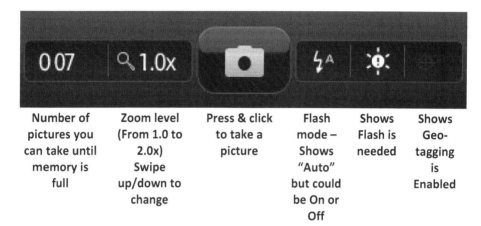

Number of pictures you can take until memory is full	Zoom level (From 1.0 to 2.0x) Swipe up/down to change	Press & click to take a picture	Flash mode – Shows "Auto" but could be On or Off	Shows Flash is needed	Shows Geo-tagging is Enabled

Your "viewfinder" gives you lots of information – to the left of the small "camera" icon is the percentage of zoon currently being used. To the right of the "Camera" icon is the flash mode.

The three available Flash modes are:

"Automatic" indicated by the Flash Symbol with the "A" next to it.

"On" indicated by the Flash symbol (will use more Battery)

"Off" indicated by the "No Flash" symbol

Changing the Default Flash Mode

When in the **Camera**, press the Menu key and select "**Options**"

Use your finger to press and click on the current **Default Flash Settings** (shown as "Automatic" in the image).

Select from "**Off**", "**On**" or "**Automatic**" (the default).

Press the **Menu key** and "**Save**" your settings.

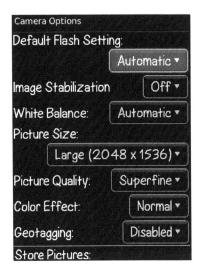

Adjusting the Size of the Picture

The size of your pictures corresponds to the number of pixels or dots used to render the image. If you tend to transfer your BlackBerry pictures to your desktop for printing or emailing, you might want a bigger or smaller picture to work with.

From the camera screen press the **Menu key** and select "**Options**." Scroll down to Picture Size and select the size of your picture; Small, Medium or Large.
Press the **Menu key** and "**Save**" your settings.

TIP: If you email your pictures, then you will be able to send them faster if you set your picture size to Small.

Geotagging Your Pictures (Adding a GPS Location)

To enable or disable "Geotagging" – which is the assigning of the current GPS (Global Positioning System) longitude and latitude location (if available) to each picture taken on your BlackBerry camera.

TIP: You can learn how to get **flickr** installed on your BlackBerry on page 185.

Why would you want to enable Geotagging?
- Some online sites such as Flickr (photo sharing) and Google Earth (mapping) can put your geotagged photo on a map to show exactly where you took the picture.

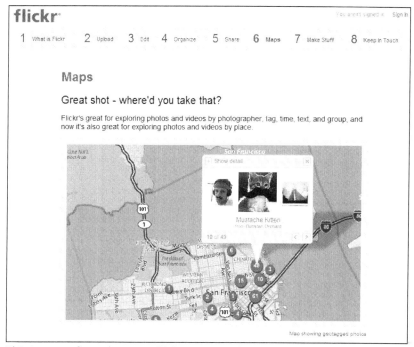

This is a map from the **www.flickr.com** site showing what geotagging your photos can accomplish – essentially it will allow you to see exactly where you snapped your photos and help organize it.

Other programs you can purchase for your computer can organize all your photos by showing their location on a map (to find such software, do a web search for 'geotag photo software (mac or windows).'

To turn on or off Geotagging, from the camera screen, press the **Menu key** and select "**Options**".

Roll down to "Geotagging" and set it to "Enable"

Make sure your GPS is enabled on your BlackBerry – see page 356.

You will then see this warning message, make sure to roll down to the "Don't ask this again" checkbox and check it by clicking the trackball or pressing the Space key.

You know when Geotagging is turned on if you see the white plus sign with circle around it and the three 'waves' to the right of it in the lower right of your Camera screen.

When Geotagging is turned on, but your BlackBerry does not have a GPS signal to tag the pictures, you will see a red plus sign with circle around it and a red X in the lower right corner.

Adjusting the White Balance

Usually the automatic white balance works fairly well, however, there may be times when you want to manually control it.

In this case you would select from the manual options for White Balance in the same Camera Options screen.

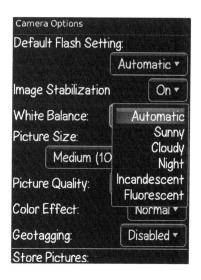

Adjusting the Picture Quality

While the BlackBerry is not meant to replace a 7 or 8 mega pixel camera, it is a very capable photo device. There are times when you might need or desire the change the picture quality. Perhaps you are using your BlackBerry camera for work and need to capture an important image. Fortunately, it is quite easy to adjust the quality of your photos. Realize, however, that **increasing the quality or the size will increase the memory requirements for that particular picture.**

In one "non-scientific" test, changing the picture quality resulted in the following changes to the file size of the picture at a fixed size setting of "Large (1600x1200)":

Normal:	**Image File Size: Approximately 50k**
Fine:	**Approximately 2X larger than "Normal"**
Superfine:	**Approximately 3X larger than "Normal"**

Start your **Camera**.
Press the **Menu key**, select "**Options**"
Scroll to "**Picture Quality**."
The choices "**Normal**," "**Fine**" and
"**Superfine**" will be available. Just press
and click on the desired quality, press the
Menu key and save your settings.

Using the Zoom

As with many cameras, the BlackBerry gives you the opportunity to zoom in or out of your subject. Zooming on the BlackBerry could not be easier.

Frame your picture and gently scroll up on the screen. The Camera will **Zoom** in on the subject.
If your status bar is showing on the bottom, you will see the Zoom level displayed to the left of the "camera" icon with a **1.0x** up to **2.0x** indicating the power of zoom chosen.

To Zoom back out, just scroll down. It takes a little getting used to – but zooming with your finger is very precise and works quite well. TIP: You can also zoom in x0.1 increments using your Volume Up and Down keys.

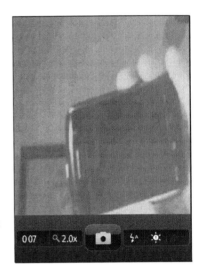

Managing Picture Storage

Your BlackBerry comes with an 8 GB Media card installed. If you find that you need to increase your storage capacity – you can purchase a 16 GB Media card. For more information on inserting the media card, please see page 314. See below for help on storing pictures on the media card.

If you do not have a media card, then you will want to carefully manage the amount of your BlackBerry's main "Device Memory" that is used for pictures.

Selecting Where Pictures are Stored

The default setting is for the BlackBerry to store pictures in main Device Memory, but if you have a Media Card inserted, we recommend selecting that instead.

To confirm the default picture storage location, press the **Menu key** from the main **Camera** screen and scroll to "**Options**" and press and click.

Scroll down to the "**Store Pictures**" and select "**On Media Card**" if you have one, or "**In Device Memory**" if you do not have a media card.

Look at the folder icon at the bottom and make sure the folder name ends in the word "**/pictures**". This will help keep pictures together with pictures, videos with videos, music with music, and make it easier when you want to transfer pictures to and from your computer.

Using the Optional Media Card

At publishing time, your BlackBerry can support up to a sizable Micro SD Media Card.   To give you some perspective, a 4.0 GB card can store over 30 times that of a BlackBerry with 128MB ("megabytes") of internal 'main memory.' This is equivalent to **several full length feature films** and **thousands of songs**. Learn how to install a Media Card in the chapter beginning on page 286. Verify your card is installed as described on page 287. Since program files can only be stored in Main memory, we recommend putting as much of your Media files on the Micro SD card as possible.

To Store Pictures on the Media Card

TIP: You may be prompted to save pictures to your Media card the first time you start your camera after you insert a new Media card. In case you did not get this choice, read on to
Navigate to the main screen of the **Camera** application and press the **Menu key** and scroll to "**Options**" and press and click.
Change the option in the "**Store Pictures**" field to "**On Media Card.**"

Viewing Pictures stored in Memory

There are two primary ways to view stored pictures.

Option #1: Viewing from the Camera program

Open up the Camera application and press the Menu key
Scroll down to **"View Pictures"** and navigate to the appropriate folder to view
your pictures.

Option #2: Viewing from the Media menu

Navigate to the Media icon and press and click.
Scroll to **"Pictures"** and press and click. Your initial options will be "**All
Pictures**," or "**Picture Folders**"
Press and click the appropriate folder and navigate to your pictures.

 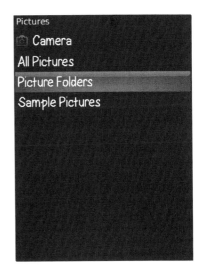

Picture Soft Keys

Like many of the other programs we have seen so far, the BlackBerry Storm adds "Soft Keys" at the bottom of the picture to make some of the more popular commands right at your finger tips.

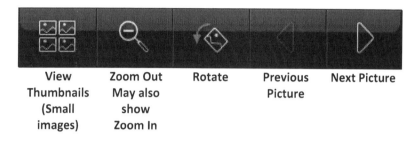

| View Thumbnails (Small images) | Zoom Out May also show Zoom In | Rotate | Previous Picture | Next Picture |

You can "View thumbnails" of all your pictures, "Zoom out or in", "Rotate" the picture or advance through your pictures by just pressing and clicking the corresponding "soft key."

To view a Slide Show

Follow the steps above and press the **Menu key** when you are in your picture directory.

Scroll to "**View Slideshow**" and press and click.

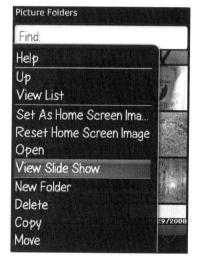

Scrolling Through Pictures

One very cool feature of your BlackBerry Storm is that you can scroll through your pictures just by swiping your finger across the screen.

Just click on any picture to bring it into the "full screen" mode.

Next, just swipe your finger to the left or right to advance through the pictures in that particular folder.

Adding Pictures to Contacts for Caller ID

As discussed previously, you can assign a picture as a "Caller ID" for your contacts. Please check out our detailed explanation on starting on page 216.

Transferring Pictures To or From Your BlackBerry

There are a few ways to get pictures you have taken on your BlackBerry off it and transfer pictures taken elsewhere onto the BlackBerry.

Method 1: Send via Email, Multi-Media Messaging, or BlackBerry Messenger. You can email or send pictures immediately after you take them on your camera by press and clicking the "Envelope" icon as shown on page 307. You may also send pictures when you are viewing them in your Media application. Press and click the Menu key and look for menu items related to sending pictures. Or, look for a "soft key" at the bottom of the screen like below.

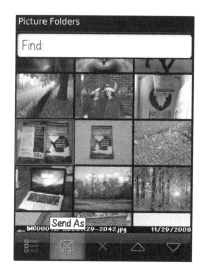

Method 2: Transfer using Bluetooth. If you want to transfer pictures to/from your computer (assuming it has Bluetooth capabilities), you can. We explain exactly how to get this done in the Bluetooth chapter on page 334.

Method 3: Transfer using your Computer with Special Computer Software
Transferring pictures and other media to your computer is handled using the Media section of your desktop software. On a Windows™ computer, this software is called "BlackBerry Desktop Manager" (see page 60) on an Apple™ computer, the software may be called "PocketMac for the BlackBerry™" (see page 85) or "The Missing Sync for BlackBerry."

Method 4: Transfer using "Mass Storage Mode" This assumes you have stored your pictures on a media card. (What's a media card? See page 314.) The first time you connect your BlackBerry to your computer, you will probably see a **"Turn on Mass Storage Mode?"** question. If you answer "Yes", then your Media Card looks just like another hard disk to your computer (just like a USB Flash Drive). Then you can drag and drop pictures to/from your BlackBerry and your Computer. For more details see page 288.

Chapter 20:
Fun with Videos

Having Fun with Videos

In addition to your Camera, your BlackBerry also comes with a built-in Video recorder to catch your world in full motion video and sound when a simple picture does not work. Your Media icon also can play all videos you record or transfer to your BlackBerry from your Computer.

Some BlackBerry providers will include a free 8.0 GB media card in your BlackBerry. With this extra storage, and the media capabilities of the BlackBerry, one might even suggest: *Why do I need an iPhone or iPod?* **I've got a BlackBerry!**

Adding Videos to Your BlackBerry

Check out page 71 to learn how to transfer videos and other media (pictures, songs) to your Media Card. If you are a Windows™ computer user, then check out the built-in Media transfer and sync capabilities to BlackBerry Desktop Manger software on page 302. If you use an Apple Mac™, please refer to page 85.

Your Video Recorder

One of the new features of your BlackBerry is the inclusion of a Video Recorder in addition to the Camera. The video recorder is perfect for capturing parts of a business presentation or your child's soccer game. Videos can be emailed or stored on your PC for later use – just like pictures.

To start the Video Recorder:

> Push the MENU key and scroll down to the **"Applications"** folder and press and click.
> Scroll to the **"Video Camera Icon"** and press and click.

> The BlackBerry should detect that you have a Media Card installed and ask you if you want to save your Videos to the card – we think it is a good idea to say "yes" to this option.

Use the screen of the BlackBerry as your viewfinder to frame your picture.

When you are ready to record – just press the record button. When done – just press the "pause" button.

You will then see the options at the bottom of the screen to either "Email" the video, "Save" it or "Delete" it.

> To see the Menu "Options" just press

the **MENU** button from within the Video Camera Application and choose:

- Help
- To View your Videos
- To "Send as Email"
- Enter the "Options" menu
- Switch to the "Camera"
- Show the Keyboard
- Switch Application or
- Close the program

Adjust your Video Options by selecting **"Options"** from the MENU. You can adjust the video light – either having a constant light from the Flash or turn this "Off." You can also adjust the **"Color Effect"**:

i. Normal
ii. Black and White
iii. Sepia (Old-fashioned Brown tone)

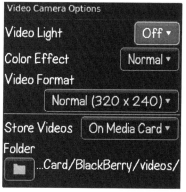

You can also adjust the Video Format for Normal (320 x 240) or to send as an MMS (176 x 144 pixels -- lower quality and smaller file size). Finally, you can choose to store your videos "On Media Card" or "In Device Memory" – Definitely choose "On Media Card" if you have one – this will give you more space.

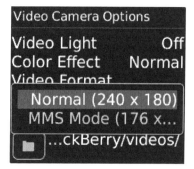

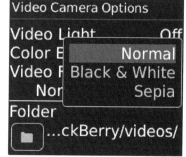

Converting DVD's and Videos to Play on the BlackBerry

One of the things that you can use your BlackBerry for is as a portable Media Player to help entertain your kids or yourself when you travel. If your car is equipped, you can even send the audio via Bluetooth right to the car stereo and so everyone can "listen" to the movie.

To convert a DVD, you first need to copy the DVD onto your computer. Then use a video encoder program to "transcode" the video (convert it to be viewable on your BlackBerry).

Please Respect Copyright Laws

As people who make our living from intellectual property (BlackBerry books, videos, etc.), we strongly encourage you to respect the copyrights of any material you are attempting to copy to your BlackBerry.

For security and copyright reasons, some DVDs cannot be copied onto a device like the BlackBerry. Make sure before you buy a video encoder or converter program that it supports the file formats that will play on your BlackBerry. Many of the User Enthusiast Forums like www.pinstack.com, www.crackberry.com or www.blackberryforums.com offer tutorials for Video Conversion. (We did not include details here because the process varies based on which Operating System you are running on your BlackBerry.)

Supported Video Formats for the BlackBerry

Because of the fast changing formats supported by different versions of the BlackBerry Operating System software, we have not included a list here. However, you can find the most up-to-date list on blackberry.com in their Knowledge Base. Do a search for "supported video formats storm". This is a link that worked when we were writing the book:
http://www.blackberry.com/btsc/articles/216/KB05419_f.SAL_Public.html#7

Playing a Video

Press and click on your **Media** icon. Press and click on the "**Video**" icon and choose the folder where your video is stored.

The video player screen looks very similar to the Audio Player screen – just press and click the screen to pause or play and use the volume controls on the side of the BlackBerry.

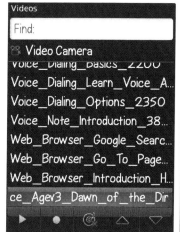

Video Player MENU options – just press the MENU button and the following "Options" are lists on the MENU

Help – Displays contextual help with Video Player

Video Library – Displays the content of your Library

Repeat – Replays the last viewed Video

Show Playlist – displays all items in the Playlist

Activate Handset – Plays the Audio of the Video through your Headset

Switch Application – Allows you to go to any other "Open" application.

Close – Closes the application

Chapter 21:
BlackBerry as a Tethered Modem

Getting Set Up

Some BlackBerry phone companies, such as Verizon in the USA, actually have simple setup script files ("Verizon Access Manager") that you can download and install on your computer to do all setup required to use your BlackBerry as a Tethered (connected) Modem.

Sometimes, these files are contained on the CD that is in the box with your BlackBerry. If not, you can download these programs for free from your phone company's web site.

We highly recommend that you check with your carrier to see if they have such software before you try to manually configure your BlackBerry as a Modem, it will be much easier for you.

Alltel Download Link: http://alltelrim.quicklinkmobile.com/ (10 digit Alltel MDN number required)

AT&T/Cingular Download Link: http://www.wireless.att.com/communicationmanager

Sprint/Nextel - Link: http://www.nextel.com/en/software_downloads/index.shtml?id9=vanity:downloads

Verizon Download Link: http://www.vzam.net/# (10-digit Verizon Wireless number required)

Don't see your BlackBerry carrier listed? Please check with your carrier's help desk, support line or web site.

Using your BlackBerry as a Modem Usually Costs Extra

Most, but not all, wireless carriers charge an extra fee to allow you to use your BlackBerry as a "Tethered Modem" or "Dial-Up Networking" or "Phone as Modem." You may be able to connect using your BlackBerry as a modem, however, unless you have specifically signed up for the "BlackBerry as Modem" or similar data plan. We have heard of users getting a surprise phone bill in the hundreds of dollars, **even when they had an "unlimited BlackBerry data plan"** (This particular carrier did not include BlackBerry modem data in the unlimited plan.)

TIP: TURN IT ON AND OFF WHEN YOU NEED IT Some carriers allow you to turn this BlackBerry As Modem Extra Service on and off. Check with your particular carrier. Also, beware that changing turning this modem service on and off might extend or renew your 2 year commitment period. Ask your phone company for their policies. Assuming there are no extra hidden costs or commitments, you could just enable it for a scheduled trip and then turn it off when you return home.

GOOD RESOURCE: We also want to thank Research In Motion, Ltd. and BlackBerry.com for valuable information contained in their extensive **"BlackBerry Technical Solution Center"**. We strongly encourage you to visit this site for the latest information on using your BlackBerry as a Modem and anything else! Visit: http://www.blackberry.com/btsc/supportcentral/supportcentral.do?id=m1 and search for "modem how to."

> **SEARCH TIP:** When searching the knowledgebase, do not enter your specific BlackBerry model, but the series. For example, if you have an Storm, then enter storm or 9500 series, or just leave that out of the search.

> **SEARCH TIP:** To locate the modem instructions for your particular BlackBerry, you will need to know the network – EDGE, GPRS, CDMA, EVDO on which your BlackBerry operates. Your BlackBerry Storm™ runs on both the EDGE/GPRS networks and the CDMA/EVDO networks.

NOTE: Not every BlackBerry wireless carrier supports using your BlackBerry as a modem. Please check with your carrier if you have trouble.

Chapter 22:
Connect with Bluetooth

Bluetooth

The BlackBerry ships with Bluetooth 2.0 Technology. Think of Bluetooth as a short range, wireless technology which allows your BlackBerry to "connect" to various peripheral devices without wires.

Bluetooth is believed to be named after a Danish Viking and King, Harald Blåtand (which has been translated as *Bluetooth* in English.) King Blåtand lived in the 10th century and is famous for uniting Denmark and Norway. Similarly, Bluetooth technology unites computers and telecom. His name, according to legend, is from his very dark hair which was unusual for Vikings. Blåtand means dark complexion. There does exist a more popular story which states that the King loved to eat Blueberries, so much so his teeth became stained with the color Blue.

Sources:
http://cp.literature.agilent.com/litweb/pdf/5980-3032EN.pdf
http://www.cs.utk.edu/~dasgupta/bluetooth/history.htm
http://www.britannica.com/eb/topic-254809/Harald-I

Understanding Bluetooth

Bluetooth allows your BlackBerry to communicate with things like headsets, GPS devices and other hands-free systems with the freedom of wireless. Bluetooth is a small radio that transmits from each device. The BlackBerry gets "paired" or connected to the peripheral. Most Bluetooth devices can be used up to 30 feet away from the BlackBerry.

Using Bluetooth on your BlackBerry

In order to use Bluetooth on your BlackBerry, it must first be turned on. This is done through the Settings folder and the Setup Bluetooth icon.

Turning On Bluetooth

Scroll through the application icons and press and click on the "**Setup**" folder, or you may need to go to the radio tower icon (if it's called **Manage Connections**)

Next, you should see an Icon that says **"Setup Bluetooth."** Go ahead and press and click on that icon.

The small Bluetooth icon will now be showing next to the battery meter in the Homescreen.

If you don't see a "**Turn On Bluetooth**" or "**Setup Bluetooth**" icons, then press and click on the "**Manage Connections**" icon.

The Press and Click on **"Set Up Bluetooth."**

Configuring Bluetooth

Once Bluetooth is enabled, you will want to follow the steps below to take full advantage of the Bluetooth capabilities of the BlackBerry.

There can sometimes be two or three ways to get into the Bluetooth setup and options screens. This depends a bit on your BlackBerry software version and BlackBerry carrier (cell phone) company.

Navigate to the Bluetooth Option screen with one of the methods below:
Method 1: Press and click on the **Setup** folder. Then scroll to "**Setup Bluetooth**" and press and click. If you see the Window asking you to either search or be discovered, just press the **"Escape"** key. Then, you can press the **MENU** key and scroll down to **"Options." Method 2:** Scroll to the "**Options**" icon from your Homescreen. Then, scroll down to **"Bluetooth,"** press and click and then press the **MENU** Key.
Method 3: Scroll to the "**Manage Connections**" icon, press and click on it then scroll to "**Set up Bluetooth**" at the bottom, then press and click the **Menu** key and select "**Options**"

If you have already paired your BlackBerry with Bluetooth devices, you will have seen those devices listed (we will cover pairing below.)

To change your Device name (the way other Bluetooth devices will see your BlackBerry) press and click where it says "**Device Name**" and type a new name (not necessary).
To make your BlackBerry "Discoverable" to other devices press and click next to "**Discoverable**" and select "**Yes**" (the default is "**No**") As we note below, you should set this back to "**No**" after you finish "pairing" for increased security.
Make sure that it says "**Always**" or "**If Unlocked**" after "**Allow Outgoing Calls**"
Set "**Address Book Transfer**" to "**Enable**" (Depending on your software version, you may see the options of "**All Entries**" – same as "**Enable,**" "**Hotlist Only**" or "**Selected Categories Only**" – depending on your preferences). This option allows your address book data to be transferred

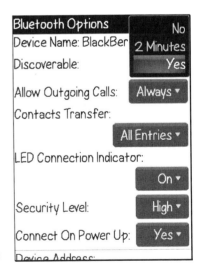

to another device or computer using Bluetooth.

To see a blue flashing LED when connected to a Bluetooth Device, make sure the LED Connection Indicator is set to **"On."**

Bluetooth Security Tips:

Here are a few security tips from a recent BlackBerry IT Newsletter. These will help prevent hackers from getting access to your BlackBerry via Bluetooth:

Never pair your BlackBerry when you are in a crowded public area.

"Disable" the **"Discoverable"** setting after you are done with pairing your BlackBerry.

Do not accept any "pairing requests" with "unknown" Bluetooth devices, only accept connections from devices with names you recognize.

Change the name of your BlackBerry to something other than the default "BlackBerry 9530" – this will help avoid hackers from easily finding your BlackBerry.

Source: http://www.blackberry.com/newsletters/connection/it/jan-2007/managing-bluetooth-security.shtml?CPID=NLC-41

Supported Devices

Your BlackBerry should work with most Bluetooth headsets, car kits, hands free kits, keyboards and GPS receivers that are Bluetooth 2.0 and earlier compliant. At publishing time, Bluetooth 2.1 was just coming on the scene; you will need to check with the device manufacturer of newer devices to make sure they are compatible with your BlackBerry.

How to Pair Your BlackBerry with a Bluetooth Device

Think of "Pairing" as establishing a connection between your BlackBerry and a peripheral (Headset, Global Positioning Device, external keyboard, Windows™ or Mac™ computer, etc.) without wires. Pairing is dependent on entering a required **"Pass key"** which "locks" your BlackBerry into a secure connection with the peripheral. Similar to getting into the "Bluetooth options" screens, there could be several ways to get into the "Bluetooth Setup" screen to "pair" your BlackBerry and establish this connection.

First, put your Bluetooth device (e.g. Headset, GPS unit, computer or other peripheral) already in "Pairing" mode as recommended by the manufacturer Also, have the "Pass key" ready to enter.

Navigate to the Bluetooth Setup screen with one of the methods below:
Method 1: Press and click on the **Options** icon. (May be inside the "Settings" icon). Then scroll to "Bluetooth" and press and click.
Method 2: Scroll to the **Set Up Bluetooth** icon and press and click on it.
Method 3: Scroll to the **Manage Connections** icon, press and click on it then select "**Setup Bluetooth**"

The BlackBerry will ask you to "Search for devices from here" or ""Allow another device to fine me." Choose the option you desire and then press and click "**OK**".

IMPORTANT: If you are pairing your BlackBerry with your computer, then you need to make sure that both your BlackBerry and your computer are in "**Discoverable**" mode. Set this in the "**Bluetooth Options**" screen by setting "**Discoverable**" to "**Yes**" or "**Ask**". (The default setting is "No" which will prevent you from pairing.)

When the Device is found, the BlackBerry will display the Device name on the screen. Press and click on the device name to select it.

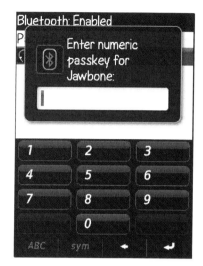

You will then be prompted to enter the 4 digit Pass Key provided by the manufacturer of the Bluetooth peripheral. Enter in the Passkey and then press the Enter key. (Many default passkeys are just "0000" or "1234")

You will then be prompted to accept the connection from the new Device (TIP: If you check the box next to "**Don't ask this again**" you will only have to do this once.)

Your device should now be connected and paired and ready to use.

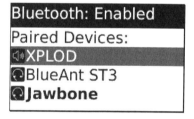

Answering and Making Calls with the Headset

Some Bluetooth headsets support an "**Auto Answer**" protocol which will, as it sounds, automatically answer incoming calls and send them right to the headset. This is very helpful when driving or in other situations where you should not be looking at your BlackBerry to answer the call. Sometimes, you will need to push a button – usually just one – to answer your call from the headset.

Option #1: Answer Directly From the Headset Itself

When the call comes into your BlackBerry, you should hear an audible beep in the headset. Just press the multi-function button on your headset to answer the call. Press the Multi function button when the call ends to disconnect.

Option #2: Transfer the Caller to the Headset

When the phone call comes into your BlackBerry, press the **Menu key**.
Scroll to "**Activate (your Bluetooth headset name)**" and the call will be sent to the selected headset.

In this image, the headset name is "Jawbone"

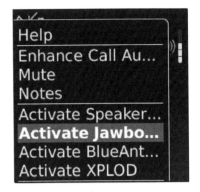

Bluetooth Setup Menu Commands

There are several options available to you from the Bluetooth menu. Learn these commands to be able to take full advantage of Bluetooth wireless technology on your BlackBerry.

Bluetooth Menu Options

Navigate to the **Options** icon and press and click.
Scroll to "**Bluetooth**" and press and click. You will now see the list of paired devices with your BlackBerry.
Highlight one of the devices listed and press the Menu key. The following options become available to you:
Disable Bluetooth – another way to turn off the Bluetooth radio – this will help to save battery life if you don't need the Bluetooth active
Connect / Disconnect– press and clicking this will immediately connect/disconnect you to/from the highlighted Bluetooth device
Add Device – to connect to a new Bluetooth peripheral
Delete Device – removes the highlighted device from the BlackBerry
Device Properties – To check whether the device is trusted, encrypted and if "Echo control" is activated

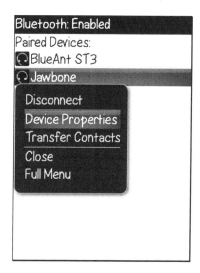

Transfer Contacts – If you connected to a PC or another Bluetooth Smartphone, you can send your address book via Bluetooth to that device
Options – Shows the Options screen (covered above)

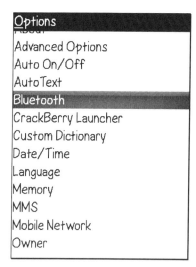

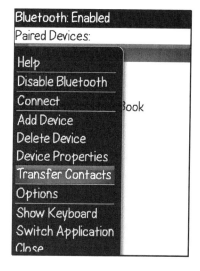

Send and Receive Files with Bluetooth

Once you have paired your BlackBerry with your computer, you can use Bluetooth to send and receive files. At publishing time, these files were limited to media files (videos, music, pictures) and address book entries, but we suspect that you will be able to transfer more types of files in the future.

To send or receive media files on your BlackBerry:

Start the **Media icon** by press and clicking on it.

Navigate to the type of file you want to send or receive – Music, Video, Ringtones, or Pictures

Navigate to the folder where you want to send or receive the file – either "**Device Memory**" or "**Media Card**"

If you are **sending a file** to your computer, then scroll to and highlight the file, select "**Send using Bluetooth**". Then you will need to follow the prompts on your computer to receive the file. NOTE: You may need to set your computer to be able to "**Receive via Bluetooth**".

If you are **receiving a file** (or files) on your BlackBerry, then you need to select "Receive via Bluetooth". Go to your computer and select the file or files and follow the commands to "**Send via Bluetooth**". You may be asked on the BlackBerry to confirm the folder which is receiving the files on your BlackBerry.

> NOTE: You can send (transfer) only media files that you have put onto your BlackBerry yourself. The "Pre-Loaded" media files cannot be transferred via Bluetooth.

Bluetooth Troubleshooting

Bluetooth is still an emergent technology and, sometimes, it doesn't work as well as we might hope. If you are having difficulty, perhaps one of these suggestions will help.

My Pass key is not being accepted by the device?

It is possible that you have the incorrect pass key. Most Bluetooth devices use either "0000" or "1234" – but some have unique pass keys.

If you lost your manual for the Bluetooth device, many times you can use a web search engine such as Google or Yahoo to find the manufacturer's web site and locate the product manual.

I have the right passkey, but I still cannot pair the device?

It is possible that the device is not compatible with the BlackBerry. One thing you can try is to turn off encryption.

Press and click Options, then Bluetooth and then highlight the problem device and press and click. In "Device Properties" Then disable Encryption for that device and try to connect again.

I can't share my Address Book?

Inside the **Bluetooth setup screen**, press the **Menu key** and select "**Options**". Make sure that you have enabled the "**Contacts Transfer**" field.

Chapter 23:
Surf the Web

Web Browsing on Your BlackBerry

One of the amazing features of Smartphones like the BlackBerry is the ability to browse the web with ease and speed right from your handheld. More and more web sites are now supporting mobile browser formatting. These sites "sense" you are viewing them from a small mobile browser and automatically re-configure themselves for your BlackBerry so they load quickly – some, even quicker than a desktop browser.

Locating the Web Browser from the Homescreen

Web browsing can actually start with a few of the icons on your Homescreen. The easiest way to get started is to find the "Browser" icon – it looks like a globe.

Use your finger to navigate to the **Browser icon** and press and click. It might say "BlackBerry Browser" or "Internet Browser" or even something different like "mLife" or "T-Zone".

You will either be taken to directly the "Home" screen of your particular carrier or to your list of Bookmarks. (You can change this by going to your "Browser > Options Screens" – learn more on page 343)

The Browser Menu

Like most other applications, the Heart of the Browser, and its capabilities, lies in the Menu options available to you.   One push and one press and click and you are off to specific sites, bookmarked pages, recent pages, your internet history and more.

New Features in the BlackBerry Browser: The "**START PAGE**"
New in this version of the BlackBerry Browser (OS v4.7) is a new "Start Page" which allows you to type in a web address. (On older BlackBerry Models, you had to select "Go To…" from the menu in order to type a web address).
On this "Start Page" view, you see a place to type a web address, a web search box (Google, Yahoo!, etc.), Bookmarks and History of recently visited pages below.

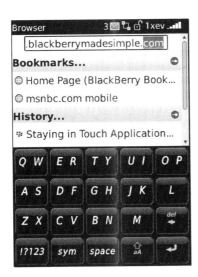 

Just press and click on of the bookmarks or type in a new Address and press and click. (Remember, just use the Space Key for the "." in the address.)

Menu Options:

While in the Browser application, press the **Menu key**
The following options are available to you:
Help – See on-screen text help for the Web Browser, useful when you forget something and need quick help
Column View/Page View – Toggles between the two views. Column view offers are more zoomed in view, Page view gives you a view of the entire page (more like a PC Web Browser.)
Zoom In – Allows you to Zoom In multiple times to see text more clearly

Zoom Out – Allows you to Zoom Out to see more of the page

Find – Lets you search for text on a web page

Find Next – Searches for the next occurrence of the last "Find."

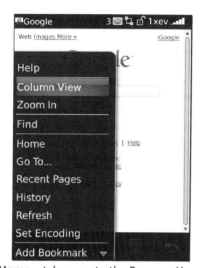 

Home – takes you to the Browser Home Page – You can set or change the Home Page inside the "Browser > Options" screen (See page 343 for details)

Go To… – allows you to type in a specific web address for browsing (See page 339 for details)

Start BB Connection – Takes you "Online" if you were viewing an "Offline" saved Web page.

Recent Pages – allows you to view the most recent web pages browsed

History – shows your entire web browsing history

Refresh – updates the current web page

Set Encoding – This is an advanced feature to change character encoding of web browsing. (Probably won't need to change this).

Add Bookmark – sets the current page as a "Favorite" or "Bookmark." **(Extremely useful)** (See page 341 for details)

Bookmarks – lists all your Bookmarks **(Extremely useful)** (See page 344 for details on using Bookmarks, Page 343 for details on organizing Bookmarks with folders)

Page Address – Shows you the full web address of the current page (See page 341 for details)

Send Address – Send the current page address to a contact (See page 341 for details)

Options – Set Browser Configuration, Properties and Cache settings.

Save Page – Save the page as a file and puts it in your Messages icon (your Email inbox)

Switch Application – Jump or multi-task over to other applications while leaving the current web page open.

Close - Close the Web Browser and exit to the Homescreen.

Using the "Go To" Command (Your Address Bar)

The first thing you will want to know how to do is get to your favorite web sites. In one of the author's cases, it is Google.com. On your desktop computer, you simply type the web address or ("URL") into your browser's "Address Bar". You won't see an Address Bar on the BlackBerry. Instead you have to use the "Go To..." menu command or "." (period) shortcut key to type in your web address.

Using the "Go To" Command (Shortcut key: ".")
Open the Browser by press and clicking on the Browser icon.

Press the MENU Key and select **"Go To..."**

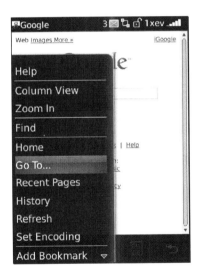 

The Address bar comes up with the "**http://www.**" in place waiting for you to type the rest of the address.

Simply type in the web address (remember, pushing the SPACE bar will put in the "dot" (.)

Press the ENTER key when you are done and the Browser will take you to the web page entered.

Once you have typed in a few web addresses using the "Go To..." command, you will notice that they appear in a list below the web address next time you select "Go To..." You can select any of these by scrolling   down and pressing and clicking on them.

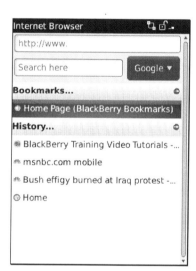

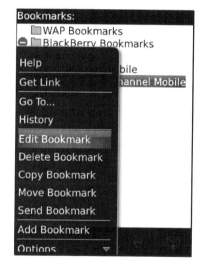

TIP: You can save time by "Editing" a bookmark. If you want to enter a web address that is similar to one that you a bookmark, you should highlight the previously entered address, press the Menu key and select "Edit Bookmark"

To Copy or Send the Web Page you are Viewing

Open the **Browser icon** and press the **Menu key**.

Scroll down to "**Page Address**" and press and click.

The web address is displayed in the window. Scroll down with your finger for options.

Scroll to "**Copy Address**" and press and click. This will copy the Web address to the clipboard and can easily be pasted into a Contact, an Email, a Memo or your Calendar.

Alternatively, scroll to "**Send Address**" and press and click. This will allow you to send the particular Web Address information via Email, MMS, SMS or PIN messaging. Just select the form and then the contact.

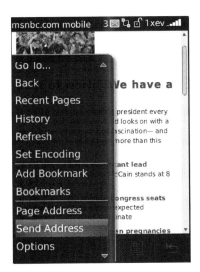

Setting and Naming Bookmarks (e.g. Local Weather)

TIP

You can instantly "**Find**" bookmarks by typing a few letters of the bookmark name – just like you lookup contacts in your Address Book. *Keep this in mind as you add new bookmarks.*

One of the keys to great Web Browsing on your BlackBerry is the liberal use of Bookmarks. Your BlackBerry will come with a couple of bookmarks already set. It is very easy to customize your bookmarks to include all your web favorites for easy browsing.

Adding and Naming Bookmarks To Easily Finding Them

Let's setup a bookmark to find our local weather instantly.

Open the Browser and use the "**Go To...**" command (or "**.**" Shortcut key) to input a favorite Web Page. In this example, we will type: www.weather.com

Type in your zip code or city name to see your current weather.

Once the page loads with your own local weather, press the Menu key and select **"Add Bookmark"** (or use the "A" Shortcut key).

The Full name of the Web address is displayed. In this case you will probably see "TWC Weather" – you will want to re-name it (see below).

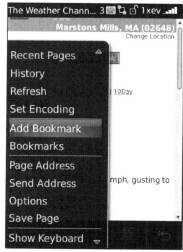

In this case (and most cases) we recommend changing the bookmark name to something short and unique.

(Note: if you bookmarked 4 different weather forecasts, the 'default' bookmark names would all show up as "The Weather Channel" – sort of useless if you want to get right to the "10 Day" forecast).

Keep these things in mind as you rename your bookmarks:

(a) **Make all bookmark names fairly short.** You will only see about the first 10-15 characters of the name in your list (because the screen is small).

(b) **Make all bookmark names similar but unique.** For example if you were adding 4 bookmarks for the weather in New York or your area, you might want to name them:

"NY – Now",
"NY – 10 day",
"NY – 36 hour",
"NY – Hourly".

This way you can instantly locate all your forecasts by typing the letters "NY" in your bookmark list. Only those bookmarks with the letters "NY" will show up.

Browser Options: See Bookmark List or Home Page

You might prefer to see the bookmark list rather than a "home page" when you open the Browser. The reason is simple: this will allow you to use the "**Find**" feature in the bookmark list to instantly locate the bookmark and press and click on it.

Benefits: It ends up being much faster to get to favorite web pages that are bookmarked like local weather (hourly, 7 day) or your favorite search engine ("Google").

Your BlackBerry may automatically open up to your Bookmarks list, but you may prefer to see a selected home page instead. You can use these instructions to make that change as well.

Press and click on the **Browser** icon.
Press the **Menu key** and select "**Options**."
Press and click on **"Browser Configuration"**

Scroll all the way down to the "**Start Page**" near the bottom and press and click on the options. You will most likely see three options "**Bookmarks Page**" (list of bookmarks), "**Home Page**" (the web site you have listed as your home page, which you do on this screen) or "**Last Page Loaded**" (keeps the last web page in memory and brings it back up when you re-enter your Browser).

To select bookmark list, choose "**Bookmarks Page**" and make sure to "Save" your settings.

Using Your Bookmarks to Browse the Web

Press and click on your **Browser icon**.

If you don't see your Bookmark list automatically when you start your browser, press the **Menu key** and scroll down to "**Bookmarks**" and press and click.

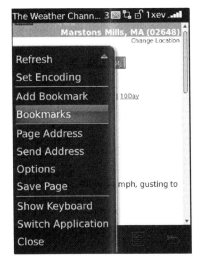 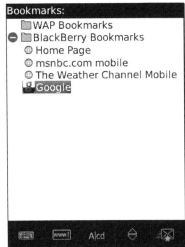

All of your Bookmarks will be listed, including any 'default' bookmarks that were put there automatically by your phone company.

You might want to press and click on a particular folder to open all the bookmarks contained within or if you see the bookmark you need, just press and click on it.

However, if you have a lot of bookmarks, then you should use the "Find:" feature and type a few letters matching the bookmark you want to find. See the image above – typing the letters "go" will immediately "**Find**" all bookmarks with "go" in the bookmark name (like "Google.")

Once you get familiar with your bookmark names, you can type a few letters and find exactly what you need.

Search with Google

Google also has a mobile version that loads quickly and is quite useful on your BlackBerry.

To get there, just go to www.google.com in your BlackBerry web browser.

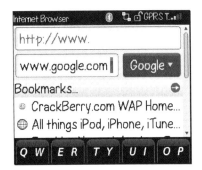

You also have a built in search bar right under the address bar which you can set for Google or Yahoo or other built in search engines. Just press and click on the dropdown arrow to the right of the search bar.

 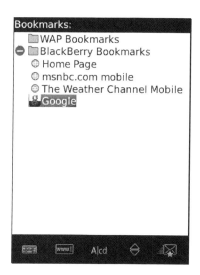

We highly recommend creating easy-to-use bookmarks this and all your favorite web sites (Learn more on page 341).

Just like on your computer, type in your search string and hit the ENTER key (saves time from scrolling and press and clicking on the "Search" button). If you wanted to find and even call pizza restaurants in a certain zip code or city, then you would type in "pizza (and your zip code or city)" See below.

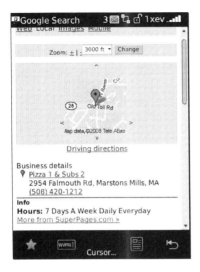

To Find a Quick Map of Your Search

If I want to find out where the "Pizza" place is that I just called, I can just press and click from my search results on the name of the restaurant.

Once I press and click on the link, Google will bring up a quick map of the location of the Pizza Place.

If I were to press and click on "Driving Directions" I could find a quick path from my current location to the restaurant – all on my BlackBerry!

Finding Things Using Google Maps

Later in this book, we describe in detail how to obtain and use Google Maps on your BlackBerry. Please go to page 361.

Web Browser Tips and Tricks

There are some helpful shortcuts to help you navigate the Web faster and easier. See page **Error! Bookmark not defined.**.

We have included a few for you below:

To insert a **period "."** in the web address in the "**Go To…**" dialog box, press the **SPACE key.**

Go to Browser>Menu Key>Options>Browser Configuration>Browser Identification> then, set this to either Firefox or Internet Explorer. Now every website will think you're a pc rather than a phone.

To stop loading a web page, press the **ESCAPE key**.

To close a browser, press and hold the **ESCAPE key**.

Chapter 24:
Add or Remove Software

Downloading and Adding New Software Icons

One of the very cool things about your BlackBerry is that, just like on your computer, you can go on the Web and find software to download. You can download everything from Ring Tones to Games to Content that is "pushed" like your email to your BlackBerry on a regular basis.

Adding Push Content to your Device

NOTE: Each Carrier/Phone Company is slightly different.

WEB SITE DISCLAIMER: As with all web sites, they change frequently. The web site images you see below may look the same on your BlackBerry, or may look totally different. If they look different, please try to look for links with approximately the same name.

Start your **Web Browser** on the BlackBerry as you normally would.

Press the **Menu key**, select "**Go To...**" and enter http://mobile.blackberry.com/

Next, Press and Click on the "News and Weather" icon on the BlackBerry Home Page.

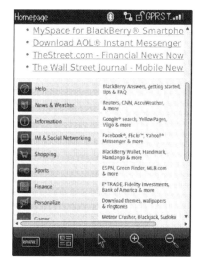

Several News sites allow you to now put an Icon on Your Homescreen that will automatically launch their news site. For our purposes, let's say we wanted to put the icon for the New York Times on the Homescreen.
Just scroll down to the New York Times icon and select **"Download."**

Choose which Icon you wish on your homescreen and press and click the screen.

Select **"Download"** to put the icon on your BlackBerry.

Once the program has successfully installed you will see a screen that looks like this.

To find the New York Times Icon, just go to your "Applications" screen and

then to the  "Downloads" folder. Inside you should see the Icon for the New York Times.

Changing Your Default Downloads Location

The default location to place all icons you download to install on your

BlackBerry is the "Downloads" folder.

You can change this location by pressing the Menu key from your Home Screen and selecting "Options."

Then press and click on the button at the top under "Set Download Folder" to change it to a new location.

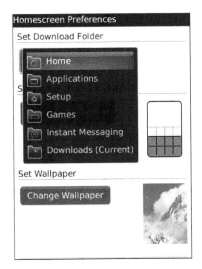

TIP: Select "**Home**" if you want your new icons easily accessible!

Downloading and Installing Games on your BlackBerry

The BlackBerry can truly me a Multi-Media Entertainment device. Sometimes, you might want to play a new game on your BlackBerry. While your BlackBerry may have come with a few games, there are many places on the Web where you can find others.

The best place to start looking for additional games is the Mobile BlackBerry site listed above.

Usually, the place you want to find games is listed as "Games and Entertainment."

Just press and click on the Games and Entertainment Icon and everything from "Free" games, to "Classic" games or "Demo" games might be available – the content changes often.

Then, just download and install exactly as you did above when installing the "Web Push" icon. Initially, the program file will go into your "Downloads" folder as stated above. You can always move the icon for the game into your "Games" folder – just take a look back at page 121 to see how to do that.

Where to Find More Software:

There are quite a few places to find Software and Services. The first place we recommend is the Partners section of www.blackberrymadesimple.com. You can get there directly by entering www.blackberrymadesimple.com/partners into your computer's web browser.

New "BlackBerryApp" Store
At publication time, BlackBerry had just announced that they were launching an 'on-the-BlackBerry' mobile software store. This will compete with the Apple iPhone AppStore. This should be a great place to find software, but the authors have not had a chance to really test it yet.

Web Stores
You can usually purchase software from these stores.
www.crackberry.com
www.shopcrackbery.com
www.bberry.com
www.eaccess.com
www.handango.com

Online Reviews of Software, Services, Ringtones, Themes, Wallpaper, Accessories and other BlackBerry-related news and Technical Support.
www.allblackberry.com
www.bbhub.com
www.berryreview.com
www.blackberrycool.com
www.blackberryforums.com
www.boygeniusreport.com
www.howardforums.com (The RIM-Research In Motion Section)
www.pinstack.com
www.RIMarkable.com

BlackBerry Official Partners
BlackBerry Solutions Guide
https://www.blackberry.com/SolutionsGuide/index.do
Software and services you will find in the Solutions Guide will be more focused toward business users than individuals.

The "Built for BlackBerry" Software Site
http://na.blackberry.com/eng/builtforblackberry/

Removing Software Icons

You have a couple of ways to easily remove any software icon that you have installed on your BlackBerry, and you can remove some of the pre-installed icons.

Probably the easiest way to do this is from the home screen. You can also delete applications from your "Options" icon.

Option 1: Delete Icons from the Home Screen

Highlight the icon you want to delete and press the Menu key.

Select "**Delete**" from the menu.

You will receive a warning:

Press and click on "Delete" to confirm.

NOTE: Not every icon can be deleted.

Option 2: Delete from the Options Icon.

Press and click on your Options icon.

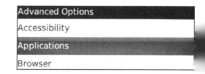

Then press and click on "**Advanced Options**." Now, press and click on "**Applications**" to see this screen.

Then type a few letters of the application icon you want to delete to find it, or you can scroll down the list and highlight it. Once highlighted, press and click the Menu key and select "Delete" as shown. You will be asked to confirm your choice, select "Delete"

You may be told that the BlackBerry needs to restart or reboot to complete deleting the icon – press and click OK or Yes to finish the process. TIP: If you are removing a number of icons, you won't need to reboot until you remove them all.

Note: If you have a Windows™ computer, you can also use the "Application Loader" icon built into BlackBerry Desktop Manager to remove icons. Check out our free Desktop Manager videos at www.madesimplelearning.com or www.blackberrymadesimple.com to see exactly how to get this done.

Chapter 25:
Maps & Directions

BlackBerry Maps, Google Maps, Bluetooth GPS

In addition to the myriad of possibilities in which your BlackBerry can manage your life, it can also literally "take you places." With the aid of software that is either pre-loaded on the BlackBerry or easily downloaded on the web you can find just about any location, business, or point of attraction using your BlackBerry.

Enable Your GPS (Global Positioning System) Receiver

In order to have your precise location tracked on mapping software, and in the camera if you turn on "Geotagging" (see page 310), you will need to turn on GPS location on your BlackBerry.

Start your Options Icon.

Click on "**Advanced Options**"

Click on "**GPS**" from the list.

Make sure that next to GPS services, the setting is "**Location ON**" as shown.

You can leave Location Aiding as "**Enabled**."

Finally, press the Menu key and select "**Save**."

Using BlackBerry Maps

The BlackBerry ships with the BlackBerry Maps software – a very good application for determining your current location and tracking your progress via your GPS (Bluetooth or built-in) receiver.

To Enable GPS use on BlackBerry
Maps (Use either Bluetooth GPS
Receiver or a Built-In GPS)

Press and click the **Maps** icon in the
applications menu and then press the
Menu key.

NOTE: If you use a Bluetooth GPS or
have a GPS built in, then you will need
to press and click on "**Options**" and
press and click in the first field "**GPS
Device**." Select your Bluetooth GPS
receiver that you just paired with
your BlackBerry and the GPS
commands will now be available to
you.

To view a particular map from a contact

From the **Map** icon, press the **Menu key** from the main map screen and
select "**Find Location**".

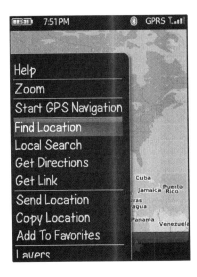
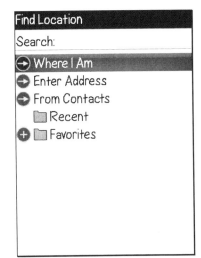

You can search based on your current location or you can **"Enter an Address,"** search **"From Contacts"** or look at recent searches.

Then, on the next screen scroll down to **"From Contacts."**

Select the Contact and press and click and a ten a map of their location will appear on the screen.

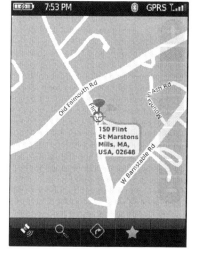

Videos are an easy way to Learn: www.MadeSimpleLearning

To Get Directions

Press the Menu key from the map screen and select "**Get Directions**." Select a **Start** location by scrolling down **to "Where I Am," "Enter Address," "From Contacts," "From Map," "Recent" or "Favorites."** Repeat the steps now for the "**End Location.**"

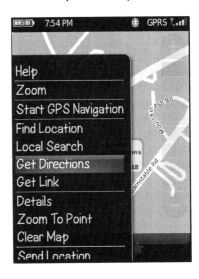

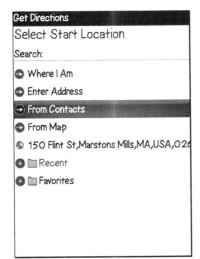

When done, press and click on your "Start Location."

You can choose whether you want the **"Fastest"** or **"Shortest"** route and whether you want to avoid highways or tolls. Then, just press and click on **"Search"** to have your Route displayed for you. If you press and click **"View on Map"** you will see a Map View of the route.

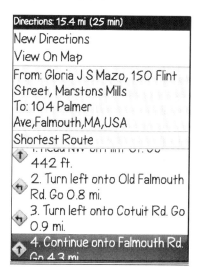

You can start your GPS by pressing the "soft key" at the bottom left of the screen. At publishing time, the GPS will track you along the route but it will not give you voice prompts or turn-by-turn voice directions.

You can also Press the gold star which will set the location as a "Favorite" in your BlackBerry.

BlackBerry Maps Menu Commands

There is a great deal you can do with the BlackBerry Map application. Pressing the Menu key offers you many options with just a scroll and a press and click. From the Menu you can do the following:

Videos are an easy way to Learn: www.MadeSimpleLearning

Zoom – takes you from street level to the stratosphere (Keyboard Shortcut Keys: "L" = Zoom In, "O" = Zoom Out)

Start/Stop GPS Navigation – to end GPS tracking (only with GPS enabled)

Find Location – Type in an address to jump to that address.

Local Search – Search for restaurants, stores or places of interest near your current location

New Directions - Find directions by using your location history or typing in new addresses.

Get Link – To connect to a Web Site to find an address

View Directions – if you are in Map Mode – this switches to text

Zoom to Point – Show the map detail around the currently selected point in the directions. (Only when viewing directions.)

Clear Map – Erases the current map or route on the screen

Send Location – Send your map location via email

Send Directions – Sends your directions to an Email, SMS, MMS or Messenger contact.

Copy Location – To add your current location to your address book or another application.

Add to Favorites – To all your current location as a "Favorite" for easy retrieval on the Map.

Layers – Show "layers" of recent searches, favorites or links on the map

Options – Change GPS Bluetooth device, Disable Backlight timeout settings, Change Units from Metric (Kilometers) to Imperial (Miles), enable or disable tracking with GPS and show or hide title bar when starting.

About – Show information about the current provider of the mapping data and software.

Show Keyboard – To enter text or numbers

Switch Application – Jump over to any other application (Multi-Task).

Google Maps: Downloading & Installing

If you have ever used Google Earth you have seen the power of satellite technology in mapping and rendering terrain. Google Maps Mobile brings that same technology to handheld devices including the BlackBerry.

With Google Maps you can view 3-D rendered satellite shots of any address – anywhere in the world. To get started with this amazing application, you need to first download it onto your BlackBerry.

Press and click on the **Browser** icon from the application menu.

Press the Menu key and scroll to the "**Go To**" command and press and click. TIP: Use the shortcut hotkey of "**.**" (period) for "**Go To**"

Enter in the address to perform an "Over the Air" ("OTA") download right onto the BlackBerry: http://www.google.com/gmm
Press and click on "**Download Google Maps**" and the installation program will begin.

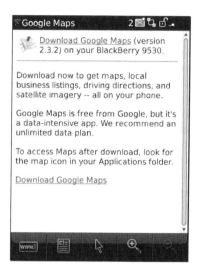 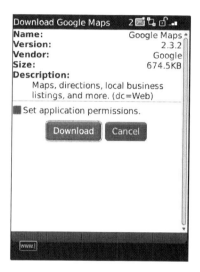

Then press and click the "**Download**" button on the next screen

Finally you will see a screen that the application was successfully installed. Select "**OK**" to close the window or "**Run**" to start Google Maps right away or press and click on the Icon on the BlackBerry which should be in the "Downloads" folder. You might get prompted to Reboot your Device – if so, just press and click on "Reboot" and then try to run the program.

The first time you start up Google Maps Mobile, just press and click the icon (it may be located in your "Downloads" folder). Then read the terms and conditions, then click on "**Accept**" in order to continue.

Google Map Menu Commands

Google Maps is full of great features – most of which are accessed right from the menu. Press the Menu key to see it.

One of the very cool new features is "Street View" which Google Maps tells you about at the first screen.

When you first start up Google Maps, it will try to determine your locations based on the built in GPS or the cell tower closest to your phone.

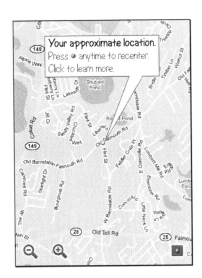

Search / Finding an Address ("Location") Or Business

Finding an Address or Business is very easy with Google Maps.

Start the Google Maps application by press and clicking on the icon. Press the Menu key and choose "**Search**", Press and click on "**Enter new search**" or scroll down to press and click on a **recent search** below.

Just type about anything in the search string – an address, type of business and zip code, business name and city/state, etc. If we wanted to find bike stores in Winter Park, Florida, we would enter "**bike stores winter park fl**" or "**bike stores 32789**" (if you know the zip code). Then, press the MENU button and select "Ok" – or just press the ENTER key on the keyboard to begin the search.

Your search results will show a number of matching entries, just scroll the up/down and touch to select an entry then press and click the screen to see details.

Press the button at the bottom which says "See on Map" to see the search results on the map.

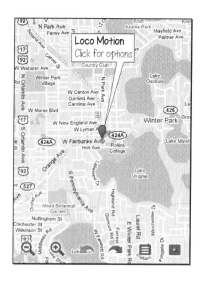 

To see the new "Street View" – just press and click on **"Street View"** from the Menu:

Google Map Shortcut Keys

To use these, you need to press the Menu key and select "Show Keyboard." Then press and hold the "!?123" to show the keypad.

4   Previous search results

6   Next search results

Toggle between Map View and
      Search Results List

2   Toggle between Satellite and
      Map Views

1   Zoom Out

3   Zoom In

*   Favorites List / Add a New
      Favorite Location

9   Mobile Search Options

0   Show / Hide Location
      (if available)

Getting Directions with Google Maps

Press the MENU key and select **"Get Directions"**

Set your **"Start Point"** – the default will be **"My Location"** and then set your **"End Point."**

Press and click on **"Show Directions"** to display turn by turn directions to your destination.

Chapter 26:
Other Applications

As if your BlackBerry doesn't do enough for you, RIM was very thoughtful and included even more Utilities and Programs to help keep your organized and to help manage your busy life. Most of these additional programs will be found in the "Applications" folder.

Calculator

There are many times when having a "Calculator" nearby is handy. I usually like to have my 13 year old "Math Genius" daughter nearby when I have a math problem to figure out, but sometimes she does need to go to school and isn't available to help. So, I rely on the Calculator on my BlackBerry.

To start the "**Calculator**" program, just go the **"Applications"** folder and press and click. One of the icons should say **"Calculator."**

Just input your equation as you would on any Calculator program.

One handy tool in the "Calculator" program is that it can easily convert amounts to Metric. Just press the MENU button and scroll to **"Convert to Metric."**

Clock

While having a Clock is nothing new for a BlackBerry, the features and the ability to customize the clock – especially when the BlackBerry is on your bedside table – is new and appreciated.

To start the "Clock" application, just go once again to the **"Applications"** folder and find the icon for the Clock. On some devices, the clock icon might just an icon in the menu – not in a folder. By default, the clock is initially set to an "analog" face – but that be changed.

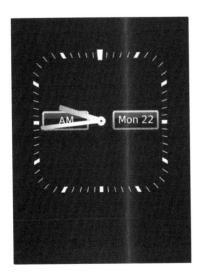

The first feature to look at is the "Alarm." The easiest way to bring up the settings for the "Alarm" is to simply press the MENU button and click "Set Alarm." The Alarm menu will appear in the center of the screen. Just press the desired field and then just scroll up or down in that highlighted field to change the option. In the farthest field to the right, after it is highlighted just scroll and select **"Off," "On"** or **"Weekdays"** for the alarm setting. Press the Escape key to save your changes.

Also built into the Clock application are a stopwatch and a timer which can be started by selecting them from the MENU.

The clock can be changed to a Digital Clock, a Flip Clock or an LCD Digital face by selecting the clock face from the **"Options"** menu.

 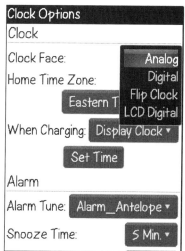

Bedside Mode:

One of the nice new features of the "Clock" application is the **"Bedside Mode"** setting. Since many of us keep our BlackBerry by the side of our bed – we now have the option of "Telling" our BlackBerry not to flash, ring or buzz in the middle of the night. We just have to activate "Bedside Mode" by pressing the MENU key and selecting **"Enter Bedside Mode."**

The Bedside Mode Options can be configured by pressing the MENU key in the "Clock" application, and then scrolling down to **"Options."** Down towards the bottom of the options menu are the specific **"Bedside Mode"** options. You can disable the LED, the radio and dim the screen when "Bedside Mode" is set.

Voice Notes Recorder

Another useful program in your "Applications" folder is the Voice Notes Recorder. Say you need to "dictate" something you need to remember at a later time. Or, perhaps you would rather "speak" a note instead of composing an email. Your BlackBerry makes that very easy for you. Just navigate to the "Applications" folder and select **"Voice Notes Recorder."**

This is a very simple program to use – just press and click the screen when you are ready to record your note. Press and click it again when you are done. You will then see options along the lower part of the program which will allow you to: continue recording, stop, play, resume, delete, save or email the voice note. Just press and click on the corresponding icon to perform the desired action.

Password Keeper

It can be very hard in today's "Web World" with different passwords and different password rules on so many different sites. Fortunately, your BlackBerry has a very effective and safe way for you to manage all your Passwords – the **"Password Keeper"** program.

Just go back to your **"Applications"** folder and navigate to the **"Password Keeper"** icon and press and click. The first thing you will need to do is set a program password – pick something you will remember!

Once your password is set, you can add new passwords for just about anything or any web site. Press the MENU button and select **"New"** and add passwords, user names and web addresses to help you remember all your various login information.

Chapter 27:
Searching for Lost Stuff

TIP: Finding Calendar Events

With the **Search** icon, you can even answer the questions like:
When is my next meeting with Sarah?
When did I last meet with her?
(For this to work, you need to type people's names in your calendar events like "Meet with Sarah" or "Lunch with Tom Wallis"

Understanding How Search Works

Once you get used to your BlackBerry, you will begin to rely on it more and more. The more you use it, the more information you will store within it. It is truly amazing how much information you can place in this little device.

At some point, you will want to retrieve something – a name or a word or phrase – but you may not be exactly sure of where you placed that particular piece of information. This is where the "Search" icon can be invaluable.

Finding the Search Icon

In your applications menu there is a **Search** Icon.

From your Homescreen of icons, just scroll to find the **Search Icon**. It may be located within the "Applications" menu and usually looks like a magnifying glass.

Search across Several Icons:

It is possible that the desired text or name could be in one or several different places on your BlackBerry. The Search tool is quite powerful and flexible. It allows you to narrow down or expand the icons you want to search. If you are sure your information is in the calendar, then just check that box, if not, you can easily check all the boxes using the **"Select All"** from the menu.

Press and click on the **Search** Icon and the main search screen is visible.

By default, only the **"Messages"** field is checked

To search all the Icons for your Name or Text, press the **Menu key** and scroll to **"Select All"** and press and click.

Also, if you hide the keyboard, you can press the **"Select All"** or **"Deselect All"** in the soft keys on the bottom.

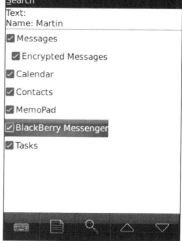

Searching for Names or Text

In the **"Name"** field, you can search for a name or email address. The **"Text"** field allows you to search for any other text that might be found in the body of an email, inside a calendar event, in an address book entry, in a memo or task.

If you decide to search for a name, then you can either type a few letters of a name, like "Mar" or press the Menu key and "**Select Name**"

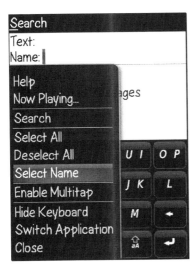

If you are looking for a specific text, like a word, phrase or even phone number that is not in an email address field, then you would type it into the "**Text**:" field.

When you are ready to start the search, press the Menu key and click on "**Search**."

The results of the search are displayed with the number of found entries. The image to the right shows that there were four total matches found, three in the Messages (Email) and one in the Contacts.

Then, just press and click on the corresponding "plus" sign to expand the search results.

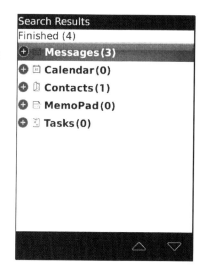

Search Tips and Tricks

You can see that the more information you enter on your BlackBerry (or enter on your desktop computer and sync to your BlackBerry), the more useful it becomes. When you combine a great deal of useful information with this Search tool, you truly have a very powerful handheld computer.

As your BlackBerry fills up, the possible places where your information is stored increases. Also, the search might not turn up the exact information you are looking for due to inconsistencies in the way you store the information.

TIP: You can even search Notes added to Calendar Events

Remember to add notes to your calendar events and the 'notes' field at the bottom of your contacts. You can do this right on your BlackBerry or on your computer and sync them. Use the Search icon to find key notes later on your BlackBerry right when you need them.

Search Tips:

Try to be consistent in the way you type someone's name – for example, always use "Martin" instead of "Marty" or "M" or any other variation. This way, the **Search** will always find what you need.

Occasionally check your address book for "Doubles" of contact information. It is easy to wind up with two or three entries for one contact if you add an email one time, a phone number another and an address another – try to keep one entry per contact. It is usually easier to do this cleanup work on your computer, and then sync the changes or deletions back to your BlackBerry.

If you are not sure whether you are looking for "Mark" or "Martin," just type in "Mar" and then search. This way, you will find both names.

Remember, if you want to find an exact name, then scroll to the "**Name**" field, press the Menu key and choose "**Select Name**" to select a name from your address book.

Do your best to put consistent information into calendar events. Example: if you wanted to find when the next Dentist appointment for Gary was, you could search for "Gary Dentist" in your calendar and find it. But only if you made sure to put the full words "Gary" and "dentist" in your calendar entry. It would be better to just search for just "dentist."

If you wanted to find a phone number and just remembered the area code, then you would type that area code into the "**Text**" field and search the Address Book.

If you wanted to find when the name "Gary" was in the body of an email, not an email address field (To:, Cc:, From:, Bcc:) then you would enter the name in the "**Text**" field, not the "**Name**" field on the Search screen.

TIP: Traveling and want to find locals?

Let's say you are traveling to New York City and want to find everyone in your BlackBerry address book with a "212" area code. Type in "212" in the "Text" field and then check the "Address Book", click **"Search,"** to immediately find everyone who has a 212 area code.

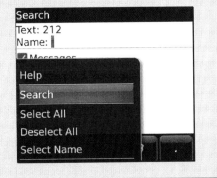

Chapter 28:
Fixing Problems

Your BlackBerry is virtually a complete computer in the palm of your hand. Sometimes it needs a little 'tweaking' in order to keep it in top running order. This chapter has some of the most valuable tips and tricks to fix problems and keep your BlackBerry running smoothly.

Clear Out the Event Log

This tip is courtesy J. Wilson from Verizon Wireless Technology Support team. Your BlackBerry tracks absolutely everything it does in order to help with debugging and troubleshooting in what is called an "Event Log." It helps your BlackBerry run smoother and faster if you periodically clear out this log.

Bring up the keyboard by pressing the Menu key and selecting "Show Keyboard"

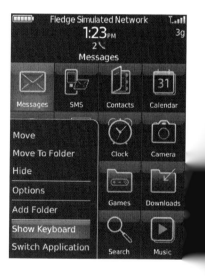

Tilt your blackberry sideways to bring up the landscape QWERTY mode full keyboard.

Press and hold the **!?123** key in order to see the number keys and basic symbols.

Now type "**/**"/ to see the Event Log screen as shown.

Press the menu key and select "**Clear Log**" in order to erase all the log entries.

Then confirm your selection on the next screen.

Once the log is cleared out, press the Escape key to return to your Home Screen.

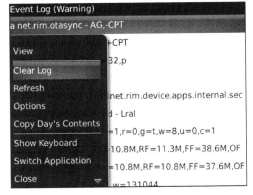

Radio Turn Off by itself?
Travel away from Network Signal?

Thanks to the engineers at RIM (Research In Motion - BlackBerry's maker, if you travel away from a wireless signal for a significant amount of time (a few hours), your BlackBerry will automatically turn off the radio to conserve battery strength. This is because the radio consumes a lot of power when it is trying to find a weak or non-existent wireless signal.

The nice thing is that all you need to do is turn your wireless radio back on by hitting the Menu key and selecting the "Manage Connections" icon.

Signal Strength Only 1-2 Bars?

You may have already figured this out, but signal strength is usually stronger above ground and near the windows, if you happen to be inside a building. It is usually best outdoors away from large buildings. We once worked in an office building that was on the very edge of coverage, and we all had to leave our BlackBerry devices on the window sill to get any coverage at all! We're not sure why, but sometimes just turning your radio off and on will recover a stronger signal.

Manage Connections to turn your Radio Off/On (Airplane Mode)

Many times the simple act of turning your radio off and back on will restore your wireless connectivity.

To do this, first go to your Homescreen. From your Homescreen press and click the "**Manage Connections**" Icon, then press and click on **"Turn all Connections off."**

Now, press and click on "Restore connections."

Look for your wireless signal meter and upper case **1XEV or EDGE or GPRS**. Check to see if your Email and Web are working.
See page 19 for more on how you read the wireless signal meter letters.

Register Now

From your Homescreen, tap the **Menu** key and press and click the "**Options**" icon.
Press and click on "**Advanced Options**"
Now select "**Host Routing Table**"

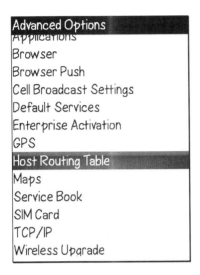

In the Host Routing Table screen you will see many entries related to your BlackBerry phone company. Press the Menu key and select "**Register Now.**"

If you see a message like "**Request queued and will be send when data connection is established**" then skip to the next step.

Save Battery Life and Ensure the Best Signal

Press and Click on "Mobile Network Options" from the "Manage Connections Screen."Make sure your Data Services are "On" and then go down to "Network Technology." If you are using your BlackBerry on a CDMA Network (Like Verizon) set this to 1XEV – since you will use the network exclusively in the US. If you travel outside of the US, change this to either "Global" or "GSM/UMTS." The problem is that if you are set to "Global" all the time, your phone will continually "search" for both types of cell signals, more quickly draining your battery.

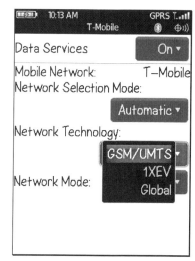

Hard Reset (Remove Battery)

Turn off your BlackBerry by pressing and holding the power button (the Red

Phone Key).

Remove the battery cover. After your BlackBerry is off, then turn it over and press the two release buttons on the lower parts of the sides of the battery cover and slide them towards the top.

Gently pry out and remove the battery (look for the little indent in the upper right corner to stick in your finger tip).
Wait about **30 seconds**.

Replace the battery – make sure to slide in the bottom of the battery first, then press down from the top.

Replace the battery door, by aligning the tabs then sliding it so it press and clicks-in and is flat.
Power-on your BlackBerry (it may come on automatically). Then wait for the hourglass – similar to a soft-reset wait.

Now, if it's not already turned on, tap the **Menu key** and press and click the **radio tower** icon which says **"Manage Connections"** and then **"Restore Connections."**

If email and/or the web browser are still not working, and you are using your BlackBerry with a BlackBerry Enterprise Server, please contact your organization's help desk or your wireless carrier's support number.

If email and web are not working and you do not use your BlackBerry with a BlackBerry Enterprise Server, then proceed to the next step.

Send Service Books (For BlackBerry Internet Service or "Personal Email" Users)

This step will work for you only if you have "Setup Internet E-Mail" or "Setup Personal E-mail" on their BlackBerry or using their wireless carrier's web site. [What is Internet/Personal Email? See page 43]

Press and click the Menu key and press and click on the "**Setup Wizard**" or "**Manage Personal E-Mail**" or "**Set Up Internet Mail**" icon. (Each carrier is a bit different.)

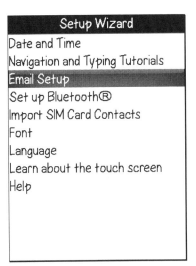

Note: If you have not yet logged in and created an account for your BlackBerry Internet Service, you may now be asked to create an account to login for the first time.

If you already have an account (or after you create your new account), you will be automatically logged in and see the screen below. Scroll down and press and click on the "**Service Books**" link.

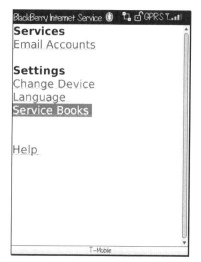 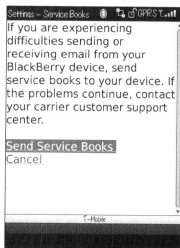

On the next screen, press and click the "**Send All**" link.

After press and clicking "**Send All**" you should see a "**Successfully Sent**" message:

If you see any other message indicating the message was not sent, then you may want to verify that you have good coverage at your current location. You may also want to repeat some of other the troubleshooting steps described above.

After the service books have been sent, you will then see an "**Activation Message**" in your Messages email inbox for each one of your Internet Email accounts setup or integrated to your BlackBerry. Each message, when opened, will look similar to this one the shown here.

From: Activation Server
Congratulations!
Dec 22, 2008 10:17 AM

Congratulations, you have successfully setup gary@blackberrymadesimple.com with your BlackBerry device. You should begin receiving new messages in approximately 20 minutes.

Still cannot fix your problems?

Visit the **BlackBerry Technical Knowledge Base**. See how to find it on page 71. Or, you can ask your question at one of the BlackBerry user forums like www.crackberry.com or www.pinstack.com.

Chapter 29:
Boost Your Battery

As everyone knows, your Battery is critical to the operation of your BlackBerry. But what you may not know is what happens when it gets too low, how often you should charge it, if there are extended life batteries available, or even what things that cause it to be drained more quickly. In this chapter we will give you an overview of battery-related information.

How often should you charge your BlackBerry?

> We recommend charging the battery every night. Using your phone is the fastest way to consume your battery life, so if you talk a lot on your BlackBerry, you definitely want to charge it every night. Another big drain on your battery is using the speaker to play music or video sound – especially at higher volumes.

> **TIP:** Just plug in your BlackBerry charger cable where you set your BlackBerry every night. Before setting the BlackBerry down, just plug it into the charging cable.

What happens when the battery gets low?

> **Low Battery Warning:** If the battery gets to only 15% of its full charge, you will hear a beep and see a warning message saying "Low Battery" and the battery indicator will usually change red. At this point, you will want to start looking for a way to get your BlackBerry charged – either by connecting it to your computer with a USB cable, or the regular power charger.

> **Very Low Battery:** When the battery gets down to 5% of its full charge you are in a "Very Low Battery" condition. At this point, in order to conserve what little remaining power there is, the BlackBerry will automatically turn off your wireless radio. This will prevent you from making any calls, browsing the

web, sending/receiving email or any messages at all. You should try to charge it immediately or turn it off.

(Almost) Dead Battery: When the BlackBerry senses the battery is just about to run out altogether, then it will automatically shut off the BlackBerry itself.

This is a preventative measure, to make sure your data remains safe on the device. However, we recommend getting the BlackBerry charged as quickly as possible after you are in this condition.

Can I re-charge my BlackBerry in the car?

Yes, the easiest way to do this is to purchase a car charger from a BlackBerry Accessory Store. To find a car charger; type in "blackberry car charger" in your favorite web search engine. REMEMBER: If you are coming from an "older" BlackBerry, the Storm uses the new Micro USB charger and your older chargers will not fit.

The other way to charge your BlackBerry is to use what is called a "vehicle power inverter" that converts your vehicle's 12V direct current (DC) into Alternating Current (AC) to which you can plug in your BlackBerry charger. The other option with a power inverter is to plug your laptop into it then connect your BlackBerry with the USB cable to the laptop (a true "mobile office" setup).

Can I re-charge my BlackBerry from my computer?

Yes, as long as your computer is plugged into a power outlet (or vehicle power inverter) and your BlackBerry is connected to your computer with a USB cable.

Tips and Tricks to Extend my Battery Life

If you are in an area with very poor (or no) wireless coverage, turn off your radio with the "Manage Connections" icon. When the radio is searching for the network, it uses a lot of battery.

Use your headphones instead of the speaker to listen to music or watch videos.

Use your speakerphone sparingly; it uses much more energy than either the regular speaker or your earphones / headset.

Decrease the backlight brightness or reduce the timeout.

You can do this in your Options icon > Screen/Keyboard as shown to the right.

If possible, set your profiles (see page 138) to ring and/or vibrate less often. You might want to turn off the vibration for every email you receive. This may help you live a more 'calm' and 'peaceful' life – you check your BlackBerry for new messages, not when every single one arrives.

Use data intensive applications sparingly. Such applications make a lot of use of the radio transmit/receive and will use up the battery more quickly. Examples are mapping programs which transmit large amounts of data to show the map moving or satellite imagery.

Send email or text instead of talking on the phone. The phone is probably the most intensive user of the battery life. If possible, send an email or SMS text message instead of making a call. Lots of time this is less intrusive for the recipient and you may be able to get an answer when a phone call might not be possible – e.g. in a meeting, etc.

Chapter 30:
Simple Video Tutorials

BlackBerry Made Simple Short Video Training
Perfect for You and Your Entire Organization

At publishing time, we were just getting started on our Storm™ video tutorials. By the time you read this, we should have at least an initial set of core videos to help you get more out of your Storm™.

BlackBerry Video Tutorials

(c) 2008 BlackBerry Made Simple

Click Below to Start Watching the Video Tutorials on your Computer

Storm COMING SOON	Bold	8800 Series	Curve	Pearl
9500 Series	9000 Series	8800 / 8820 (Wi-Fi) / 8830 World Edition	8300 / 8310 8320 (Wi-Fi) / 8330	8100 / 8110 8120 (Wi-Fi) / 8130

Pearl 'Flip' COMING SOON	Curve 8900	8700 Series	77/75/72/6xxx	7100 Series
8200 Series	8900 Series	8700 c/g/e 8705e / 8707g / 87xx	77xx / 75xx / 72xx 67xx / 65xx / 62xx	7100 g/i/x 7130 c/e/q / 71xx

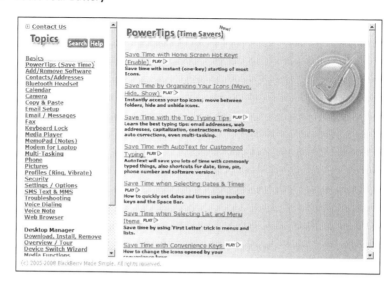

We keep our videos short and to-the-point – most are just 3 minutes long.

Gone are the days of trying to puzzle out how to do something. You can just watch and learn by seeing the expert do it on their BlackBerry.

We listen to our customers and watch development with new BlackBerry models to add new videos frequently. When you check out the site, it's quite likely there will be a number of new videos on the BlackBerry and other devices. Maybe even an iPhone!

Upcoming Books from BlackBerry Made Simple

Keep your eyes on www.MadeSimpleLearning.com and on www.amazon.com for all our newest "Made Simple" books.

Thanks Again!

Again, we sincerely thank you for purchasing this book and hope it has helped you really learn how to get every last drop of productivity and fun out of your BlackBerry™!

If you have any suggestions or ideas for improvements, we welcome them anytime, just email them to us directly from your BlackBerry at info@blackberrymadesimple.com.

INDEX

Videos are an easy way to Learn: www.MadeSimpleLearning.com

3693466

Made in the USA